The Parish of

and St. Joseph.

Stanford-le-Hope, Essex 1913-2013

Published by
Dynan Publishing

Kevin Redmond with foreword

by Fr. Paul Dynan

Current church of Our Lady and St. Joseph *Front Cover Top*

Original church of Our Lady and St. Joseph *Front Cover Bottom*

ISBN 978-0-9573479-0-8

Acknowledgements

A little girl is concentrating. In front of her lie the pieces of a jigsaw puzzle. She is five years old, but already she knows that the best strategy is to start with the edges and corners and then to fit in the middle pieces. She is our much loved granddaughter.

Over the past year or so, her grandfather has been completing a similar jigsaw. As he compiles a history of our parish he knows that the straight edges are supplied by previous writers, including C.R. (Bob) Sharp, Peter Preston and Sister Monica Cremin. There are also parish records, the detailed entries of the diocesan archive and the vivid memories of parishioners.

These fit neatly together, and [illegible]ll that is left are the few pieces in the middle, the bits that have to [illegible]itten by the author. Except that he knows he is not really the autho[illegible] has merely managed to finish the jigsaw.

I would like to thank my wife, Felicity, [illegible]indness and patient support. There simply would not have been a [illegible]ut her.

Special thanks are due to Mary Pollard, who wro[illegible]ter on Tilbury, and who gave access to her M.A. dissertation o[illegible] of Mercy. Mary's history of St. Joseph's School was extensively [illegible] this book.

The 'author' wishes to express appreciation of the great courtesy and assistance extended to him by the Diocesan Archivist, Father Stewart Foster.

We wish to acknowledge the considerable help offered to us by Lee Moore, for typesetting the book and the overall organisation of its layout.

Jay Dynan provided the photographs of the interior and exterior of our modern church.

Our thanks are also due to Michael Dynan who acted as facilitator for the production of the book.

The local press readily agreed to use of material from their newspapers, and these included *The Thurrock Gazette*, *The Echo* and *The Brentwood News*.

The real credit for the creation of this book should go to the priest who suggested it and who gave encouragement at every stage, Father Paul Dynan.

KSR : 2012

Table of Contents

Foreword

This book has been published in the period leading up to the celebration of the Centenary of the Parish of Our Lady and St. Joseph, Stanford-le Hope, Essex. The reason for compiling a history of the first hundred years of the parish is to put on record the development of the parish from its origins. The book also fulfils a desire to pay tribute to those who have contributed to the building-up of the parish during its history, through to the present day. Of particular mention are the pioneers of the earliest days of the parish, as well as the outstanding contribution made by the Sisters of Mercy over the years, all of whom are owed a tremendous debt of thanks,

In the autumn of 2010 Bishop Thomas McMahon appointed me Parish Priest of Stanford-le-Hope. A short time after my arrival, I contacted Fr. Stewart Foster, Diocesan Archivist, to ascertain the official dates of the parish and he informed me that Stanford-le-Hope parish had been established on 22nd June 1913. This was in keeping with the discovery of a framed Papal Blessing in the presbytery, which had been obtained during the Pontificate of His Holiness Pope John XXIII, to mark the occasion of Golden Jubilee of the parish in 1963.

A programme of events to celebrate the Centenary in 2013 included writing a history of the parish to coincide with the planned liturgical and social events. When I first raised the prospect of compiling such a book with Kevin Redmond, the material we had available was to say the least "thin on the ground" and rightly Kevin expressed the fear that there might not be sufficient material for a book. However, through the tremendous help and support we obtained from Fr. Stewart Foster in the Diocesan Archives, support and encouragement from many parishioners and Kevin's own hard work, we came to realise that, not only would there be more than enough material, but it might prove a case of what to include and what to leave out.

I would like to take this opportunity to express my deep gratitude to Kevin, who took on the mantle of collecting and collating the available historical material, as well as interviewing parishioners and others to obtain first hand knowledge about the history of the parish.

There is, quite rightly, a separate section of official acknowledgements where all those who have helped will be thanked, but I wish herein to record my own sincere thanks to the author who has spent untold hours both in the archives and his home, working through available documents and putting together what, I am certain you will agree, is an extremely interesting and thoroughly well presented history of the parish of Stanford-le-Hope.

Fr. Paul Dynan BA, STB, MA, FIBMS

Parish Priest, Stanford-le-Hope

Introduction

On a winter's evening a few years after the turn of the twentieth century, a group of six boys walked along a footpath from Grays to a small, black barn in Stanford-le-Hope. It was Christmas Eve and the snow was falling. With them was their Parish Priest, Father Charles Carless. At midnight, for the first time in over three hundred years, a public Catholic Mass was said in Stanford-le-Hope. Father Carless, a Catholic priest based in Corringham, possessed the vision and determination to set the story of our parish in motion.

Present at the Mass were just twenty-two people. The barn's roof could not keep out the flurries of snow, but that did not seem to deter this small group of people. After the Mass they returned to their homes, and the boys took the long walk back to Grays. Father Carless, in a strange echo of the first Christmas, slept on a heap of straw in a corner of the barn.

Unexpectedly, the names of the six boys from Grays have survived : Bart Hastings, Jack Byron, Ernest Crouch, George Crooks, Jeremiah Fyffes and a boy known only as Martin. Ernest was later to become the first Sacristan in Stanford-le-Hope.

The year was 1909, midway through what we tend to think of as the Edwardian Golden Age, between the death of Queen Victoria and the outbreak of the First World War.

Chapter One : The Early History of Stanford-le-Hope

Whilst excavations of archaeological sites have not centred on the original village of Stanford-le-Hope, there is evidence of human settlement in the area which considerably predates Saxon times. The name Stanford, or stone ford, is clearly of German derivation, a reflection of the Saxon settlements which spread across England in what is sometimes called the Dark Ages. The second part of our name "le-Hope" suggests the influence of Norman French, although "Hope" could well be another Old English word, referring both to an inlet and the upper part of a wooded valley.

The ford itself could have been over a meandering stream, the Hassingbrook, which once formed the boundary between Mucking, Stanford and Horndon on the Hill. If so, then any Hope or inlet on the stream would scarcely have been large enough to warrant a mention. Just off the Thames coastline, however, is a stretch of water long recognised as a safe anchorage for boats navigating the Thames. It is known as the Hope or Haven. There is therefore the possibility that the name of our village derives from the happy coincidence of a useful ford and a safe area to anchor ships on the tidal Thames. More prosaically, there is a small river, the Hope, which flows through the parish, but it is impossible to determine whether the river's name preceded that of the village or was derived from it.

For all practical purposes, however, it would be sensible to refer to the years immediately following the Norman Conquest of England as the time when the recorded history of our area might be outlined with any accuracy. This was a time of great upheaval for the relatively small land-owning class, who saw their lands and estates taken away and given to Norman lords, some of whom became the wealthiest people to have lived in England in the past thousand years.

For the ordinary people, however, there was less disruption to their way of life. Their lives before the Norman invasion had been hard under their Saxon lords and their way of life remained so. The Anglo-Saxon Chronicle records that William the Conqueror was a man "of great sternness", and we must assume that the Norman aristocracy had little time for the needs of the Saxon peasantry. Indeed, the Norman interest in hunting and the chase led to many laws protecting the game that they hunted for sport, and Saxons were faced with severe penalties if they took such animals from the woods and forests that covered much of England.

Gradually the forests around Stanford were cleared, and the clay soil turned over for farming. The ordinary people worked the land owned by their local lord and were given small plots of land in exchange, on which they grew their subsistence crops. The tolls and dues paid to the lord of the manor would have varied from one area to the next, but all would have been heavily weighted in favour of the lord and at the expense of those who lived on his land.

At the time of the Domesday Survey in 1086, the main village of Hassingbrook was divided into two parts, a large estate of some 1500 acres and a smaller area of just over 150 acres. These two parcels of land, previously owned by Saxon freemen, were handed over to William the First's half-brother, Bishop Odo, who leased them to Norman gentry. Over the course of time, these lands became three distinct Manors, Hassingbrook, Abbot's Hall and Cabborns.

Hassingbrook comprised the land to the northern part of Stanford. Owned for many centuries by the Montchensy family, and later by Richard Campion, who was Sheriff of London and Lord Mayor in the sixteenth century, it was the largest of the three Manors. In 1746, it was valued at £400,000.

Abbot's Hall was owned by Waltham Abbey, after which it was probably named. After the Dissolution of the Monasteries, Henry VIII gave it to Walter Farr and his wife, Fridiswide, in 1543, when it became known as the Manor of Stanford-le-Hope. The great Manor House was destroyed by fire in the nineteenth century.

Cabborns later became Manor Farm, and its Manor was pulled down just before the Second World War.

Other local areas mentioned in the Domesday Survey include Fobbing (Phobbinge) which was transferred from a Saxon thane to the Norman Count Eustace, Horndon on the Hill (Hordinduna) divided into four plots, Orset (Orseda) which was two areas of land, and Corringham. The Norman lords moved in and the land was divided between them, with Bishop Odo being granted considerable property. There is little good that can be said about this violent half-brother of William the First, who fell out with the king amid charges of fraud and rebellion and was imprisoned for five years until William's death.

The Church exercised considerable influence over the people of England and, in a time when such diseases as the Plague spread unchecked across the land, there was always the prospect of sudden death. It is probable that many of the labouring classes would have recognised the description given by Thomas Hobbes in the seventeenth century, when he described the life of man without good government as “Nasty, brutish and short”.

Not that life was without its diversions. Local historians point with some pride to the significant part played by the villagers of Stanford, Corringham and Fobbing in what became known as the Peasants’ Revolt. This spread across Essex, Kent and East Anglia in 1381, almost overthrowing the monarchy. In an attempt to raise money for the battles of the Hundred Years War against France, there were eight separate taxes imposed on ordinary people between 1371 and 1381. A commissioner for the latest poll tax, Thomas Bampton, visited Brentwood to carry out the necessary paperwork, but an estimated 5,000 people from this area marched over and sent him packing.

When a Chief Justice returned from London with some soldiers to restore order, he was attacked by the crowd and made to swear on the Bible that he would never again be involved in such matters. Three of his retinue were beheaded and the peasants began their revolt. Local Essex manor houses were attacked, and the estate records burned as a sign that there was to be a new order in England. Many lords were forced to rewrite agreements with their tenants, on more favourable terms. The whole of Colchester fell to the rebels, and many priests supported their parishioners, whose lives were so impoverished.

The rebels marched on London, led among others by Thomas Baker of Fobbing. The young king, Richard II, met the rebels and promised reforms if they would return to their homes. The king did come to visit them, but at the head of a well-disciplined army who crushed the rebels and killed many of them. The rebellion was over, although many labourers saw their lot improve when the Black Death created a shortage of labour in the South of England. Landlords now had to offer better terms to ensure that their lands were properly managed.

Within a century, the Tudor period saw a reshaping of the rural scene to a pattern we would recognise today. The local strip farming of feudal times was replaced by enclosures, with a pattern of fields and hedgerows, woodland and open heaths. Today, of course, fewer people live and work on the land, but the rural landscape itself has not changed greatly in the past four hundred years.

Stanford remained a rural village over the centuries. In the 1763 Parliamentary election, when only landowners were permitted to vote, there were only four electors in the village. By 1830, the population was listed as 330, with eight electors. A trade directory of 1848 reveals the range of activities carried out in the village. There were nine farmers, a surgeon, a shoemaker, a blacksmith, a builder and wheelwright, a shop, a post office, a small school and two public houses.

The arrival of the railway in 1854 was to begin the changes that would see Stanford develop into the area we know today. The census returns show a steady increase in the population of Stanford, although some of our older parishioners still refer to the village of Stanford-le-Hope, where they grew up.

1861 census	608	people
1891 census	1093	people
1901 census	1715	people
1911 census	2547	people

And so the scene is set for the start of our parish's history. The next century was to see substantial changes, as the population grew beyond all expectations, and the lives of the people were to change almost beyond recognition.

(With special thanks to Aubrey Saunders : *A Short History of the Church and Village of Stanford-le-Hope*)

The generation of people we now call the Edwardians is just beyond our reach today, but we feel we have so much in common that we might almost know them. Yet it was a very different world from our own.

Many people regarded Catholicism with some suspicion and the anti-Catholic clauses of the 1689 Bill of Rights and the 1701 Act of Settlement remained in force. Even after the Catholic Emancipation Act of 1829, and the gradual emergence of a more public and confident Catholic population, there was an air of reserve and caution towards Catholicism from the professional classes and downright hostility among many working class communities.

Most of the adult population were denied the right to vote in parliamentary elections. Universal education of children had been introduced as late as 1870, and was still patchy in some areas of Britain. There was no financial support for those on hard times, although thousands of workhouses were built in the nineteenth century and society distinguished between the *deserving* and the *undeserving* poor. Life expectancy for the working class remained obstinately at the Victorian average of 40, although the new Liberal government of 1906 tried to improve the nation's health, introducing medical inspections in schools.

A decade later, when conscription to the armed forces was introduced in the First World War, the proportion of men turned down because of poor health was so high that the age limit was raised to 41 and subsequently to 51 for military service and 60 for civilian war work. Large numbers of those selected died from disease rather than as the result of enemy action.

Even the details of daily life in Edwardian England show us what a different world it was. As we begin to experience today the economic measures introduced by our current national government, we would not recognise the lives that social reformers discovered when they investigated the lives of ordinary working people living in towns at the dawn of the twentieth century. Researchers funded by the Rowntree Foundation reported on conditions in these terms:

> A family living upon the scale allowed for (the wages paid for unskilled labour) must never spend a penny on railway fare or omnibus. They must never go into the country unless they walk. They must never purchase a halfpenny newspaper or spend a penny to buy a ticket for a popular concert. They must write no letters to absent children for they cannot afford to pay the postage . . . The

> children must have no pocket money for dolls, marbles or sweets. The father must smoke no tobacco, and must drink no beer. The mother must never buy any pretty clothes . . . Should a child fall ill, it must be attended by the parish doctor; should it die, it must be buried by the parish. Finally, the wage earner must never be absent from his work for a single day.

A more localised account of such poverty is contained in the Statement of Adoption of Grays Thurrock Free Library, written in 1893. Recognising that it would be all but impossible to buy reading material for the new library, the authorities asked for help from generous donors who lived in more affluent areas. To further this cause, they outlined the level of poverty in the area.

> In proportion to its population Grays is one of the poorest places in the Kingdom, in proof of which it may be mentioned that, whereas the average rateable value per head is £5 for England and Wales, the total rateable value of Grays is only £31,250, which, with a population exceeding 13,000, averages only £2 8s 0d per head or less than half the usual figure. A considerable population of *very poor* persons, as well as a large number of the labouring classes earning moderate wages, have been brought into the parish by the creation of the great Docks at Tilbury, but as these Docks are situated outside the parish boundaries, they contribute absolutely nothing to its revenues, though adding greatly to its burdens.
>
> The rapid increase of population in our midst, which has risen from 3,000 in 1871 to over 13,000 now, has necessitated the erection of two large Board Schools, and the creation of a School Debt, which after many instalments have been repaid, still amounts to upwards of £13,000. In addition to this it has become needful to construct a most expensive system of sewers and sewage disposal, for which the Local Board has been compelled to borrow no less than £42,000.
>
> The parish indebtedness therefore amounts to the large sum of £62,000, or more than double its rateable value, and equal to nearly £5 per head.
>
> The rates are nearly 8 shillings in the pound, and will have to be advanced by another sixpence in the pound next year.
>
> From these causes it is hopeless for this Committee to expect large voluntary subscriptions from the few employers of labour in the parish, who find themselves already labouring under exceptionally heavy rating burdens, and we venture to think that our municipal poverty affords us reasonable ground for troubling non-residents with an appeal for help in the commencement of our undertaking.

> Gifts of Books, old or new, Reviewers' Copies, Publishers' Surplus Copies or Soiled Copies, indeed, all Literature suitable for the shelves of a Free Library, will be thankfully received and acknowledged by the Committee.

The opening of the little library appears to have been mired in debt and for the next decade there was little, if any, improvement in the community's level of poverty, as a 1902 letter indicates. The letter, from a Mr. G.H. Silverwood, was addressed to the man reputed to be the richest man in the world, Andrew Carnegie. Born in Scotland in 1835, he moved as a child to the United States. From humble beginnings he built a vast industrial empire, mostly in steel production, and sold all of his holdings in 1901, donating most of this money to charitable causes until his death in 1919. It is believed that he founded over 2,800 libraries.

> SIR,
> I venture to address the following statements and remarks to you in the hope that you may be induced thereby to take an interest in this our Town, and may be disposed to help it, as you have so munificently helped others, which, I make bold to say, are not more needy and more deserving than Grays, qualities which it is known appeal successfully to your aid.
>
> Grays is a town of some 14,000 inhabitants, situated 20 miles east of London, on the north bank of the Thames, and served by the London, Tilbury and Southend Railway. It is one of the centres of the Portland Cement industry, and has extensive brick and whiting works. Owing to its proximity to Tilbury Docks a large proportion of dock labourers and bargemen reside here.
>
> From this you will gather that the residents are mainly, I might say almost exclusively, of the labouring class. Indeed with the exception of the retail tradesmen, a few of the lower dock officials, and the usual sprinkling of doctors, lawyers, schoolmasters and ministers of religion, there is practically no middle class. As a proof of this I might mention that the total number of houses in the town is 2,487, of which only 451 have a rateable value of £15 and over; and the average weekly earnings of the inhabitants probably do not exceed thirty shillings.
>
> Thirty years ago Grays was only a waterside village with a population of about 2,000, and the main increase has taken place during the last twenty years. This received its greatest impetus from the construction of Tilbury Docks, when fully 2,000 navvies invaded the Town and district. At this time there was no local governing body, and when the first local Board was formed in 1886 it found itself face to face with a most deplorable state of affairs – hundreds

of jerry-built houses run up by speculative builders, no roads or footpaths, and worst of all no system of sewerage.

You will, therefore, readily understand that the Town was put to great expense in the way of providing school accommodation, constructing sewerage works, making up roads and footpaths etc. So heavy indeed is the financial burden upon us (the total indebtedness amounting to £96,147 16s. 5d., nearly £7 per head) and so low is the total rateable value (£41,339 10s. 0d., barely £3 per head of the inhabitants) that for several years past the local rates have averaged close upon 10 shillings in the £, and on some occasions have exceeded this sum, yet in spite of this the Local Council contributes 50 guineas per annum to the Passmore Edwards Cottage Hospital; the working men arrange an annual demonstration and make regular collections in the various works for the same Institution, and seven years ago the inhabitants generally decided by a considerable majority to still further tax themselves that they might provide for their own good and that of their children a Free Library, and it is on behalf of this Institution that I, as Chairman of the Committee, make this appeal to you.

Our accommodation consists of a Reading Room and a Lending Library. The former measures 27 feet by 15 feet and in the winter evenings it is so crowded that men frequently have to leave owing to their inability to find a seat or even room to stand and read. A room formerly used as a Kitchen has been fitted up to serve as a Lending Library. We now possess 1,884 volumes. I might add that Mr. Passmore Edwards has signified his interest in, and appreciation of our work by presenting us with 500 volumes, and various neighbours have given small parcels of books. Our work is suffering from want of more ample accommodation, and we are quite unable to help ourselves.

The Public Libraries Act permits the Council to levy a rate of 1d in the £ to support our Institution, and this produces £172 per annum, out of which we have to pay the Librarian's salary, rent etc., purchase newspapers and add new books.

To sum up, Sir, I set before you as an object worthy of your consideration the provision of a building which shall afford suitable accommodation for a Public Reading Room and a Free Library in this struggling town of 14,000 inhabitants, which possesses no public buildings but a Fire Station and a Police Station, and no adequate facilities for indoor recreation and intellectual improvement.

I need scarcely add that should you desire it, a small deputation from the Committee will be pleased to wait upon you and supply you with any additional information you may wish to have.

Mr. Silverwood was also Headmaster of Palmers Endowed School, which developed and extended during the twentieth century, eventually moving to a new site to become our local Sixth Form College.

It is difficult not to be moved by the difficult conditions under which these people lived, and the noble efforts even the poorest made for self-improvement. The image of a crowded Reading Room, where working men would stand in the evenings after a day's manual labour, is a haunting one. It certainly had an effect on Andrew Carnegie, who responded to the plea with the gift of three thousand pounds to build a new Free Public Lending Library in Grays.

Grays Free Library : Opened November 1903

The story of Catholicism in our area had begun in 1903, when a few Catholic families joined together to build a church. They were given a plot of land in Herd Lane, Corringham, by Messrs Kynoch. This family owned an explosives factory, built on the marshes below Fobbing in 1898. The isolated site of the factory was chosen deliberately, as there was some risk of an accident which would have taken many more lives in a populated area. The Kynochs brought some 80 workers down from Birmingham, many of them of Irish descent, and the firm was anxious to provide a regular Catholic service for their employees. In the initial stages of the company's development there was a dispute between the company and the government about the agreed contracts and some of the work people left. In later years, however, the company thrived and expanded rapidly, particularly during the First World War.

Kynochtown School : Opened in 1899 for the children of the factory workers

A Mr. Curtis, the part owner of a brick yard near Fobbing Creek, Curtis and Scott, provided the bricks for the new church. Whilst the church was being built, the Parish Priest in Barking, the Rev. Dean Clemens, rode over on horseback once a month to say Mass, hear Confessions and conduct baptisms at the house of Mrs. Carmen, which served as a Mass centre. The doughty priest would stay overnight then ride back to his parish the following day.

The new church was dedicated to St. Francis de Sales, the French priest and visionary who had worked to convert people back to the Catholic faith. Interestingly, he is the patron saint of writers.

The priests from Barking continued their journeys on horseback to visit the church until 1907. Diocesan records reveal that in 1906 Father Van Meenan in Tilbury had some responsibility for the Catholics at Corringham, but that he wished to relinquish this as he had too much work to do. He reported in March 1906 that there were only 50 Catholics in the area and that interest on the loan to build the small church was being paid by Mr. Curtis, on condition that a Mass was said there at least once a month. Father Carless later commented that the mortgage was a heavy one, considering the quality of the building. The mortgage was for £1,530, and this was after the free land and the free bricks.

When Father Van Meenan stated that he could not provide Mass at both Tilbury and Corringham, he was instructed by the Westminster Archdiocese to obtain a supply priest so that both areas could be served. By July 1906, the Archdiocese was providing funds for the extra Mass to be said. In August 1906, the Franciscans were considered as possible priests for Corringham, but by November a decision was made to serve Corringham from Grays. It seemed as though Corringham was not regarded by the Diocese as an attractive venture; it was certainly a responsibility that few were willing to shoulder. By July 1907, the priest-in-charge at Corringham was named as Father Gilbert, who was based at Grays.

The first full time priest was appointed in 1910. It was Father Charles Carless, who had first said Mass in the Stanford-le-Hope barn the previous year. Father Carless was priest for the new parish of Corringham, but he had responsibility for Stanford-le-Hope, where, in Park Road, he rented both the barn which now served as a Mass centre and a nearby house in which to live. The house was leased at £36 a year from a Mrs. F.J. Kerly and the barn (and shed) were leased at £10 per year from Walter Tyrrell Esq. There was the option to purchase the freehold of the house during the first year for £700, but this was not taken up.

The Barn Mass Centre and School of St. Mary circa 1909

Although Corringham's small church was the centre of his parish and Stanford no more than a mission, it was the latter that proved to be successful, even before the church at Stanford-le-Hope was built. By 1911, Father Carless was recording that annual diocesan collections in Corringham, for the African Missions, Diocesan Education Fund, Lenten Alms and Peter's Pence, among others, were 'almost nil' and were added to the Stanford accounts.

The interior of the Barn Mass Centre
(from a painting by C.R. Sharp)

Charles William Carless, the son of a friendly society clerk, was born in London in August 1871, of part-German stock. With his brothers and sister, he grew up in Islington. The family was non-Catholic, but he was received into the Catholic Church in 1890, and subsequently trained for the priesthood at St. Edmund's College, Ware. He was a student of the Archdiocese of Westminster, part of which would become the Diocese of Brentwood in 1917.

Ordained in 1903, Father Carless was assistant priest at SS Peter and Paul in Rosoman Street, London, and then in Wood Green. After short term postings in Parsons Green, Brook Green and Rainham, he was appointed to the new Mission of Stanford-le-Hope, which also served Corringham.

There was considerable poverty in the new parish. Diocesan surveys listed it as the 'poorest mission' in the Archdiocese of Westminster. When we are able to read contemporary surveys of London life at this time, where many children went barefoot, an understanding can be formed of some of the challenges Father Carless faced.

Father Charles Carless

He experienced anti-Catholic sentiment at first hand, and often had stones thrown at him. Yet he gradually gained the respect and even the love of the local community as he walked around the area distributing groceries to the poor and needy, Protestant and Catholic alike. This same priest would climb onto the roof of the old barn to carry out repairs. Indeed, a picture of this was published in the Catholic newspaper *The Universe* as part of a fund raising exercise to gather money to build a proper Catholic church in Stanford-le-Hope.

Father Carless made frequent use of the *Catholic Times* to appeal for donations to build a church in Stanford-le-Hope. A typical appeal on 14th April 1911 shows a picture of the barn, titled 'The Temporary Church, Stanford-le-Hope' with the following text:

PLEASE HELP THIS –

THE POOREST MISSION IN THE ARCHDIOCESE

The dearest wish of the all-poor congregation is to have a suitable church, before next winter, to replace the Barn – so cold and draughty. NO OTHER CHURCH FOR MILES AROUND.
A Site has already been secured, and if every family of readers of the "Catholic Times" will send me only 6 pence, building operations can be begun at once. MASSES FOR BENEFACTORS.
This appeal is made with confidence to the generous Catholic public, ever ready to help according to their means. Please send your offering to

Yours gratefully, (Rev.) CHARLES CARLESS
STANFORD-LE-HOPE, ESSEX

The following month, there was a small news item in the *Catholic Times.*

> The Rev. Father Carless still needs help for his struggling mission, and those of our readers who have not as yet responded to his earnest appeal, which has been appearing on the Diocesan News page for some weeks past, are urged to do so at once. As an evidence of the popularity of Father Carless amongst his non-Catholic neighbours, he has just been requested to join the local Coronation Festivities Committee.

Father Carless saw the opportunity latent in this coronation. In June, 1911, he writes in the *Catholic Times*

> DEAR READER,
> Whatever your station in life, you are preparing to celebrate the Coronation of our King. If you are blessed with means, you have perhaps already secured seats to view the procession at a high price; you have made provision for the entertainment of your friends.
> **HERE** we are striving to build a *Home* for the *King of Kings*: you are all princes in the House of God, and *you* will expect to be crowned for your good works.
>
> Where there's a will there's a way,
> Please send your donation TO-DAY.
> And as you read this little verse,
> All you do is to open your purse
> With a cheerful heart
> To give us a start.
> And if not much all-told,
> The reward is a hundred-fold.
>
> Send your crown (or half crown) **NOW** – it's a good and safe investment – to FATHER CHARLES CARLESS,
> STANFORD-LE-HOPE, ESSEX

Of course, raising money was hard at a time when poverty was so prevalent, but Father Carless was not one to give up easily. As the building fund began to grow, and perhaps encouraged by his 'little verse', he plunged again into poetry to stimulate the generosity of the readers of the *Catholic Times.*

> We're getting impatient at Stanford-le-Hope
> For our present old barn's quite unable to cope
> With the needs of the this parish which grows ev'ry day,
> And it *does* seem a pity to send folks away.
>
> The sum we are asking is not very great,
> But until it is ours we must certainly wait.
> If every kind reader would send us a shilling
> The church we'd soon be completing and filling.

Six hundred and sixty gold sovereigns is not
In my estimation a very great lot
  To pay for a church to seat two hundred people,
  (You see we're content to be minus a steeple.)

We've already collected three hundred and fifty
Subscribed by good friends who're both generous and thrifty,
  For thrift in the accurate sense of the word
  Is money that people have lent to the Lord.

I want *you* to help us to get in the rest.
You'll surely say "Yes" to my urgent request.
  A shilling is all that I ask you to send
  Tho' a cheque for five pounds would in no way offend!!

Post your donation *to-day* to FATHER CARLESS, Stanford-le-Hope, Essex. There's no time to be lost.

By the beginning of 1912, Father Carless had almost reached the two thirds proportion of the construction costs that would make the building of the little church possible. Benefactors were offered Weekly Mass and daily memento if the last £20 could be found. The priest admitted that the offertory collection was so small that it did not cover existing parish costs, and so all depended on the generosity of donors.

In 1911 a site for the new church had indeed been found. It was owned by a Mr. Blyth. A Mr. and Mrs. Burgess contributed funds, as did The London and Thames Haven Oil Wharves Ltd., a large conglomerate with business premises on the banks of the River Thames. This company continued to support the parish for many years, donating a regular annual sum that must have helped the early days of the new parish. Father Carless is credited with raising most of the funding for the church himself.

After the purchase of the site, a decision was made to build the church in what was called the Byzantine style. This might suggest a building with extensive ornamentation and ambitious domes, containing lavish decoration and, perhaps, intricate mosaics. If this was not apparent in the finished church, the second decision, to build using *considere* methods certainly was. This involved the use of reinforced concrete for the main shell of the building, a process that became more prevalent as the years passed but one that was novel in the Edwardian era. We are not able to state who made this bold decision, but it would have involved Father Carless, whose close association with Stanford-le-Hope would continue until 1919, when he was sent to the coastal parish of Walton on the Naze and Frinton.

The building of our Parish Church : 1912

When the church was completed in 1913, at a cost of nine hundred pounds, it was originally dedicated to Saint Joseph. On 22nd June of that year, the first Mass was said by Cardinal Bourne and Monsignor Jackman. The parish records show that among the congregation were Mr. and Mrs. Burgess, who had helped to purchase the site, Mr. and Mrs. Booth, Mr. and Mrs. Twydell and family, Mr. and Mrs. McDade and Mr. and Mrs. Treston. It was considered that the church could accommodate up to 150 people. An estimate was made that the total number of practising Catholics in this area was between 150 and 200 people, living as far apart as the outskirts of Leigh-on-Sea and Grays. By the end of 1913, the church was insured for a total of one thousand three hundred pounds, suggesting that Father Carless had managed to call in a few favours when the original building costs had been agreed.

The opening of the church was covered by the *Catholic Times* in its issue of 27th June 1913.

> A new church, dedicated to St. Joseph, was opened on Tuesday morning by Cardinal Bourne at Stanford-le-Hope, Essex. A mission was founded there some four years ago, and when Father Carless arrived there shortly afterwards he had no better place in which to say Mass than a somewhat dilapidated barn. This served, for want of a better sanctuary, until the present time. The new church, which will accommodate 250 persons, is built in what is described as the

"Considere" style. The site for the church was presented some time ago, and now practically the whole cost of the new edifice (£900) has been collected by Father Carless. There are between 150 and 200 Catholics in the district, many of them living some distance from the village. Grays is the nearest mission on one side, and Leigh on Sea on the other. The barn is at present serving as a school for the Catholic children of the district.

The opening of Our Lady and St. Joseph's Church : 1913

When Cardinal Bourne arrived, the church, which stands near the old Parish Church on the London Road to Southend, was gaily decorated with bunting. His Eminence presided at Mass, celebrated by Father McKenna, with Fathers Gilbert and Deady as Deacon and Sub-Deacon. At the throne were Canon Edmund Egan and Mgr. Canon de Wiart, and Mgr. Jackman was Master of Ceremonies. Father Carless assisted the choir, which rendered the music effectively, with Mrs. Fitzmaurice at the organ and Mr. Fenwick as leader.

Father Carless, effectively reduced to the ranks for this first Mass in his church, must have hoped for words that would help to create positive links between the new parish and its non-Catholic surroundings. Cardinal Bourne, however, had other ideas. Citing the anniversary of the execution of John Fisher, Bishop of Rochester in 1535, for refusing to acknowledge Henry VIII as the Head of the Church in England, Cardinal Bourne focused his attention on the absolute need to challenge the religious authority of the Church of England, including "those who now possess the ancient church a few steps away". The Catholic community had a "real, compelling duty" to build churches throughout the land that would oppose the religious stance of those who still occupied the original Catholic churches, and used them to promote the mistaken view that the sovereign and not the Pope had supreme authority in ecclesiastical matters.

Cardinal Bourne saw the Church of England as too willing to forget about the circumstances which brought about its foundation, but this should not be permitted.

> Our Anglican friends would like, nowadays, to forget about Henry VIII. They try to make themselves believe sometimes that the lust and passion of Henry VIII had very little to do really with the change of religion in England. … If Henry VIII had not been a man of lust and passions he would never have thought of separating himself from the unity of the Catholic Church.

Later that day, Cardinal Bourne returned to Westminster, leaving Father Carless to establish the fledgling parish and to build friendly links with his non-Catholic neighbours.

The new church effectively changed the structure of the parish. Stanford had been the centre of a larger group of Catholics, but they had been served by their Parish Priest who was based at St. Francis de Sales, Corringham. Now the balance shifted, with the parish centering on St. Joseph's and the little church at Corringham becoming less significant.

Father Carless was now able to move from rented accommodation in Park Road, where he had kept a small chapel and administered baptisms. He found a house in Scratton Road, nearer to the new church.

The church soon became known as Our Lady and Saint Joseph's. It saw its first marriage on January 13th 1914. Henry Martin and Josephine Carmen were married. It seems probable that the bride's family were the ones who had offered their house as a Mass centre before the building of the church of Saint Francis de Sales in Corringham. There were on average 40 adults attending Sunday Mass in the new church, but Father Snell recorded that there were 'hardly any' Communions. The priest felt obliged to explain this to his Diocese.

> With regard to Communions, the absence of an early Mass on Sundays, combined with the long distance many come, retards the frequency of Communions. A certain proportion come to Communion on Feast Days of importance, occurring on a weekday.

Father Carless did not choose to elaborate on what he called 'a certain proportion'.

Interior of the new Church in 1915

It has to be acknowledged that the interior of Our Lady and Saint Joseph's Church was quite spartan in appearance, and there was little attention paid to heating. There was a fine altar of marble and other stone, given to the church by an anonymous donor as thanksgiving after his wife had recovered from a serious illness. There were the simple chairs for the congregation. The walls, floors and ceiling, however, bore testament to the building method chosen, and were bare concrete. The ceiling was as flat as the floor for the architects had designed a flat roof to the building, an unusual choice to those with a passing knowledge of English climate. In the wintertime, the interior of the church was very cold indeed, although perhaps no colder than that old barn first used in 1909. People do seem to have been hardier then, when central heating was merely something archaeologists unearthed in the excavations of Roman villas.

Detail of the Altar at our Church : 1917

Parish finances were in a precarious position and nothing went to waste. Financial returns included income from the sale of grass, seventy five pence. With an annual offertory income of some thirty six pounds, or about seventy pence a week, the parish relied on much of its income from the saying of special Masses. At Corringham, annual offertory income averaged no more than seven pence a week. Yet somehow money had to be found to meet the expenses of the parish, and even the smallest details of expenditure were faithfully recorded. One entry made in 1912 recorded the sum of £1.35 for the conveyance of the priest on '9 wet Sundays' as he moved between Stanford and Corringham to say Mass. As there is no other reference to dryer days, we must infer that these were cost free and the priest was obliged to walk around his parish, no small task given its growing size.

Fortunately, the parish was able to rely on donations from what was known as The Gillow Trust. When John Gillow died in the village of Stock in 1894, his will established a charitable foundation to help the Archdiocese of Westminster. He offered a substantial home, Lilystone Hall to the Archbishop to use as a country residence, but this was politely declined. This fine family home, now a listed building, contained a chapel that was used as the village's Catholic church until the local school was converted to St. Joseph's Church, Stock. Regular payments from the Trust in the early years of our parish helped in its struggle to become solvent.

With two main church buildings to maintain, there was a lot of responsibility on the Parish Priest. In the first year of the new church in Stanford, St. Francis de Sales itself needed repairs to its exterior, caused by what Father Carless called 'stormy weather'. Of course by then there were storms elsewhere, and later that year most of Europe was involved in the Great War. Although the area was less threatened by the immediacy of the war than in World War Two, it was now necessary to insure the church and school against bomb damage. With the exaggerated fears of the new military flying machines, the parish had to pay more for this insurance than for the more mundane fire insurance.

The area saw a large, if temporary, increase in population when war work increased at the explosives factory at Kynochtown. Many hundreds of women were now employed, working twelve hour shifts, and no less than 6,000 additional men were taken on. A target for Zeppelin air raids, it posed many hazards for its workers. Those who became overwhelmed by the chemicals in the air inside the factory were allowed to go outside and lie down in the fresh air until they recovered. Undeterred by such trifles, in July 1915 the company successfully applied for the construction of an additional factory to manufacture cordite.

A model village of forty houses was built, together with a school, shop and an institute, which was opened as a working men's club. The village postmaster who owned the shop was quoted as saying

> We are the Post Office, the Butcher, the Baker and the Candlestick Maker. It has taken some time for the Post office to find us at the end of the earth here, but we've got a real postal address and soon we shall have a real railway.

Kynochtown Shop and Post Office

The parish supported those who at first volunteered and then were conscripted to fight for their country, contributing to the upkeep of a Soldiers' Club Room in Stanford and subscribing to the running of the local volunteer force. Although the parish still relied heavily on the Gillow Fund to keep its finances in order, it was possible for Father Carless to report at the end of 1915 that whilst the parish did not have any money, neither did it owe any. The financial deficit in Stanford was exactly balanced by the small credit account at Corringham. Times were moving on in other ways too, for the priest recorded the sum of ninety-five pence paid out that year for Motor Hire when he visited the sick of the parish.

The boundaries of the new parish began to expand, attesting to the success of the Stanford-le-Hope Catholic community and their priest, Father Carless. Included now were Basildon, Bulphan, Corringham, Fobbing, Horndon on the Hill, Kynochtown (later Coryton), Laindon, Linford, Mucking, Nevedon, Pitsea, Shell Haven, Thames Haven and Vange. In 1921, the village of Orsett was added to the parish, and the infirmary there paid fifteen pounds per year for the services of a priest.

We must assume that these villages were rather smaller than many of them are today, although the distances between them would have been just the same. Indeed, by 1925 Father Snell estimated the size of the parish as one hundred square miles. The parish itself was supervised by

Canon McKenna of Westcliff. Supervision later passed to Tilbury and then to Grays.

The little school attached to the church had also grown, at least in numbers. By 1917, it had one hundred pupils, with 51 Catholics and 49 non-Catholics. The school buildings, like the church itself, were insured against attacks from enemy aircraft. This aspect of modern warfare was only in its infancy, although there were over fifty air raids recorded on Britain during the First World War and over five hundred people were killed.

The parish continued its support of the Soldiers' Club in Stanford, with an annual subscription of sixty pence. In 1917, the parish received an unexpected contribution to its funds in the form of a fifty pounds donation for Services to the Troops. This made a substantial difference to parish finances, although the arrangement was a temporary one, as Father Carless carefully recorded.

If the church was the hub of the parish, Father Carless was on the move again. The new presbytery was now on Southend Road, opposite the church, but there was still no permanent home for the Parish Priest. Although further land was bought by the parish from 1915 onwards, there were no funds for a permanent presbytery by the time that Father Charles Carless left Stanford-le-Hope in 1919 for his new parish of Walton-on-the-Naze and Frinton-on-Sea. The Sunday offertory remained fixed at seventy pence a week, from a Catholic population of 80 adults and 70 children.

In 1923, Father Carless became Parish Priest of Custom House. He was also Port Chaplain to the Royal London Docks. His charitable work continued amongst the poor. Those who remembered his distribution of food to the poor in Stanford-le-Hope would not have been surprised that his later years were characterised by similar charity. Recorded in diocesan archives as 'an assiduous visitor', he used his private income to assist those in poverty.

One story records that when he became concerned about the gambling amongst men in one of his parishes, which was depriving poor families of much needed income, he organised his own betting syndicate, accepting wagers from the men but distributing any winnings to their wives. Not surprisingly, the Bishop of Brentwood had to instruct him to stop this project as it was not in the best interests of the Church. The name of the parish is now lost. This is such a good story that we might almost wish that Stanford-le-Hope were the parish.

At his death in February 1939, The Tablet commented that Father Carless had been 'full of schemes and projects for the better social life of his poor congregation. Father Carless seldom appeared to rest from his spiritual duties.'

Father James Campbell

Father Carless was replaced as Parish Priest by Father Campbell, who remained in post until November 1920. James William Campbell was born in Queenstown, County Cork, Ireland in 1884, the second of eight children. His father, James Hugh Campbell, was the Town Clerk, a magistrate and variously Vice Consul for Venezuela and Vice Consul for Spain. When the Cunard shipping company abandoned the port of Queenstown as a base for its fast steamers, James Hugh Campbell wrote a book in protest against the decision. *The Cunard Company and Irish Interests*, Dublin 1910, castigated the steamship owners for their abandonment of his home town.

James Campbell, his son, was educated at St. Sulpice in Paris, having been accepted as a student sponsored by the Archdiocese of Westminster.

Father Campbell was ordained in Paris in 1909. He served in no fewer than seven parishes before coming to Stanford-le-Hope, where he was the Parish Priest for just over eighteen months. It does not seem to have been a happy time for either Father Campbell or his parishioners. There were many disagreements that resulted in letters to the Bishop of Brentwood. Some parishioners complained about the frequency of Mass, or rather its infrequency. They made charges about the church being locked, the lack of opportunity for Confessions and the attitude of their new Parish Priest. On his part, Father Campbell singled out individual parishioners for criticism, characterised many of his congregation as trouble-makers and was reported to have commented 'very strongly from the Altar-rails on the lying slanders of certain people who had reported him to the Bishop'. The following year, Father Campbell left Stanford-le-Hope.

After one month as Parish Priest in Witham, Father Campbell applied to join the foreign missions in China. By 1924, ill health caused him to return home to Ireland. After postings in Portsmouth, Grayshott, Alderney and Didcot, he became chaplain of Saint Anne's Nursing home in Wokingham, Berkshire, where he died in November 1940.

Father Charles Snell

If Father Carless had done much to help create the parish of Stanford-le-Hope, much of this work was consolidated by Father Charles Snell, who was appointed on November 10th 1920 and remained Parish Priest until his death in February 1949. He thus saw the turbulent decades of the nineteen twenties and thirties, and the trials of the Second World War and its aftermath.

Charles Lionel Henry Snell was born in Dalston, Stoke Newington on November 10th, 1887. He was the third of five surviving children in a non-Catholic family. His father, Ernest Joseph Snell, was a bank clerk from Tiverton, Devon. Charles Snell was educated privately and then worked for a number of foreign banks in London. In 1910, he was received into the Catholic Church, and was confirmed the following year. Charles Snell continued working in the City, studying Latin and other subjects in the evening at St. Augustine's House of Studies, Walworth. In 1913, when he was almost 26, he entered St. Edmund's College, Ware, and he was ordained priest just before the end of the Great War in May 1918.

When Bishop Ward selected the seminarians to serve in the newly created Diocese of Brentwood, he chose this student whose practical and infectious enthusiasm for the Church had impressed his fellows at St. Edmund's College.

Father Snell was appointed as assistant priest at St. George's, Walthamstow in June 1918, and served briefly in Leigh-on-Sea in 1920 before taking charge of Stanford-le-Hope in November 1920, becoming the Parish Priest in January 1921. Father Snell remained in Stanford-le-Hope for the rest of his life. As our Parish Priest for over twenty-eight years he is by far the longest serving priest in the history of the parish.

When Father Snell first came to Stanford-le-Hope, it was just two years after the end of the Great War. Many people had hope for a brave new world. Social change was in the air, and our parishioners, along with the rest of the country, must have expected radical improvements in their way of life. Lloyd George had famously promised "A land fit for heroes" and there was a groundswell of optimism running through the country. Britain was one of the victors in the First World War, it now had the largest navy in the history of the world and was still head of the largest empire there had ever been.

Father Charles Snell

Yet those expectations were soon to be dashed. The control of power that had been taken by the government during the course of the war was soon released and power returned to special interest groups such as mine and factory owners and transport companies. Without wartime regulation, Lloyd George's promise soon sounded grandiose and unrealistic. The wave of new house building came to a stop when the money ran out and by 1922 all the dreams of a new world had evaporated. Even the Empire was experiencing growing unrest, and the troubles in Ireland proved to be the precursor of many struggles for independence as Britain began to realise it could not keep people subjugated by force.

Much has been said about the lost generation, the soldiers who died and the families they would have had in the years after the war. Britain lost some 250,000 men and the world now seemed full of badly injured ex-servicemen. Many of the young women who were to marry those killed in the war chose not to marry and there was a curious gap of young men that was noticeable for many years in workplaces and leisure crowds.

There were a few social changes. The school leaving age was raised, although only to 14. After their major contribution to the war effort, there was now serious talk of votes for women, but they had to wait until 1928 before they were to be treated the same as men. During this decade, however, many people went hungry and the years after the 1929 Wall

Street Crash would swell the ranks of the unemployed, the poor and the hungry.

As for Stanford-le-Hope, it had troubles of its own. The Bishop of Brentwood had expressed doubts about the viability of the parish and had considered closing it down entirely. If Stanford-le-Hope is now celebrating its centenary, it nearly didn't see its first ten years as an independent parish. Father Snell managed to persuade the Bishop to give him the chance to consolidate the work of Father Carless. A grant of one hundred pounds per year was made by the Diocese to assist the venture.

In the meantime, the Parish Priest was obliged to continue his nomadic existence. Father Snell lodged at The Laurels in First Avenue, and then moved to a one room bed sit in Third Avenue, where he remained until the parish presbytery was at last built.

Permission to build the presbytery had to be obtained from the Bishop of Brentwood. In his submission to the Bishop in March 1921, Father Snell promised that no debt would be incurred. No building work would begin until all the funding had been provided and the design of the presbytery would be subject to two constraints. The first was that the presbytery would harmonise with the existing church; the second that the servant's quarters (presumably a reference to a female housekeeper) would be entirely separated from the rest of the house.

A week later, Father Snell felt compelled to strengthen his submission by referring to the major sources for the funding. These were two directors of the London and Thames Haven Oil Wharves, Mr. Burgess and Mr. Angilogoff, described by Father Snell as 'splendid Catholics'. Their company wished to promote the development of Stanford-le-Hope and had already donated a large tract of land as a recreation ground for the village. Father Snell advised the Bishop that the company was building some 100 homes in the area and these directors would be able to negotiate the building of the presbytery 'at cost'.

Father Snell asked the Bishop to allow him to conduct the work of the building from Stanford-le-Hope directly, rather than going through the bureaucracy of the Brentwood Diocese. He now stated that he would not 'actually have the cash' for the project, raising the prospect of loans and debts and concerns about who would hold responsibility for these. Mr. Burgess was described as 'frantically keen' on the building of the new presbytery, although he expressed the view that Father Snell should try to find some of the funds himself. This was to prove something of a stumbling block.

Father Snell's attempts to raise money from additional sources did not meet with early success. Although he contacted well-known Catholics seeking help, he was obliged to admit that "I … have had no response whatever so far." He asked the Bishop if he would put his own name on the subscription list, stating that this would give added status to the appeal. He was aware that at a time of great poverty the Bishop expected his clergy to solve such difficulties without seeking diocesan backing, but it does not seem that the Bishop was eager to become involved. In effect, Father Snell was in a quagmire. Help would be forthcoming from wealthy Catholics only if he could raise some of the funds himself, his own efforts to do this were marginal at best and the Bishop did not wish to become directly involved.

Mr. Burgess summed up the problem in May 1921.

> The house is not for me but for the Church and you, and if you cannot first get the assistance of your own Authorities to enable you to get a start, it seems rather out of place to invoke my aid.

There is no indication here of the 'frantic' keenness of this benefactor to see a presbytery built. The presbytery was finally paid for by a loan of £1,185 from the Diocese of Brentwood. Some of the original supporters of the scheme did provide private contributions, but it became Father Snell's direct responsibility to fund the interest payments on the commercial loan and to attempt to repay the capital. His attempts to find private funding to reduce the debt were not successful, and some parishioners cruelly reminded him that before his arrival there was no debt to worry about.

A local benefactor, Mrs. Barnescone, furnished the presbytery at a cost of three hundred pounds. The Bishop of Brentwood formally opened the presbytery on 14th June 1923, and it has been the base for our Parish Priests ever since. The church and its new presbytery were bounded by the small village of Stanford-le-Hope on one side and by open country on all other sides, a rather different aspect than the one we see today.

In 1923, Father Snell estimated the total population living in the parish as about six thousand. There were just one hundred and sixty Catholics in the parish, with 111 adults and 49 children. This may partly explain the decline in the numbers of children attending school, as the school now had only fifty children, half the number recorded five years before. There was still a mix of Catholic children, 39, and non-Catholics, 11. The school had two classrooms separated by a glass partition, a large playground, a small room with a sink, two cloakrooms and five lavatories.

The priest's inventory of the school stated that it had desks and accommodation for 100 children together with '<u>all</u> the necessary furniture for the proper and efficient education of children'. These are listed as books, easels, blackboards, piano, museum cases, teacher's desk or rostrum, cupboards, pictures, rulers, pens and ink. Perhaps defeated by the task, Father Snell adds 'etc., etc., etc., etc.'

Father Snell's work in establishing the permanence of his parish at Stanford-Le-Hope was rewarded by a steady increase in the number of his parishioners during the nineteen twenties and thirties. With Linford, East Tilbury, Corringham, Fobbing and Horndon-on-the Hill part of the growing parish, Father Snell was allocated an assistant priest to help him in his work. From 1932 to 1937, his assistant was Laurence Gilmartin, from 1937 to 1941 the assistant was Michael Hopkins, and during the rest of the war years he was helped by Eric Goldingay and, briefly, by John Boyle. Eric Goldingay, later Canon Goldingay, was to become the first Parish Priest of the Blessed (later Saint) Anne Line in South Woodford.

Father Snell made some attempts to improve the interior of the originally very bare church. At a religious level, Sanctuary lamps were installed in the church, one hanging from the roof in the centre of the church and one on the pier on the Gospel side of the Altar rails. Over the High Altar itself, there was a large painting of the Sacred Heart. The artist was Mr. Pernuddocke, a member of a non-Catholic religious order that had been established in the area. By 1924, statues of the Sacred Heart and Our Lady were installed at either end of the Altar rails. Stations of the Cross now adorned the walls of the church.

Outside the church, wooden gates were built as an entrance to the church grounds. An Angelus Bell was installed over the Sacristy. But the most striking feature was a life-size crucifix that was erected on the corner of the church property. Originally a wayside shrine in Belgium, the figure of Christ was severely damaged during the First World War and was thought to be beyond repair. Father (later Monsignor Canon) Van Meenan managed to salvage it and brought it to Brentwood. Initial examination suggested it was beyond repair, but fortunately Father Snell persuaded the Diocese to give it to the Stanford-le-Hope parish. Father

Snell and a leading parishioner, William McDade, worked together to restore the figure. Missing parts were recarved and the many cracks and splits were filled with red lead. When the restored figure was repainted and placed on a new cross built by Mr. McDade, it was placed under a roof shelter as protection against the elements. Subsequent repainting was carried out by Mr. McDade's daughter, Margaret. As C.R. Sharp commented in his excellent brochure produced to mark the Golden Jubilee of the parish in 1963:

> That is how the figure of Christ, that looked down on scenes of war and desolation in a ravished Belgium, came to Stanford to look down on the peaceful scene of an English parish.

Meanwhile, Father Snell and his parishioners were busy raising money to build a church at Vange, which then formed part of the parish. By 1924, enough money had been raised to buy a site and build a small church at a cost of five hundred pounds. The church was dedicated to the Sacred Heart. To begin with, Mass was said at the new church once a month, but this soon became a weekly service. With just the one priest, this reduced the number of Masses that could be said at Stanford-le-Hope. Even though the Stanford-le-Hope parishioners were less than happy with a single Sunday Mass in their own church, it was thought better to accept this than to deprive the Vange congregation of their own weekly service. The Sunday Mass at Vange was said at 9.00 and the Stanford-le-Hope Mass at 10.30. Before the 1932 arrival of the first curate, Father Gilmartin, who could then assist with the saying of Mass, this must have called for some pretty nippy legwork from Father Snell.

In 1927 a fine marble altar, The Altar of Our Lady, was built, the gift of a parishioner, Mrs. Barnescone, who died before the work was completed. Father Snell estimated that there were now 320 Catholics in the parish, and a total population of just over ten thousand. In just a few years, the potential congregation had doubled and the area itself now had nearly twice as many residents.

In the same year, Father Joyce took charge of the parish for a while during the temporary indisposition of Father Snell. A native of County Kilkenny, John Joseph Joyce was born in 1894, the youngest child of Martin and Margaret Joyce. In the 1901 census, his mother was recorded as a widow and a farmer. She then lived with her family in Chapel Lane, Urlingford. After his initial education at Mount St. Joseph Abbey in County Tipperary and St. Kieran's College, Kilkenny, he was accepted as a student for the Diocese of Ossory. In January 1919, he successfully applied to Bishop Ward at the new Diocese of Brentwood, and was ordained the following month. The day after his ordination, he became assistant priest at Leyton.

Father Joyce took temporary charge of our parish from May to August 1927. He was appointed to take temporary charge of Saffron Walden in September 1927 and was appointed as the Parish Priest of Burnham-on-Crouch in October 1927. 1927 was quite a year for Father Joyce. Unfortunately, his health was not good and he had to resign from his post in 1935. By November of that year, Father Joyce was appointed as assistant priest at St. George's, Walthamstow, where he remained until his death in 1947. After a Requiem Mass celebrated by Father Kieran Joyce, a close relative, he was buried in the family plot in Urlingford, County Kilkenny.

During the nineteen twenties and thirties, many parishioners had commented on the very cold temperatures at Our Lady and St. Joseph's Church in the winter months. The concrete floor allowed cold to seep up from the ground, and such heat as there was escaped readily from the flat concrete roof. In 1938, Father Snell had this roof built over with a pitched roof that provided some degree of insulation. The work cost a thousand pounds, the money being provided by a single donation from a friend. After the war, the concrete floor was finally laid with wooden blocks, although this parquet flooring was not installed until after the departure of Father Snell's successor, Father Watson, in 1953.

The size of the congregation and that of the local population continued to increase. By 1932, there were 530 Catholics in the district and people living in the parish now numbered some twelve thousand six hundred. The average Sunday attendance at Mass was just under four hundred, divided between two Masses at Stanford, one at Vange and one at the new chapel at Horndon on the Hill. Father Snell's interest in the welfare of young people extended beyond his responsibilities in the church and the school. He became a member of the Recreation Ground Committee for the Stanford-le-Hope area, where he served enthusiastically for many years as the Bishop's nominee.

The school was also thriving. With the transfer of children from an earlier charitable project at Horndon on the Hill, there were now 155 pupils in the Junior School and the recently added Senior School. 80% of the pupils were from Catholic families. Strenuous efforts were made by Father Snell and others to have the school officially recognised by the Board of Education. This would serve to improve the status of the school and raise its standards by the employment of qualified teachers and the guidance of government education experts. The Sisters of Mercy at Wanstead were invited to take on the role of teaching in the school and they would become the school's first qualified teachers.

The wider picture was less encouraging. After the Wall Street Crash of 1929, the United States had begun to call in the loans made to Europe during and just after the First World War. One consequence of this was a big reduction in money available to stimulate the economy and a more parsimonious attitude towards those receiving the low levels of state benefit. With over three million people registered as unemployed, such benefits as existed were controlled by a stringent Means Test. The lot of ordinary working people would not improve in Britain until fears of impending war led to a drive towards rearmament and a gradual increase in wages. The doctor was still an unaffordable luxury for most, to be used only in a dire emergency. Many doctors hired men to call at the family homes of those they had treated, to collect something on account on a Friday, the national pay day. Whilst poverty did not match the conditions recorded in late Victorian and Edwardian times, and mortality rates were improving, most working class people in England had a poor diet, indifferent living conditions, a low standard of education, and little enough help from the state in old age. Perhaps there was a recognition of the desperate condition of many people in the parish when Father Snell answered the diocesan enquiry about whether the tabernacle in the church was proof against fire and theft with the words 'Against fire but hardly against theft in these days'.

The population of the district and the number of Catholics continued to grow in number. By 1935, there were 600 Catholics in a total population of thirteen thousand. Sunday Mass was attended by an average of 338 people and the school, while still viable, had seen a slight decrease in its numbers to 123 pupils. The Parish Priest and his curate were kept busy. The wards at the Orsett Infirmary were visited every week, there were new responsibilities in Vange, and the Sisters of Mercy were able to instruct the children there in weekly catechism. With the sick to be visited, the poor and needy supported and new Catholics welcomed into the parish, there was not much time for leisure. And then there was the ever-pressing matter of the finances. Father Snell had taken out a £3,000 loan to help pay for the improvements to St. Joseph's School, and it was his responsibility to manage and reduce the loan.

In 1939, the parish capital debt which stood at £2,700 was reduced by some £200 when the Bishop of Brentwood donated that amount. Father

Snell was effusive in his thanks to the Bishop for his generosity. At the same time, Father Snell contributed one thousand pounds himself, to reduce the overall debt to some fifteen hundred pounds. The Bishop agreed to pay off the outstanding sum over a period of nine years, although he made it quite clear that in his view this debt should really be paid by the Parish Priest of Stanford-le-Hope.

Debt continued to be an issue. On February 17th 1939, when Father Snell asked the Bishop's permission to carry out some improvements to the church, he was quick to point out that there would be no debt incurred in the work. The improvements comprised two new stained glass windows in the Sanctuary, one of St. Joseph and one of Our Lady of Lourdes, the replacement of a plaster figure of Our Lady by a marble figure, to be placed on the Lady Altar, renovations to the church roof and the provision of some heating in the church. All of this was to be paid for by the donations of local parishioners. The Bishop gave his permission for these alterations, but stipulated in a letter to Father Snell that he would hold him personally responsible 'for any balance of debt there may be when the work has been completed'.

Even here, Father Snell was beset with difficulties. A previous bequest from a lady who helped to fund the work of Miss Green's Horndon 'Priory', to pay for a priest at Horndon, was used for the new purpose of repairing and renovating the church roof. This later caused some diocesan alarm, until it was discovered that the reallocation of the money had been approved by the original donor.

During the nineteen thirties, Father Snell actively supported the Children's Open Air Mission, a charity founded in 1882 by the Rev. Edward Canney and Mr. Walter Hazell. Its aim was to send delicate children who lived in the slums of central London for a holiday to the sea or countryside. It was our Parish Priest's responsibility to find lodgings for some 50 children, many of them convalescing, during their stay in the countryside of Stanford-le-Hope.

In April 1939, a few months before the outbreak of the Second World War, Father Snell wrote to the Bishop to tell him, somewhat belatedly, of this charitable venture (he had been involved in the project for ten years). He also made reference to the Irish nurses at Orsett hospital, who were now able to travel by car to weekly Mass in Stanford-le-Hope. These twenty-five nurses were able to make the journey because Essex County Council had agreed to provide a car each Sunday.

The parish continued to flourish in the years leading up to the Second World War. When the war started, there was the possibility of evacuation for the children of the parish, together with some of their mothers and the Sisters of Mercy, but eventually this did not happen. At about this time, Father Snell's health began to deteriorate quite rapidly. Although only fifty three years of age, he went on extended sick leave to Tiverton in Devon, where he stayed at the Convent of Our Lady. He met with and helped evacuees from Dartford in Kent and occasionally helped the local priest with the pastoral care of Catholic evacuees from the Diocese of Brentwood.

Father Snell's temporary replacement, Father Michael Hopkins, became concerned in 1941 about a group of Irishmen who had arrived from Ireland to do war work at the Shell Oil Company in Coryton. The problem was that the men were compelled to work on Sundays, making it difficult for them to attend Mass at the usual times. The earliest Stanford Sunday Mass was 8.30, but the men had to be at work by 8.00 a.m. Father Hopkins realised that rearranging the time of the earliest Mass would make it difficult for the parishioners living in Corringham to get a bus to take them to church (always assuming that they would be happy to attend a Mass that would be early enough to allow the Shell workers to be at work by 8 o'clock in the morning). The solution was for Father Hopkins to say three Masses on the Sunday, an arrangement that required, and received, the approval of the Diocese.

Father Snell returned to our parish in May 1942 and in October made new arrangements for the Sunday parish Masses to accommodate the parishioners in East Tilbury. This would allow the hundred Catholics living in the area, and soldiers based at Coalhouse Fort, to attend Mass in a room provided by the Bata Shoe factory. The Girls' Club there was described as 'large and dignified and eminently suitable' and it already contained a suitable altar. Apart from the soldiers at Coalhouse Fort, there were numerous members of H.M. forces stationed in nearby camps, and these too could benefit. The only alternative was to hold such a Mass at Chadwell St. Mary, a journey of over three miles from the Bata factory with no public transport available. The Mass was said once a month, at the expense of the parishioners at Horndon on the Hill, who lost their Sunday Mass on the days of the East Tilbury Mass.

The following year marked the Silver Jubilee of Father Snell's ordination. A Solemn High Mass was said to celebrate the occasion on 9th May, 1943. The lunch that followed was a ticket only function and its success was a measure of the high regard in which Father Snell was held, both by his parishioners and the wider community of Stanford-le-Hope.

As the years of the war passed, additional economy measures were introduced in the area. When the bus service between Corringham and Stanford was withdrawn, there was a problem for Corringham parishioners who found the journey to Stanford quite difficult. Father Snell proposed his own war-time measure as a solution: the saying of Mass in what was once the Church of England Parish School in Corringham. The school had closed as far back as 1890. The local parson, Rev. Nottage, was happy to offer this facility, and Father Snell was keen to accept, pointing out to his Bishop that the old school was a good 1,000 yards from the Protestant church on glebe land and had not been blessed or consecrated by a Protestant Bishop and so could be considered acceptable. The room could accommodate some 40 people, and might hold up to 60 on a Sunday.

In May 1943 the war came to Stanford-le-Hope, when six church windows were damaged by bomb blast. There was no possibility of acquiring leaded lights during the war, and Father Snell thought it better to wait until after the war rather than put plain glass in the windows. The local paper chose this moment to announce that the total number of bombs dropped on the Grays Thurrock area since the start of the war was 50,286.

During the war, a number of German prisoners of war attended Sunday Mass at Our Lady and St. Joseph's. They were brought over in a lorry from Orsett, where they were being held. The universality of the Latin Mass meant that the Germans had no problems with understanding the Mass itself, but the gospel readings for the day were read out first of all in English and then in German, courtesy of a German officer. Some of the younger parishioners were surprised to see Germans among the congregation. Nearly seventy years later, when asked how many prisoners of war were at these Masses, our parishioners were a little vague but the general view was that there were "an awful lot of them". Working on the land and in some construction work, the Germans made a real contribution to the neighbourhood, helping to build the temporary houses across the road from the church, homes which remained for many years after the war.

Although the church suffered some small measure of bomb damage, the war itself left the church and its surroundings largely unscathed. By 1945, the major sign of change was the absence of the school playground railings, donated to the war effort. The inside of the church received a coat of cream distemper, and the trees and shrubs outside the church had grown and become more established.

Now that the war was over, the men and women of the parish were able to renew their support for the parish itself, and the Catholic organisations became much more active. This also served to ease some of the burden carried by Father Snell, although his assistant priests, Father Goldingay and, later, Father Evers did much to lighten the load of this dedicated Parish Priest.

Unfortunately, Father Snell was not able to regain his health, and on February 13th 1949 he died in his presbytery after a long illness. His Requiem Mass was conducted by an old friend and colleague from St. Edmund's College, Bishop John Petit. The homily was given by Bishop Beck, who had recently been appointed to assist Bishop Arthur Doubleday, the ailing Bishop of Brentwood.

Chapter Four : The Nineteen Fifties

Father John Watson

Father Evers looked after the running of the parish until Father Snell's replacement was appointed. John Frederick Aloysius Watson was born in Buxted, Sussex in October 1908. He was the eldest child of Frederick and Mary Watson, who lived at Heron's Ghyll farm. His father was a gamekeeper on the estate and subsequently became bailiff, but he died in January 1917 of an illness contracted during active service in the First World War. His son John was educated at the convent at Heron's Ghyll, Notre Dame School in Leicester Square, London and, after his father's death, at St. Helen's School, Brentwood. In 1922, he entered St. John's Seminary, Wonersh as a junior seminarian, and was ordained at St. George's Church, Walthamstow in July 1933 by Bishop Doubleday.

Before the Second World War, Father Watson served as assistant priest at East Ham. In June 1939, he was commissioned as a Chaplain in the Territorial Army, and when war broke out in September 1939 he was attached to the Second General Hospital of the 54 East Anglian Division, based in Huntingdonshire. Two years later he was in Malaya. With the fall of Singapore in February 1942, he was captured by the Japanese and became a prisoner of war. Father Watson was one of only eight British Catholic Chaplains to the Forces captured and imprisoned in the Far East. Later in the war, he took part in the notorious 'Death March' through Burma during the building of the Thailand Burma railway, when over a quarter of Allied prisoners died. In August 1945, Father Watson was released from this terrible ordeal to return to England.

The details of his ordeal during the war were obtained from the diocesan archive in Brentwood, for Father Watson never spoke openly about the suffering he endured. Just before his death in July 1966, he attributed his poor health to the treatment he had received as a prisoner of war.

Immediately after the war, Father Watson became the first resident priest at Canvey Island and in 1946 he was appointed priest-in-charge at Canvey Island. He then served as assistant priest in Dunmow, Custom House and Grays before he was appointed as Parish Priest of Stanford-le-Hope in March 1949.

Father John Watson

The Diocese was aware of the suffering he had experienced in the war. When, in May 1949, he requested permission from the Bishop to say three Masses on a Sunday, he was following in the footsteps of many previous incumbents. However, in granting this permission, for the first time the Bishop of Brentwood warned against the dangers of overtaxing himself, and exhorted him to find additional supply priests whenever possible to lighten his load.

Of course, if one load was to be lightened, there was always another one just around the corner. In November 1949, the Diocese inaugurated a new drive for the Brentwood Schools Building Fund, to build new schools for Catholic children and to refurnish those schools in need of repair. The 'good news' was that the Bishop had donated the sum of £20,000 to stimulate the growth of the fund; the 'bad news' was that the parish of Stanford-le-Hope would be expected to contribute the sum of £370 every year towards the fund.

In July 1950, Father Watson paid the first half-yearly contribution of £185 after receiving what the Bishop called 'the somewhat peremptory character of my reminder to you'. Plans were already well established to build a big Catholic secondary school in Dagenham, where pre- and post-war housing estates had created an enormous surge in population. Essex County Council had already given the Diocese some temporary primary school accommodation for 320 children in the growing area of Debden, but the Diocese knew that if it wanted permanent Catholic schools it would have to build them itself. The Ministry of Education had imposed restrictions on loans for the building of faith schools, and the Bank of England had followed suit.

Despite the difficulties that the diocese faced at a national level, at a local level there was a greater understanding of the need to involve religious organisations in the planning of new towns that were springing up around London. One of the first acts passed in Clement Attlee's post-war Labour government, was the New Towns Act of 1946.

One of the many aims of the Act was to create 'overspill' new towns to try to alleviate the shortage of housing in London following the Second World War and the bomb damage inflicted on its residential developments, many of them in a pretty poor state. In November 1946, Stevenage in Hertfordshire became the first of eight designated 'new towns' that were designed and built between 1946 and 1951.

In 1948 the government granted provisional approval for Basildon to follow suit. Lewis Silkin, Minister of Town and Country Planning, came to Laindon in September 1948 and addressed a large gathering with the words:

> Basildon will become a city which people from all over the world will want to visit. It will be a place where all classes of community can meet freely together on equal terms and enjoy common cultural recreational facilities.

Basildon was officially designated a new town in January 1949.

When the town planners began to draw up a draft master plan for Basildon, the Bishop was asked what his requirements would be for new churches to serve the area. This necessarily involved local Parish Priests, and Father Watson was asked to participate in the planning discussions. His suggestion that a priest in any new church would also need a house to live in was well received by Brigadier Knapton, who led the planning team, and a house was duly provided. The Church had obviously come a long way from the early days of the Stanford-le-Hope parish, when the provision of a suitable presbytery took years to arrange and involved many disputes about who would pay.

Father Watson had other interests as well. He was moved by the work of Father Malcolm Cowin, the newly appointed Catholic priest of Wymondham in Norfolk, who had also been incarcerated as a prisoner of war by the Japanese. When his new church was built, Father Cowin proposed a permanent memorial to the Far East Prisoners of War (FEPOW) within the new Norfolk church. Father Watson was tireless in raising money for this memorial. His Norfolk colleague said a daily Mass for the War Dead until he left that parish in 1965.

Father Watson's more immediate memorial at Stanford-le-Hope was the installation of the wooden floor to our church, which lifted the temperature and the morale of his congregation. It was finally laid just after Father Watson moved on to become Parish Priest of Southend-on-Sea in March 1953, where he served until his death in July 1966.

Father John Hibbert

The very day that Father Watson left for his new position in Southend-on-Sea, Father John Hibbert arrived to become the new Parish Priest at Stanford-le-Hope. It was a few months before the coronation of Queen Elizabeth II and the first ascent of Mount Everest.

Father John Hibbert

John Cyril Wortley Hibbert was born in April 1905 in Leytonstone. His father was an accountant in an insurance company. The father died in 1912, at the age of thirty-seven. John and his younger brother were brought up by their mother, Gladys Mary Wortley, who was received into the Catholic Church the year after her husband's death. After some years of study and contemplation, John Hibbert was accepted by Bishop Doubleday as a student for the Diocese of Brentwood, and he entered St.

John's Seminary Wonersh in 1926. He was ordained by Bishop Doubleday in May 1932.

His first appointment was as assistant priest in Billericay in July 1932 and then in March 1933 he became curate at Manor Park. From 1937, his Parish Priest was Father (later Cardinal) John Carmel Heenan. Father Hibbert made a name for himself as a good organiser of the cricket team and parish socials. Cardinal Heenan later recorded that Father Hibbert was 'a splendid assistant'.

Like his predecessor at Stanford-le-Hope, Father Watson, Father Hibbert was commissioned as a Chaplain to the Forces. This was in October 1939, just after the outbreak of the Second World War. He served with the British Expeditionary Force at the fall of France in June 1940, coming under heavy bombardment from the steadily advancing German forces. Father Hibbert managed to return to England through the port of Bordeaux before it was captured, but the ordeal cost him dearly. He was diagnosed with shellshock and was finally released from military service in July 1941. Returning to his mother's house in Billericay, Father Hibbert covered short term absences of local priests, but in December 1941 an attempt to appoint him as assistant priest in Leyton came to nothing because his health was too poor.

By June 1942 he had recovered sufficiently to become assistant priest at Canning Town, but he took on the role of chaplain to the Franciscan Missionaries of Mary, who had been evacuated from Canning Town to Haslemere, Surrey. After the Second World War, Father Hibbert was assistant priest at Chingford and then Barkingside, before moving on to become priest-in-charge at Hainault.

A parishioner wrote this about Father John Hibbert.

> Father Hibbert was appointed Parish Priest in 1953. His aged mother came to live with him as his housekeeper – in fact he was the carer. He was a kind, caring priest, who did not make her feel that she was a burden. She was a poor cook so assistant priests, who were often Missionary priests doing short supply, fared badly and used to resort to the convent.
>
> After his mother died, Father John employed an elderly Irish woman as housekeeper. Unfortunately, she suffered from a personality disorder and when Father John was absent she took total control, much to the discomfort of the assistant priest. A Sister teaching in the school hall, which was very close to the presbytery kitchen, often

upset her as she interpreted their rote learning as defaming her character. Off she would go to the Police Station to complain.

Vatican II brought about many changes, and the celebration of Mass facing the Congregation was an ordeal for Father John. His very able assistant priest, Father John Timmins, was a wonderful support and with lots of encouragement it was an easy transition.

Father Archibald O'Brien came to live with Father John and the partnership between Father John, who was a staunch Englishman, and Father Archie, who was a staunch Irishman, was phenomenal. At that time, Orsett Hospital had a high percentage of Irish nurses. Father John's relationship with them very quickly changed from acquaintances to close friends, as a result of Father Archie's influence.

Father John was by nature fairly impatient but he spent many holidays in Ireland patiently fishing, and while in the Green Isle he would visit many of the nurses' families.

When Father Archie got ill Father John cared for him, until it was necessary for him to be admitted to hospital. Father Archie's replacement was Father Joseph Haugh, who was loaned from the Diocese of Killaloe for about three years.

Father Hibbert arrived at a time of substantial growth in the population of Stanford-le-Hope and the surrounding areas. There was a surge in private house building, and East Ham and West Ham, together with our own Thurrock Council, were building large council estates. There was an unexpected increase in the numbers of children in the local schools, including St. Joseph's, and the size of the church congregation grew steadily. Not for the first time in our recent history, the social consequences of large scale house-building had not been adequately assessed, and the community had to do the best it could until a fuller response could be made to look after the interests of the many people who now moved into the area.

The parishioners in Corringham still lacked a suitable base for the saying of Mass. There had been a series of temporary arrangements over the years, but in late 1954 the British Legion Hall in Corringham became available. Father Hibbert recorded that it measured 120 feet by 52 feet and was for sale for £900. Hardly modern estate agent language, but it has to be admitted that the hall was quite basic, and it never became a congenial Mass centre in terms of the accommodation it provided. Nevertheless, there was at last a properly designated building for the Catholics of Corringham after nearly forty years. Father Hibbert managed to arrange a loan of £725 from the Diocese of Brentwood (at two and a half per cent interest). The new Mass centre became known as St. Teresa's Hall.

There was briefly the possibility of further expansion in Fobbing, when Father Hibbert was urged by the Bishop to investigate the possibility of a chapel in the village. The Parish Priest discovered that there were only 'ten or twelve' Catholics in the village and that they were all able to attend Mass at Stanford or at Sacred Heart, Vange. In addition, the village was designated as an agricultural area and Thurrock Council was not planning any expansion onto Green Belt land. The plan was quietly shelved.

In the meantime, money remained very tight, with the parish barely able to pay its way. When the Diocese increased Stanford's annual contribution towards the Diocesan Development Fund to £500, Father Hibbert had to reply "I hope you had your tongue in your cheek when you wrote that".

In March 1957, the Bishop of Brentwood decided that the parish would dispense with a resident curate, and Father McDermott was sent to Aveley to fill a temporary vacancy. There was no suggestion that Father McDermott would return or that Stanford would see another curate in the future. Without the assistance of a curate, Father Hibbert was obliged to take on additional work. He was helped by a steady succession of assistant priests, some of whom came just to say the Sunday Mass, some of whom were able to stay for weeks and some who stayed on for a few months. Records show that these assistants hailed from Italy, France, Germany, Spain, United States of America, China, Goa, Vietnam and Ceylon, and these were joined by English and Irish priests returning from the African missions.

Amongst the many assistant priests, one is particularly remembered. This was Father Paul Nguiem-Gia-De who served in Stanford-le-Hope from 1955 to 1956. His cheerful and happy manner gave no clue to the fact that in Vietnam he had been hunted by the communists with a price on his head. He had travelled from village to village saying Mass in a parish the size of England and Wales, disguising himself as a peasant to evade capture, and had often been under fire.

Father Hibberts's experience as an army chaplain seems to have developed the organising zeal noted before the war at Manor Park. He now set about the task of organising the parish societies to help him with the work of the steadily growing parish community. At Sunday Mass in Stanford-le-Hope it was necessary to arrive early to be sure of a seat, and many would stand at the back of the church and fill the aisles along both sides. The seating itself now changed, with pews of oak replacing the chairs, and new gas heaters were hung on the walls to take the edge off the winter cold.

In 1958 a chapel was added to the convent of the Sisters of Mercy, and Mass was said there every day of the year. In the same year, a pilgrimage to Aylesford was organised by the parish, and this proved to be so successful that another took place the following year, a practice we have seen mirrored in the most recent years of our parish. Father Hibbert's energy and organisational skill were rewarded by the appointment of an assistant priest in the early part of 1959, Father O'Brien, who remained in the parish until he died in 1961.

This was a time of prodigious fund-raising within the parish, when it seemed that every parishioner was in some way involved. There were many schemes to gain money for the parish, so many indeed that our earlier historian, C.R. Sharp, referred to them as 'too numerous to mention'. The annual bazaar was the main event, and would usually raise the sum of £300, a mighty sum of money in those days when the average house cost about two thousand pounds and an average salary was just over one hundred and fifty pounds a year. Whatever we hope to raise in such events today, no-one seriously sets the target at twice the average annual salary. Of course, we were living in the age described by the then Prime Minister, Harold Macmillan, with the statement 'You've never had it so good' and as many as one in three families now owned a car.

Towards the end of 1960, Father Hibbert returned from a holiday in Ireland with a painting of Our Lady of Perpetual Succour, Mater de Perpetuo Succursu, which had been given to him by a friend. It is based on an early medieval Byzantine icon, itself believed to refer to St. Luke's painting of Our Lady. It served as a starting point for a perpetual Novena.

After the success of the pilgrimages to Aylesford, a pilgrimage to Igatestone Hall was organised in 1961, in honour of the Forty Martyrs of England and Wales. These Catholic martyrs were executed during the sixteenth and seventeenth century, usually on a charge of treason that would be made when they refused to acknowledge the monarch as the Head of the Church in England and Wales. In October 1970, they were canonised by Pope Paul VI. The parishioners from Stanford-le-Hope were pleased to acknowledge that their 1961 contingent formed one of the largest present on the pilgrimage. The number of Catholics in the area had now risen to some fifteen hundred, and St. Joseph's School had three hundred pupils.

Further improvements were made in the church with the installation of central heating in 1961. The cost of two thousand pounds was met by an overdraft facility at the bank, authorised and guaranteed by the Bishop.

In 1962, planning began for a pilgrimage to Lourdes the following year, a year that was also to mark the Golden Jubilee of the Stanford-le-Hope Parish. The special Mass held to commemorate the Golden Jubilee was attended by Hugh Delargy, the Labour Member of Parliament for Thurrock from 1950 until his death in 1976. He became effectively a spokesperson for the Catholic point of view during his many years in the House of Commons. Thurrock Council was represented by Councillor W.P. O'Donoghue who proposed the formal toast to the parish of Our Lady and St. Joseph at a Jubilee Supper which followed the Mass. The commemorative Mass was so well attended that closed circuit television was used to pipe the service to the overflow congregation in the two classrooms at the rear of the church. The Bishop of Brentwood was represented by the Very Rev. Canon Goldingay.

In the same year, the parish was eagerly pursuing plans to buy some land for a chapel in East Tilbury. A site was found near to the railway level crossing, but surveyors' reports and the attitude of the Local Planning

Authority made the plan unrealistic. The chapel would be on Green Belt land, was judged to be too near to the railway line to guarantee safety, on the wrong side of the railway line and nowhere near the people it was intended to serve. One assumes that apart from that it was fine. Father Hibbert's returns to Thurrock Council in February 1963 therefore listed the properties owned by the parish as Our Lady and St. Joseph's Church, the presbytery and its garage, St. Joseph's Primary School, St. Teresa's Hall, Corringham, and the Chapel of the Blessed Sacrament at Horndon on the Hill.

In March 1965 Father Hibbert recorded in his response to the diocesan audit that he kept the Holy Oils not in the church but in the presbytery as during the cold months 'there is danger of them freezing in the church'. Many parishioners would have known exactly what he meant. It seems that the term 'central heating' was wrong on both counts.

Not that things were any more comfortable at the presbytery. Father Hibbert sent his contribution to the Diocesan Development Fund in December 1966 apologising for the amount, stating that the presbytery and some of the furniture had been infested with woodworm and extensive redecoration had been required after Rentokill had rooted out the problem.

In 1967, Thurrock Council decided to do something about the dangerously sharp corner at the junction of Scratton Road and Southend Road. The Council took some of the church land to improve the safety of the junction, but paid for all the work, rebuilt the boundary concrete wall and fence, laid a bitumen path, paid all legal costs incurred and even transplanted various flowers and shrubs.

Father Hibbert left the parish in 1967, to become the Parish Priest in East Ham. He retired from the priesthood in 1972, suffering from arthritis, and went to live with friends in County Tyrone, Ireland. He returned to the Diocese of Brentwood for the last few months of his life, and died in January 1975.

Contemporaries remember his love of golf, and a silver bowl trophy was introduced for 'high handicap clergy' as a memento to this sports loving priest.

Father Bernard Collings

Bernard Frederick Collings was born in nearby Thorpe Bay, Southend-on-Sea on June 24th, 1915. He was the youngest of five children born to

John Saxby Collings and his wife Helen. His father was a successful architect who was to design a number of churches in the Diocese of Brentwood, most notably St. Mary Mother of God, Hornchurch. Both parents became converts to Catholicism.

On his mother's side he was related to the famous Labour backbencher MP Woodrow Wyatt, who was later the chairman of the Horserace Totalisator Board for over twenty years. The family was descended from Sir Thomas Wyatt, who briefly installed Lady Jane Grey as Queen of England (The Nine Days' Queen), an exploit which cost both of them their lives.

Bernard Collings was taught at Mayfield College, Sussex by the Xaverian Brothers, a religious order named in honour of St. Francis Xavier and dedicated to education. When he left the college in 1932, he was recommended as a student for the priesthood by Father Toft, who had been the family's Parish Priest in Shoeburyness. Bishop Doubleday sent him first to St. Joseph's Junior Seminary, Mark Cross and then, in 1934, to St. John's Seminary, Wonersh. He was ordained by Bishop Doubleday at Brentwood Cathedral in May, 1940.

Father Collings returned to Shoeburyness in June 1940 and then moved the same month to the post of assistant priest at Chelmsford. He made an annual pilgrimage to Lourdes from 1947 onwards. In 1952, he was appointed as assistant priest at Saint Helen's, Westcliff-on-Sea. He became Parish Priest of Wickford in February 1955, and whilst there supervised the building of a presbytery.

On 26th July 1967 he was appointed Parish Priest at Stanford-le-Hope. During his seven years in the parish, Father Collings was assisted by a number of memorable curates. These included Father John Timmins, famous for his guitar playing, who served the parish from 1964 to 1969, Father Scrope who worked in the parish from 1969 to 1971, and Father Eamonn Magrath, 1971-1973.

October 1968: Father John Timmins plays in the garden of the Catcracker after the wedding of local girl Sandra Williams and one of The Bachelors group, Declan Cluskey. Vera Lynn is seated centre. Witnesses were Con Cluskey and Virginia Lewis, Vera Lynn's daughter.

Father Collings had many strengths, but he would have been the first to admit that keeping up to date with financial matters was not one of them.

First Holy Communion Breakfast : School Hall : 1968

The correspondence of the time is peppered with reminders about unpaid bills, which were coupled with letters from the Diocese about overdue payments. Those of you who are used to final reminders will sympathise. At least we have to deal merely with Thurrock Council or the Water Company. To keep a Bishop waiting is altogether more serious.

By June 1972, the population of the area was 30,500 and Catholics numbered 1,650. Average mass attendance on Sundays was 630, with most attending at Stanford (459). The average Sunday attendance at Corringham was 70, at Horndon on the Hill 54 and at Orsett Hospital 47.

On Saturday, 8th September 1973, the Nativity of Our Blessed Lady, the parish of Stanford-le-Hope celebrated its Diamond Jubilee. There was a special Mass and arrangements were made to ensure that all sections of the community had a part to play in the service. The parishioners co-operated to decorate the church, although there were plans to hold the service outside as a large congregation was expected. The Mass took place at 4.30 p.m. and the principal guest was the Bishop of Brentwood. He agreed to say a few words, prompted by advance details that Father Collings was able to provide about the major events in the parish during the previous sixty years. The members of the Youth Club and the St. Joseph's schoolchildren were especially prominent in the Mass.

The repeated ceremonies of the Catholic year, First Communions, Confirmations, Weddings, Baptisms, Funerals create a pattern not unlike the seasons, so that one year may occasionally seem like any other. But for Father Collings, the Confirmations in December 1973 had an additional feature. It was the year of petrol shortages, when the whole country was about to be given coupons to ration the supply of fuel for cars. Not a huge problem perhaps, but Father Collings had arranged to collect the Bishop and bring him to the parish to conduct the Confirmations. The local garage had promised the Parish Priest a few gallons, but the petrol tanker had not delivered its quota. Father Collings wrote to his Bishop in some panic, but we must assume that supplies were found as the Bishop was certainly present at the Confirmations. Of course, a certain priest from Barking, Father Clemens, who would ride out on horseback once a month to say a Mass at Corringham in the early years of the twentieth century, would have had no such problem with transport. It might have been just one horse power, but there was always one horse.

An old view of Our Lady and St. Joseph's Church : note (a) the Crucifix and (b) the boundary wall, paid for by a member of The Bachelors music group, who married parishioner Sandra Williams

A short while after this celebration, Father Collings was appointed Parish Priest at Warley, in July 1974. In that capacity, he served as the chaplain to Warley Hospital, where he soon developed a reputation for doing all that he could for the psychiatric patients in his pastoral care. He was affectionately known by his fellow clergy as 'Bunny'.

Apart from his kindness and seemingly infinite patience, Father Collings took his spiritual life and the celebration of Mass with great seriousness. He became a devoted member of the Catholic Charismatic Renewal Movement, which promoted Life in the Spirit Seminars. This inter-denominational movement emphasises the healing power of the Holy Spirit, and in its lively Masses attempts to recreate the experience of the first followers of Christ when the Holy Spirit descended on them at Pentecost.

Father Collings had a special rapport with the young, but he encouraged all of his parishioners to acknowledge their liturgical and apostolic duties. Keen to develop links with other Christian denominations, he belonged to the Ecumenical Society of the Blessed Virgin Mary, and he was a keen participant in all gatherings of clergy who served a local area.

Father Collings was an active supporter of the Women's World Day of Prayer, an ecumenical movement that is now spread across one hundred and seventy countries worldwide and which holds an annual day of prayer on the first Friday of March. As a priest in the Diocese of Brentwood, he served on the Diocesan Council of Priests and as a Diocesan Representative on the National Council of Priests.

He had many, wide-ranging hobbies. Diocesan archives record his interest in organ-building, making corn dollies, polishing stones, reading, and the making of electronic gadgets, jewellery, toys, models, pottery and wine.

The Venerable Margaret Sinclair, the Poor Clare nun from humble origins in Scotland, who died from tubercolosis at the age of 25, died in the Marillac Sanitorium at Warley Hospital in 1926. Father Collings took up her cause and became an active promoter of the Friends of Margaret Sinclair, arranging the group's first Mass at the Marillac Hospital, Warley. After this, a Mass was said every month and an Annual General Meeting held. In 1976, Pope Paul VI declared Margaret Sinclair 'Venerable' and the path to her eventual canonisation was later given encouragement by Pope John Paul II in 1982.

Father Collings died at the Marillac Hospital in August 1988, and his Requiem Mass was celebrated by Bishop McMahon at Brentwood Cathedral. In a moving obituary written by John Glynn, the final two paragraphs sum up this gifted priest.

> The presence of so many of his brother priests at Bunny's funeral was eloquent testimony to the esteem in which he was held by them. He had the gift of making friends with everyone, and never talked down to anyone. He bore his last illness with fortitude, leaving the presbytery only two weeks before he died, and determining not to be any trouble to anyone. That last fortnight he was able to spend in his own parish of Warley in the care of the Marillac Sisters who looked after him wonderfully.
>
> There was always a fund of jokes or anecdotes; even in the last days of his life he still relished telling a new story. It is that freshness and childlike eagerness to learn something new that I shall treasure. He will enjoy discovering the endless delights of heaven, with the help, no doubt, of a brand-new Morris Minor estate. May he rest in peace and rise in glory.

Father John Taylor

John Taylor was born in Walthamstow on June 24th, 1929. A convert to Catholicism, he was educated for the priesthood at St. Edmunds College, Ware. Father Taylor was ordained on May 5th 1968 at St. George's, Walthamstow by Bishop Wall. He served as an assistant priest at Leigh-on-Sea from 1968 to 1970, and at Our Lady Immaculate, Chelmsford, from 1970 to 1974. He was Parish Priest of Stanford-le-Hope from 1974 to 1979, before moving to Romford as the Parish Priest from 1979 to 1990. He returned briefly as Parish Priest to St. George's, Walthamstow, 1990-1991, before his final parish of Upminster, where he served as Parish Priest from 1991 until his retirement in 2011.

Many parishioners today have kind memories of Father Taylor. One of them wrote the following about this gentle priest.

> Father John was kind, gentle, understanding, caring, calm and unassuming. He never showed impatience or annoyance, no matter how difficult the situation. He loved people and the presbytery was often open house.
>
> Once, a very grateful parishioner gave him a sum of money to buy himself a warm winter coat. He waited for the Sales and donated the balance to the Lourdes fund for the sick; he was generous to a fault.
>
> It was during his time at Stanford that the expansion of the school occurred, due to the overspill from London. Father John was a strong supporter of a very enthusiastic PTA who saw the great need for a larger school, and he was always at hand to praise and encourage.
>
> Father John was a good preacher and had a good sense of humour. Cricket was his favourite sport.
>
> His assistant was Father Bart Lynch, who was already well established in Stanford when Father John was appointed as Parish Priest, but in a short time the latter's gentle, unassuming personality endeared him to the community. The partnership between those two priests was a very 'healthy' one and many refer to that time as 'the Golden Years'.

Father Taylor worked closely with his curate, Bart Lynch, who had been ordained in June, 1972. The two did indeed develop a most effective working relationship, and this influenced the life and work of the parish. There was an excellent rapport between the priests and their parishioners. The number of Catholics seems to have increased in these years. Although the local population remained fairly static at about thirty thousand, it was estimated that the parish now had some three thousand Catholics.

The presbytery continued to have its problems. Where Father Collings had battled against woodworm, in 1974 Father Taylor applied for a Low Interest Diocesan Loan to combat rodent infestation in the kitchen. A new floor was needed as the premises were badly affected. At the same time, repairs were necessary on the church roof. The wooden shingles had to be replaced as they were in a state of disrepair. One quotation received, for £1,419, was for asbestos slates, at a time when the dangers of this material were not fully realised. Fortunately, an architect advised the use of pine wood shingles. At the same time, the presbytery roof was given new guttering as water was leaking everywhere. Father Collings had acquired these quotations for all of the work the previous year but had not followed them up. One assumes that Father Taylor took one look on his arrival and decided to act immediately.

Another task was to reorganise the parish's finances. The Parish Finance Sub-Committee, set up by the Parish Council, examined the state of the finances, issuing an initial report in 1974. They paid tribute to the detailed records that Father Taylor had kept from June to August 1974, which at last made it possible to create a fairly detailed picture of income and expenditure. Their report was passed on immediately to the parishioners, for the situation was serious.

At a time of industrial unrest, the three day week, oil shortages and economic stagnation, inflation had raced ahead, reaching a spike of over 25% in the mid seventies. The trouble was that the offertory collections had not kept pace. The report was not couched in terms of an appeal for funds but to show the parishioners what the situation was and what was projected.

The report concluded with the following words.

> As will be seen, the parish is not really solvent. Day to day running costs are not quite covered, and so there is no margin for any capital expenditure. It is appreciated that there is no mention (in the report) of funds raised from such sources as Fetes, Bazaars, Jumble Sales etc., but equally there is no allowance for those unforeseen items of expenditure which, as we all know, occur with depressing regularity. In this connection it is worth mentioning that Stanford-le-Hope has an accumulated debt of some £4,500 in respect of diocesan levies unpaid in recent years, and the parish is also having to borrow from

> the Diocese a further amount of around £3,000 to cover essential repairs to the church and also the presbytery exterior and interior.
>
> The conclusion drawn, therefore, is that the financial state of the parish is not a healthy one. It is a problem which must urgently involve us all and we must ask everyone to give great thought to this end and be prepared to support proposals to remedy this situation.

The situation was indeed serious. The parish's main source of income, Sunday collections, averaged just £90 per week, from which so many things had to be paid, ranging from insurance premiums and basic utilities to diocesan levies and loan repayments. Even the cost of altar breads and candles had been factored into the summary. The Parish Priest could hardly be accused of living off the fat of the land; his annual salary was quoted at just £220.

Not that this prevented our Parish Priest from looking after the needs of others. Concerned about the future prospects of the housekeeper who worked at the presbytery, Father Taylor took the necessary steps to enrol her in the diocesan pension scheme so that she would have a guaranteed regular income on retirement.

Prior to the Easter services of 1976, the Bishop of Brentwood permitted his clergy to offer General Absolution at Masses. In Stanford-le-Hope, it was offered at the afternoon liturgy of Good Friday. Father Taylor noted a substantial increase in the size of the congregation and in the numbers receiving Holy Communion in the Good Friday and Easter Sunday Masses. In thanking the Bishop for helping so many back to the receiving of the Sacraments, Father Taylor concluded "I personally am convinced that nothing but good can come of having had General Absolution".

By February 1977, work was well established to build a church and hall in Corringham. It was to be known as St. Augustine's. The parish agreed a bank loan of £24,000 to cover the costs. As this was clearly a major project, Father Taylor informed the Diocese that no further building, renovation or maintenance was planned in the parish before Easter 1979. With the parish now owing substantial sums of money, it was grateful to receive an interest free loan of ten thousand pounds from the Sisters of Mercy.

In May 1977, St. Augustine's was opened by Bishop Patrick Casey, as was reported in the local press.

Opening of new RC Church

> Corringham's new Roman Catholic church was officially opened last week with a Mass of thanksgiving by the Bishop of Brentwood, Bishop Patrick Casey.
> And the occasion was marked by a get together by representatives of all the local churches.
> The Rev. Jack Hassett, Rector of St. Margaret's, Stanford, the Rev. Malcolm Cherry from Horndon and the Rev. Leonard Middleton from East Tilbury represented the Church of England. The Rev. Alan Dawson, Stanford Methodist minister, was there. The Roman Catholics were represented by Canon John Byrne of Tilbury.
> The new church, in St. John's Way, was named after St. Augustine, an early missionary to the English. The day after the opening was St. Augustine's Day.
> Corringham's Roman Catholics did not forget the Rev. Leonard Hill, who allowed them to use St. John's Church nearby for ten years, while they were without a church of their own. They presented him with a set of vestments for St. John's.

In 1977, Father Lynch left the parish for Harold Hill and his leaving do at St. Augustine's was so well attended that many parishioners were obliged to stand outside in the street to say goodbye to this popular priest. Everyone felt quite emotional at Father Bart's departure, not least the priest himself. Father Bart moved on to a few other parishes before settling in Holy Trinity at Basildon.

In December 2010, Father Bart Lynch died. The Brentwood Diocesan Directory for 2012 contains a moving account of the life of this popular and kind priest, written by his friend and colleague, Father Patrick J. Sammon.

> Hindsight, as most of us learn sooner or later in life, is a wonderful teacher. Looking back now at Bart's life, I realise that he began to take his leave of us soon after the death of his mother. I saw the change in him but missed the meaning. He was deeply devoted to his mother and she to him. Her death affected him enormously and sometimes his grief was expressed in that he spoke about her in the words of Patrick Kavanagh – "I do not see you lying in the wet clay of a Monaghan (Dublin) graveyard." He could never accept that she had gone from this world. The change in him was apparent and as time went on I noticed that he would miss appointments, e.g. invite me to visit and forget. I put this down to grief and tried to suggest that he should, perhaps, see a doctor, etc. and tried all sorts of ways

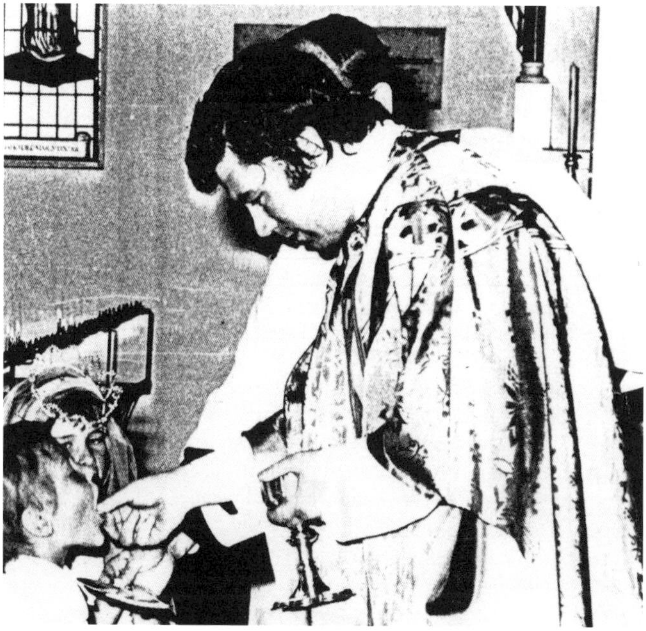

Father Bart officiates at a First Communion Service.

to help him through the grieving process. He was a sensitive, intelligent and proud man and dismissed any suggestion that there could be anything wrong. I thought his condition was due to grief and loneliness. He would not see a doctor so it was a great surprise to me when, after the summer holidays, I heard that he had been taken seriously ill en route from Ireland and was missing for some time. The illness was far more serious and different than I had first suspected. He was brought to hospital, a diagnosis made, and after that he was never the same again. Something in him died. He struggled to cope with his illness, and actually I think gave up the will to carry on. He never fully understood the seriousness of his illness and was impatient with it.

Bart's family and his early life

Bartholomew James Lynch was the eldest child and only son of Patrick and Christina Lynch. He has eight sisters. The family lived in Ballyfermot, Dublin. Bart, as he was called, was baptised at St. Kevin's, Harrington Street, Dublin and was confirmed by Archbishop John Charles McQuaid. He was educated by the De La Salle Brothers, first at primary level and later at secondary level. He was a class mate of the present Archbishop of Dublin, Archbishop Martin. After leaving school he studied horology, received a qualification and worked for some time as a silversmith. He was also an expert in judo, obtaining a black belt. He became an accomplished Instructor in Judo and was involved in training police cadets in London. He has a great love of motorbikes and, according to himself, owned a Harley Davidson!!! (and frightened elderly ladies out of their lives in Ballyfermot as he rode along the streets). His favourite act was lifting the motorcycle on the rear wheel and zooming along at breakneck speed.

He learns Latin and studies for the priesthood

For some years he had been thinking of the priesthood but had not studied Latin. A Carmelite priest referred him to the Mount Melleray Seminary, Cappoquin, Co. Waterford, and it was here that he first came as a student to the Cistercian monks to study Latin in 1965 and enter the Major Seminary in 1968. In the seminary he excelled at Basketball, was a keen sportsman, and an excellent chess player. He also was a champion debater and a formidable opponent in college debates. He loved the poetry of Patrick Kavanagh, the writings of Brendan Behan and James Joyce. He had read "Finnegan's Wake" and "Ulysses" and always celebrated Bloomsday. He was a great devotee of the cinema and theatre and saw many of the great London plays.

He was ordained to the priesthood at All Hallows College, Dublin in June 1972.

Bart maintained the reason he chose Brentwood Diocese was because he felt sorry for Canon Loughran, the Vocations Director. On visits to the seminary Canon Loughran painted a bleak picture of the shortage of priests and advised the students of plum parishes when they became priests and signed on for the Diocese of Brentwood. It seems at that point we had 100 students at varying levels of study for the diocese at minor and major seminaries. Some were known as the 'Young Disciples' or "Charlie's Angels". Bart, Canon Loughran said, was the 100th student!!!! Then someone left and numbers decreased. It was through Bart's persuasion that I signed on for Brentwood.

Father Bart's early appointments in the diocese and his pastoral care for those in hospital

In September 1972 Father Bart was appointed as an assistant priest at Wanstead, where he became known for his pastoral care in Whipps Cross and Wanstead hospitals, especially by organising spiritual and social gatherings for the many Irish nurses in the area. In November 1973 he was appointed as assistant priest at Stanford-le-Hope and again his ministry to the staff and patients at Orsett hospital was outstanding – his devotion to duty was second to none.

In September 1977, seeking to discern whether his priestly ministry would be better exercised in Ireland, Father Bart was granted permission to return to Dublin with a view to incardination into that archdiocese. He was appointed as assistant priest at Our Lady of Mercy, Artane, Dublin. However, after two years he returned to the Diocese of Brentwood.

In September 1979 he served as an assistant priest pro tem at Clacton-on- Sea. In November 1979 he was appointed as an assistant priest at St. Mary's, Hornchurch where the Parish Priest was Father Gerry Kerr and the curate Father John Garrett. In April 1982 Father Bart was appointed as assistant priest at Romford, where again he exercised his ministry at Oldchurch hospital with great devotion.

A newly appointed Parish Priest

In June 1983 he was appointed as Parish Priest of St. Dominic's, Harold Hill. He loved St. Dominic's Parish and its "wonderful people" as he called them.

In 1984 he was appointed as a member of the Diocesan Ministry to Priests' Team and carried on a "one to one" ministry with many priests. He had a wonderful gift of 'listening' and giving time to people.

In August 1990 Father Bart was appointed as Parish Priest of Most Holy Trinity, Basildon. On receiving news of this appointment, the Head Teacher of St. Ursula's Primary School, Harold Hill wrote to Bishop McMahon to express the regret of both the parish and the school at the loss of such a fine priest.

In 1991 he was appointed as chaplain to the sick on the Brentwood Diocesan Pilgrimage to Lourdes, a role he continued for several years and is fondly remembered to this day by many of the Pilgrims with whom he spent quality time.

The Silver Jubilee of his ordination

In October 1995 he was appointed as Parish Priest of Hainault. It was here, in June 1997, that he celebrated the Silver Jubilee of his ordination in a church thronged with parishioners and friends, past and present. On that occasion Bishop McMahon praised him for his 'willingness to accept any appointment he had been asked to consider': whenever he had asked him to move to another parish the answer had always been 'yes' without hesitation.

From Christmas 1997 to March 1998 he completed a sabbatical course with the Irish Missionary Union at Dalgan Park, Navan, County Meath.

Father Bart's health begins to fail

In October 2001 Father Bart was appointed as Parish Priest at Westcliff-on-Sea. It was here that his health began to fail. In September 2003 he entered Nazareth House, Southend-on Sea, for treatment and convalescence.

In March 2004 he took up residence at St. Anthony of Padua, Forest Gate. During Father Bart's stay at Forest Gate an anonymous visitor, who was working on behalf of the 'Ship of Fools' website, posted a report of the celebrant and his sermon at the Sunday Mass that he/she had attended. The priest was Father Bart who, in a five minute homily, rated 8 out of 10, 'spoke simply but to the point, but I was amazed at how many sheets of A4 paper he rustled through for a sermon that was so short… Father preached on the story of the Prodigal Son, emphasising the decision of the son to return, the welcome of the father and the attitude of the elder son. He then said we should forgive one another and also our enemies, just as God has forgiven us. Rarely has a service been so emotional and brought me frequently to tears… Were I to embrace the Roman Catholic faith… this would be my church.' For the reviewer, the most memorable point in the Mass was 'the smile (was it a bit cheeky?) on the face of the priest as he read the Gospel.'

In September 2004 Father Bart was appointed as assistant priest at SS Peter and Paul, Ilford.

In May 2005 failing health obliged him to return to Nazareth House, Southend-on-Sea.

Returning to Ireland to be near his family

In May 2010 Father Bart took up residence at Mary Mount Care Centre, Westmanstown, Lucan, County Dublin, where he could be near his family and where he was able to celebrate Mass daily.

He died there rather suddenly on 1st December 2010. His Requiem Mass was celebrated by Monsignor Armitage VG and Father Tom Jordan at Our Lady of the Nativity, Leixlip, County Kildare, on 6th December 2010. Burial took place in Esker Cemetery, Lucan, County Dublin. Inclement weather caused my flight from City Airport to be cancelled so I missed the funeral. Bart's close friends, Sheila and John Delander were there. They were loyal and true to the end, and shared his joys and sorrows down the years. He would be pleased that they were there for the final Goodbye, and would want me to thank them for their devoted friendship and care. He said of them "John and Sheila were always there for me".

Bart the priest

In conclusion I would like to say something about Bart the priest I knew. His favourite gospel passage which he often shared with me was John 14:16 where Jesus said "Love one another as I have loved you". Bart often reflected – "Christ personified the way of love" in the first and greatest Commandment. He felt that all sin was a failure to love and if you struggled to be loving people God would understand and forgive and make allowances for all our weaknesses. And no one can think of Bart without reflecting on his great love for humankind – his priestly love – his love for his mother and father, his sisters and their families, his friends, his parishioners, his commitment to his favourite charities – Christian Aid, CAFOD, River Blindness. He would often say that his neighbour is not the person next door nor did his parish end on the boundary between it and the next parish. All of humankind was his neighbour, especially those who were suffering. He always watched out for the person on the road to Jericho who was injured. This bringing together of Bart's love for everyone, and his defence of the 'little people', the 'zero people' as he called them was a striking characteristic of him as a priest. It imbued his priesthood. His daily devotion to prayer, the Divine Office, meditation, the Rosary and Mass and his love for his brother priests in the diocese were always in evidence. His great respect for and obedience to the Bishop – one could go on and on. In 44 years of knowing him I never once heard an unkind or unchristian word from out of his mouth about anyone. He always sought to seek and find the best in every human being – 'God's work of art' as he said.

MAY HIS GENEROUS SOUL REST IN PEACE

When Father Taylor left the parish in 1979, St. Joseph's Hall was packed to capacity to say farewell and, as Father Taylor left, a brand new Ford Escort was waiting for him in the car park. That the parishioners had managed to collect enough money to buy the new car outright is an indication of the love the parish had for their priest. The event was reported in the local press.

Farewell present of a car for Stanford's Father Taylor

Stanford's Roman Catholics presented their former priest with a moving present on Friday, a brand new £3,000 Ford Escort car.

Father John Taylor, now priest of St. Edward's Catholic Church, Romford, worked at St. Joseph's Church, Stanford-le-Hope, for more than five years.

His parishioners gave him the car as a thank you gift for his work in Stanford and Corringham.

> Parish Communication Officer Mr. Norbert McCabe said: "Father Taylor has to do a fair bit of travelling in his day-to-day work so we thought it would be nice to try to buy him a car.
> "He had an old faithful Triumph which wasn't that reliable.
> "We wrote to our parishioners asking for donations and received over £3,000.
> "The response was quite overwhelming. He is a quite remarkable priest and was very well loved in the parish."
> Father Taylor, who now lives in Romford, helped to get St. Augustine's Church in Corringham built, and also helped to improve St. Joseph's Junior School, Stanford.

Father Bernard McWilliams

Brian McWilliams was born in Belfast in January 1930, and grew up in Ilford, where he was educated at Saints Peter and Paul School from 1935 to 1944, followed by Clark's College, 1944-1946. He was educated for the priesthood at Campion House, Osterley, 1950-1952 and St. Edmund's College, Ware 1952-1958. Father McWilliams was ordained to the priesthood in May 1958 by Bishop Wall at Brentwood Cathedral. He served as assistant priest at St. George's, Walthamstow for a short time in 1958 and then at Holy Cross, Harlow from 1958 to 1965. In that year he was transferred to Brentwood Cathedral, where he worked until 1968, when he was appointed as Parish Priest at Burnham-on-Crouch, a position he held until 1970. He was then Parish Priest at Ilford Lane, 1970-1977, Rochford 1977-1979, Stanford-le-Hope 1979-1982, Waltham Abbey 1982-1990, and then Holy Name, Chelmsford from 1990 until his retirement in 1995. Father McWilliams is the Diocesan Registrar for Deceased Clergy. He now lives at Nazareth House, Southend on Sea, where he has served as Chaplain since 2003.

Father McWilliams spent just over three years with us in the parish, from 1979 to 1982. Those who were in the parish at the time still recall his startlingly loud voice. There was no need for any PA system when Father McWilliams was preaching; even those standing outside the church could hear his voice clearly.

Father Gerald Gostling

Gerald Gostling was born in Dagenham in January 1945. He grew up in Holy Family Parish and was educated at St. Joseph's School, Dagenham and Bishop Ward Secondary Modern School, Dagenham. He trained for the priesthood at Mark Cross, Sussex from 1959 to 1963 and St. John's Seminary, Wonersh, 1963-1969. He was ordained to the priesthood at his old school, Bishop Ward, in July 1969 by Bishop Wall. Father Gostling served as assistant priest at Upminster 1969-1972, Southend-on-Sea 1972-1975, Clacton-on-Sea 1975-1979, Rayleigh 1979-1980 and Canning Town 1980-1982. He served as Parish Priest of Stanford-le-Hope 1982-1989, Chadwell Heath 1989-1997, Clacton-on-Sea 1999-2000 and Holy Redeemer, Harold Hill 2000-2004. Father Gostling has been working in the Diocese of Dundee, South Africa, since 2004.

Father Gostling's curate at Stanford-le-Hope was Father Peter Connor who had been very recently ordained, in October 1983.

Father Gostling was the Diocesan Chaplain for the Deaf, and each year Our Lady and Saint Joseph's acted as host for parties of hearing impaired children, often arranging dormitory provision for the visitors in St. Joseph's Hall. The children were looked after on a daily basis by members of the congregation. Those who attended the special Masses will never forget the moving sight of Father Gostling delivering the entire Mass in sign language, with the children responding in the same way.

In 1983, a single storey extension was built onto the side of the presbytery. This added to the comfort of the priests in the main building, as the many regular meetings of parish organisations were now held there.

Tricia Dollard and Marian Sharp 1983
painting – mostly themselves – before their Confirmation

News came to the parish in 1986 that it was to have a Mission Week in the Spring of 1987, starting on the weekend of March 28th. A special working group was set up by Father Gostling to prepare for the Mission. It met on a weekly basis throughout the winter of 1986 and the spring of 1987. Some research was conducted by the working group on the number of people who lived in the parish. This was judged to be just short of 43,000. The UK Christian Handbook of that year estimated total weekly Church attendance as seven million, of which two million were Catholics. But how many people attended Mass in our parish? On a Saturday and Sunday in October 1986, a head count was made by Father Gostling. There were six Masses that weekend, variously held at Stanford-le-Hope, Horndon, East Tilbury and Corringham. Total attendance was 698.

In an attempt to assess the vitality of our parish, the total number of active organisations was listed by members of the Mission Working Party. It is an impressive list.

Parish Priest – Sisters of Mercy – St. Joseph's School – Knights of St. Columba – Catholic Women's League – S.V.P. – Parent Teachers

Association – Scouts – Venture Scouts – Cubs – Guides – Brownies – Youth Club – Altar Servers – Organists and Choir – Repository – Readers – Eucharistic Ministers – Altar Society – Orchestra – Parish Council – Charities Commission – Marriage Encounter – CAFOD – Missionary Society – Play School – Mother and Child Club – Society for the Protection of the Unborn Child – Snowdon Club – Judo – St. Johns – Handicapped Children Club – St. Francis – St. Lukes Hospice – Free Wheelers Drama Club – Thurrock Orchestra – Unemployment Advisory - Ecumenical Liaison Officer – Irish Dancing Club.

The Mission Team was given a set of areas to cover in preparation for the Mission itself. These comprised Visiting, Hospitality, Ecumenism, Publicity, Youth, Liturgy, Sponsorship, Prayer and Transport.

After the Mission Week, the Mission priests, Father Draper and Father Keogh, continued to meet both with the Mission Team and the parishioners to guide them on what should happen next. There was general agreement that while there were few new faces in the parish congregations after the Mission, those who had been actively involved had experienced a sense of renewal in their own faith.

In January, 1988 the parish celebrated the 75th anniversary of the founding of the church of Our Lady and St. Joseph. A festival Mass was held to celebrate the event, attended by a full church of parishioners and people from the community who wished us well. This was followed by a Cheese and Wine party in St. Joseph's Hall.

In the same year, the church building benefited from the attentions of a group of young people on the government sponsored YTEC scheme. These youngsters refurbished and repainted our church, and also managed to redecorate St. Augustine's at Corringham, and the Sacred Heart Chapel at Horndon on the Hill.

There was another celebration in the same year. The headmistress of St. Joseph's School, Sister Philippa, and her former colleague Sister Helen, who was back for a short break from her work in Kenya, celebrated the Silver Jubilee of their entry into the Sisters of Mercy. Once again, the church of Our Lady and Saint Joseph was packed to capacity on their special day. Sister Philippa retired from the school in 1992 and went to Rome to study whilst awaiting another calling, and Sister Helen returned from her work in Africa to our parish and school where she had worked on two previous occasions.

Front Row : Father Gostling, Bishop McMahon and Father Connor
Second Row : Sister Philippa, Sister Perpetua, Sister Helen and Sister Monica

Her work in Kenya had seen a great expansion, both in the building work undertaken there, and in the faith of the children she inspired. The parishioners of Stanford-le-Hope have supported Sister Helen in her missionary work, in hundreds of letters to her and in donations of money raised within the parish. In 1992, just as Sister Helen was to return from Kenya, a group of parishioners went over to Kenya to visit her, and they made a short video of her African school to show to all her many friends and supporters here in England.

During this time our curate, Father Peter Connor, was a major force within the parish, especially in his work with young people. He was a firm supporter of the Youth Club and he helped to organise a series of memorable visits to Walsingham House, the Catholic retreat centre for young people, and Allington Castle in Kent, once home to an order of Carmelite Nuns. The youngsters were accompanied by Father Connor, together with the Youth Club leaders, Sister Helen and, later, Sister Barbara.

Father Connor also took on the position of chaplain to Orsett Hospital, continuing a relationship between the parish and its local hospital which was first formalised back in 1921 when the services of a Catholic priest were requested by the Orsett Infirmary. When Father Connor left the parish in 1986, he was to be the last curate appointed to the parish. The general shortage of priests, which was becoming something of a problem for the wider Catholic community, meant that our own Parish Priest was now obliged to serve the parish on his own. This was no small task, bearing in mind the number of parishioners and the geographical size of the parish.

Father Gostling speaks with a Very Important Person

Shortly before the departure of Father Gostling, the parish suffered a major set-back. An electrical fault in the confessional started a fire that spread into the main body of the church and caused very considerable damage. The thick smoke created by the fire did more harm to the fabric of the building than the flames themselves. Worse was to follow. When the damage done to the church was investigated, another problem was discovered. The main frame of the building was diagnosed to have what was termed 'concrete cancer'. The total bill for all the work that had to be done was so high that there remained only one option: the church building would have to be completely demolished and a new church built in its place. This would at least give the parish the chance to create a church that could hold a larger congregation and, perhaps, create a place of worship that did not suffer the twin problems of condensation and cold.

The old Church of Our Lady and St. Joseph is demolished

An architect was appointed, Roger Jones of Tomei and Mackley based in Croydon, and his designs created a great deal of discussion amongst the parishioners. Some wanted a building similar to the old one, with the added benefit of a warm and dry interior. Others preferred a complete break with the past, a church that made a statement about the close partnership that exists between a Parish Priest and his congregation. The exciting new plans certainly favoured the second viewpoint, representing a considerable change in the style of the church, and all of the parishioners soon supported the proposed scheme.

The main difficulty, of course, would be finding the money for the new building. Unfortunately, the only way to help finance the capital outlay was to sell both the chapel at Horndon on the Hill and St. Augustine's Church in Corringham. The first task was completed quite quickly, with the chapel being converted into a private house. The second task, the sale of St. Augustine's Church in Corringham, had to await the completion of the new church in Stanford-le-Hope. Until the new church was ready, Masses would be said in the adjoining Hall, or in St. Augustine's Church.

In the meantime, Father Gostling left the parish in 1989 to become Parish Priest in Chadwell Heath. This popular priest found himself on the receiving end of a 'This Is Your Life' production, designed to highlight his many qualities and the particular contribution he had made to the life of the parish. It was presented by the children of the parish and St. Joseph's School, and was a clear indication of the high regard which we all had for Father Gerald Gostling.

Our new Parish Priest was Father Richard Ashton, who came to us from Holy Trinity Church in Basildon. He took on the additional responsibility of supervising the rebuilding of our church. Local builders, Hall and Riley from Westcliff, were appointed to construct the new church, and Father Richard, or Father Dick as he became known, soon established himself in the parish.

Father Dick celebrated the Silver Jubilee of his ordination on October 30th, 1991. As the new church of Our Lady and St. Joseph was not yet completed, the Mass to celebrate the Silver Jubilee was said at St. Augustine's in Corringham. It was concelebrated by Father Ashton and the Bishop of Brentwood, Thomas McMahon. Many of Father Richard's family attended the Mass, together with a great number of priests and our Sisters of Mercy. There was a social celebration afterwards in St. Joseph's Hall, next to the site where our new church was being rebuilt.

Father Dick Ashton in the parish

And on holiday

On December 8th, 1992, the church of Our Lady and St. Joseph was at last completed. It had taken three years to build. The new church could now comfortably accommodate 300 people, whereas the older building could seat about half that number. A celebration Mass was held by Father Dick. After the ceremony, he stated "Everyone says how beautiful the new church is." To mark the occasion, our Parish Priest reflected on the changes.

> Many of those who live in Stanford had been brought up with the old church. Their fathers had built it. They had been baptised and married in it and wanted nothing to do with a wooden hall or modern monstrosity masquerading as a church.
>
> To them St. Joseph's was beautiful – and real beauty in churches has to be chiefly in the lives of those who make up the church community, united in Christ.
>
> However, the three year wait turned out to be worth it. The new church of Our Lady and St. Joseph is, according to parishioners, warm, homely and beautiful!

Father Dick in the newly completed church

> But needless to say we have not yet paid for it. The idea is that we sell our outlying properties to raise the ready.

But at least we are ready before Christmas. There will be room in our new church for as many who turn up.

The real question for all of us, though, is: "What room do we have for Christ in our hearts?"

In 1993, the January 21st edition of the *Evening Echo* contained an article on the new church, written by Louise Dray.

Yellow brick church needs cash from sale of site

Follow the old Southend Road, till you come to the yellow brick church, locals will say.
But Stanford-le-Hope is like a European village now with its new £350,000 Catholic church.
Architect Roger Jones described his style: "It's definitely Italianate with the low square bell tower and colouring, a village church with a European influence."
Parish Priest Fr. Dick Ashton says money is still money, even if it's not Ecus, and prays to the Lord to revive the property market.

He needs to raise another £200,000 and must sell a prime site in Corringham Town Centre – where an old wooden Catholic church stands.
He tells you wryly: "We trust in the Lord but sometimes He takes his time!"
The debt on the last church he built, Holy Trinity, Basildon, is being paid off with the help of a few thousand a year from a club.
But he said: "We have no club here, The debt is piling up while we wait to sell. There has been some interest in the Corringham site but though it has planning permission for houses, they can't sell them at present."
His parishioners who are parents, he explains, are good and willing raisers of money but it goes on the school.

He said: "Our PTA has lots of fund raising events but we had to buy an extra classroom for the school and equipment. That comes first."
The church is formally dedicated to Our Lady and St. Joseph but is generally just known as St. Joseph's.
The old one was badly damaged by fire in October 1989 and the plan was to raise the money for a new church by reorganising the three Mass centres served from Stanford-le-Hope. One was at Horndon on the Hill and that was sold to a builder who turned it into a home for himself.

In East Tilbury, Mass is said in the village hall and the third is the wooden church at Corringham where they want to sell the site.
The scattered parish includes Fobbing and Langdon Hills and extends as far as Dry Street and along the A127 to Bulphan.

When it comes to choosing the new design, members of St. Joseph's Parish Council went round by car to see churches that Roger Jones's practice had built in Kent.
The interior furniture in modern Catholic churches is important to the symbolism in the religion.
Fr. Ashton said: "The Bishop has a good art and architecture committee and we invited the chairman, Stephen Scully, when we got the first draft of the plans.
"In effect he gave us a lesson on why church interiors are designed as they are, to better perform the liturgy.
The position of our new baptismal font, for instance, is right in the middle of the church under the skylight."
The interior charms with its sense of warmth given by the earthy colours, wooden furniture in shades of walnut from pale to dark, altar furniture of creamy Caen stone from Normandy, and the brown and green carpeting.

The walls are the same bricks inside as out and the architect says technically they are buff – but most lay people would probably describe them as pale yellow, as Fr. Ashton does.
What gives the striking look is the dark brown pointing – for which the correct description is "darker stripe contrasting band courses."

Roger Jones said as it was to be a village church, the emphasis was all on natural materials.
His firm has built a number of churches and he has studied church architecture in Italy, a country where he likes to spend his holidays.

Inevitably there was sadness among older parishioners at the loss of the original building which had been such a focal point in their lives, but they are pleased the old stained glass windows, with single figures of saints, have been transferred well into the new design.

Their former Stations of the Cross – wall plaques depicting the journey to the crucifixion which are a visual aid to prayer in every Catholic church - have been restored with fresh paint by craftsman Sid Buddle of Vange. A skilled carpenter, he is now in his 80th year.

He is also recolouring the figure of Christ on the Cross which will hang on the large crucifix outside the entrance to the church and looks like continental wood carving which should go well with the style of the new building.
Parts of the wood in the figure were frost damaged, so since that was repaired it is taking all Sid's tender loving care in the painting work.

> Other homely reminders of the demolished St. Joseph's are the holy water stoups made in pottery class at St. Anselm's, Basildon, by young parishioner John Sharp, now 24, when he was a schoolboy.
> The Bishop of the Roman Catholic Diocese of Brentwood, the Rt. Rev. Thomas McMahon, is coming to dedicate the church on February 11th, the feast of Our Lady of Lourdes.

On February 11th 1993, the church was ready for its official dedication by the Bishop of Brentwood. The following week, *The Thurrock Gazette* reported on the event.

> The new £350,000 Catholic church of Our Lady and St. Joseph was officially consecrated by the Bishop of Brentwood, the Rt. Rev. Thomas McMahon, last week.
>
> He was welcomed to the church by Fr. Richard Ashton, the Parish Priest.
>
> The consecration service was attended by representatives from a number of other churches, including the Rev. and Mrs. Reg Edmonds from Stanford Methodist church, Mrs. Jan Rylands from the Salvation Army, and the Rev. and Mrs. David Prior from St. Mary's Anglican church in Corringham.
>
> Special music and choral items were directed by Peter Preston, and the organist was Mauro Sheehan.
>
> The new church replaces the older building, built in 1913 and burned down three years ago.

Additional detail was provided by the *Evening Echo* in the same week. As might be expected from the paper's Religious Correspondent, Louise Dray reported on the words of Bishop McMahon in his dedication of the new church, the size of the congregation and the geographical range of the parish. Even in a time of rapidly rising property values, she also appears to have added £50,000 to the value of the church.

> Bishop McMahon preached on the symbolism of water when he dedicated the new £400,000 Stanford-le-Hope church of Our Lady and Saint Joseph on the feast of Our Lady of Lourdes (February 11).
> The baptismal font is in the centre of the Italianate style and he said "When we think of Lourdes we think of the healing, cleansing, life giving properties of water."
> He said we were all sick spiritually, we needed healing constantly through the grace of the church.
> In that sense, he said: "The whole world is like a hospital ward because we lack wholeness."

The Gospel was St. John 4 : 19-24 and he quoted "Whoever drinks of the water I will give will never thirst."
There was standing room only before the two-hour service began, with people from all parts of the scattered parish and 10 priests on the sanctuary.
St. Joseph's serves three Mass centres, covering an area from Dry Street, Basildon and Langdon Hills to East Tilbury, including Horndon-on-the-Hill, Corringham and Fobbing.
The old church was badly damaged by fire in 1989 and demolished in 1991.

During the two hour service, the rites included the depositing of Saints' relics in the altar, anointing and incensing the new altar, and anointing the walls.

There were many Socials, Summer Fetes and Christmas Bazaars in those days. One memorable event was the celebration to mark the fiftieth anniversary of V.E. day. It took place in the playground of St. Joseph's School, which is now the church car park, on Monday 6th May, 1995.

Our 50th VE day celebrations (with thanks to the Thurrock Gazette)

It was a very hot Bank Holiday Monday. Parishioners were encouraged to attend in period costume and about 600 people packed the area. The prize exhibit was a cardboard tank, which featured largely in *The Thurrock Gazette*. In keeping with the theme of the day, old-fashioned games were played, including Hopscotch, Nine Pins, Hoopla, Giant Ludo, Boules, Whack-a-Rat and Lotto (Bingo). There was also a Fancy Dress Competition.

Refreshments were provided by our own version of the NAAFI. Peter Preston's Musicians played on a specially constructed stage under an awning made by a Scout tarpaulin. Peter recalls "There was a sort of programme, but it ran away with itself and in the end nobody wanted to go home".

Peter Preston makes a worryingly good 'Spiv' at the V.E. 50th anniversary celebrations

People also remember evenings when meals were organised in the Parish Hall to celebrate a range of cultures. These included Spanish Tapas evenings, the Hebrew feast of Seder to mark the start of Passover, including part of the text of the Haggadah, and the Mardi Gras celebrations which the English celebrate in a more restrained way on Shrove Tuesday (Pancake Day). In a more cosmopolitan world, much of this might now be regarded as quite normal, but less than fifty years ago a Vesta curry was still considered quite exotic.

Having organised the rebuilding of our beautiful new church, Father Dick Ashton remained with us in the parish until 1998, when he moved to Canvey Island, to be Parish Priest there. He retired from the priesthood in 2000. His successor at Our Lady and St. Joseph's was Father Martin Nott.

Father Martin Nott

Father Nott was a convert to Catholicism. He studied at the Beda College, Rome and was ordained to the priesthood at St. James the Less, Colchester in July 1990 by Bishop McMahon. Father Nott served as an assistant priest at Brentwood Cathedral 1990-1993, and Rayleigh 1993-1994 before working in the Diocese of Dundee in South Africa 1994-1998.

Father Martin Nott

He was in charge at Dunmow for a short time in 1998 before moving to Stanford-le-Hope as Parish Priest the same year. Father Nott remained at Stanford-le-Hope until 2006, when he moved on to Dunmow as Parish Priest. His place was taken by Father David Clemens.

Father David Clemens

David Clemens studied for the priesthood at Campion House, Osterley 1977-1978, and at the Venerable English College, Rome 1978-1979. He left the seminary in 1979, but resumed his studies at the Beda College, Rome in 1988. Father Clemens was ordained to the priesthood in July 1992, and continued his studies in Rome. He served as an assistant priest at Leigh-on-Sea for a short period in 1993, and at Saints Peter and Paul, Ilford 1993-1995. Father Clemens was Parish Priest of Tilbury 1995-2000, before moving to serve as Parish Priest at Stanford-le-Hope 2006-2010. He has also served as Diocesan Director of the Lourdes Pilgrimage and with the Pastoral Service for the Deaf.

When Father David left Stanford, there was a major reorganisation of this part of the diocese. Father Paul arrived as our Parish Priest in October 2010. He took on a considerable responsibility, as at the same time Father Paul was appointed as Parish Priest for Tilbury. This means that his week is characterised by a continuous movement between the two parishes as he involves himself fully in the life and pastoral work of both parishes. Ask Father Paul what he thinks about this arrangement and you will always receive the same reply. With a twinkling smile, he says "It is a privilege".

Father Paul Dynan

(This article is taken from the Brentwood Diocesan Directory, 2005)

> Father Paul was ordained to the priesthood in his home parish of Our Lady Immaculate, linked with the church of the Holy Name, Chelmsford on Saturday 10th July 2004. Father Paul grew up in Manor Park, East London where he attended St. Winefride's School in Church Road and was for many years an altar server at St. Stephen's Church. Secondary education was at St. Bonaventure's School in Forest Gate where the Franciscan Friars had a marked influence on his life since he was to later join the Secular Franciscan Order and become a member of the Stratford and, later, the Abbotswick Fraternities.
>
> In his late teens Father Paul's family moved to Upton Park where he joined the choir at the church of Our Lady of Compassion, Green Street.

His career was spent exclusively working in the National Health Service. At the age of twenty-three he qualified as a Fellow of the Institute of Biomedical Sciences, specialising in Medical Microbiology and Haematology. He moved into the field of Blood Transfusion and was for many years Chief Biomedical Scientist in a busy district pathology department.

In the early days of his working life he met Connie, a nurse working at the time at the same East London hospital. They married at the church of Our Lady of Compassion and had three children, Michael, Claire and Jonathan. Following Connie's untimely death through cancer in 1988, Paul committed himself to family, parish and career. He has been a member of the Knights of St. Columba since 1982 and has held a number of offices. When the children reached adulthood he broached the subject with them of possibly leaving the hospital service and applying to Bishop Thomas to train for the priesthood.

Father Paul studied at Allen Hall in Chelsea, the seminary of the Westminster Diocese, and gained the degree of Sacrae Theologiae Baccalaureum from the University of Louvain.

His Diaconate year was spent in the newly formed Basildon Team Ministry working alongside Father Julian Wiener, Father Peter Fitch and Sister Clare Kane, OSU. The Team Ministry, whilst demanding at times, was a period of great joy and he made numerous new friends. He holds himself very fortunate to have had so many and such varied student placements during his time as a seminarian and deeply appreciates the love, help and kindness shown to him during his years as a student for the priesthood. He believes that such preparation has been invaluable in equipping him for the path ahead. Father Paul has been appointed to serve in the parish of St. James the Less and St. Helen in Colchester.

But of course a priest must spend a lot of time preparing for his ministry. One important stage is the Diaconate year that occurs in the year before ordination as a priest. Here, Father Paul reflects on what that year was like for him. This article appeared in the Summer 2004 edition of *The*

Parishioner, the magazine for the parish of Our Lady Immaculate, London Road, where Father Paul was ordained in July of that year.

Appointment
It was a pleasant afternoon on Wednesday, 25th June 2003 when I took the bus from Chelmsford to Stock for an appointment with Bishop Thomas McMahon. It was just a few weeks prior to my ordination to the Diaconate and, as one does, for some days I had been reflecting upon which of the parishes that I might be sent to for my year's placement.

Some possibilities were slightly more obvious than others. For instance, parishes which often in the past had a deacon working there for their pre-priestly ordination year – others were parishes where deacons had been working until recently and had now created a vacancy by their recent ordination to the priesthood. I had a list, one might even say a league table, of seven and I felt fairly certain that wherever Bishop Thomas was about to send me was one of those I had in the back of my mind.

After a bit of a chat, Bishop Thomas told me that there were plans to set up a "Team Ministry" in Basildon and informed me that he wanted me to go there as a deacon, to work alongside Father Julian Wiener and Father Peter Fitch, who was newly ordained. We would share the Priests' House at St. Basil's and some sisters from the Brentwood Ursuline Order would be resident in the presbytery at The Holy Trinity Church.

All I could think of at the time was "Basildon – that's not on my list!"

Having said that, I was truly pleased and excited about my placement and felt that it would indeed be an honour to be part of this pioneering ministry and to work with those that the Bishop had mentioned. I could not wait to get to Basildon and meet the parishioners and their families or visit the schools or hospitals, but protocol demanded that I waited until October the 1st before going to the parish.

It was not until some weeks after my meeting with Bishop Thomas that I was to meet the fourth member of the Basildon Team as we were to become known – the charming Sister Clare Kane.

For those who (as I was on the 25th June) are unfamiliar with the area, the district covered by the Team Ministry includes the parishes of St. Basil the Great, at the Vange/Pitsea end of the town, The Most Holy Trinity near the town centre, the parish of St. Therese of Lisieux in Laindon, four schools (one at secondary level) a large teaching hospital and a hospice. Further details can be obtained from the website on www.basildoncatholicteamministry.org.uk

Not too busy

Life at first was fairly gentle. Moving in, getting to know the area and finding out where things were and who was responsible for what. However, that is of course for all three parishes. It was what you might describe as a steep learning curve. Trying to remember the many names is one of the hardest tasks. Particularly when half a dozen people are introduced at any one of the parishes at the same moment, it takes a little time to assimilate who's who. But I did try – honestly. I tried very hard to emulate Father Brian O'Higgins who is renowned and admired by all for his almost photographic memory to remember who is who and even who their second-cousin-twice-removed is. I know how much people appreciated this.

During Mass for the first two weekends we each had to get up and say a little about ourselves and "our journey on the way to Basildon". I recall stating that I was very pleased to be in Basildon and that during my year I was looking forward to getting to know those parishioners better. When I mentioned that Father Brian O'Shea was my parish priest back home in Chelmsford my ratings soared, especially in St. Basil's Parish, as he is still to this day warmly remembered for his time spent caring for the people in this parish.

One good thing about being the first of such team ministries is that there is no "model" to follow – no accepted method of working, and so, under Father Julian's guiding hand we planned and organised who would be doing what. On the other hand, not having a "tried and tested" method to follow meant that we had to learn by trial and error about things and had to be flexible enough to allow for adjustment if things required to be modified. Having said that, the year during which I was due to be working with the Team had been designated as a year of discernment during which no major decisions were to be made. Being the deacon in this new type of team ministry was to prove a unique and rewarding experience for me.

Getting busier

Within weeks of our arrival we received a pastoral visit from the Bishop, and a group of ten young people received the Sacrament of Confirmation. A number of steering groups were established from each of the three distinct communities and these met in January. In fact a round of meetings began, culminating in May in the gathering of the three steering groups under one roof.

I learnt what it meant to be available to minister to the bereaved and conduct funerals, as well as to officiate at baptisms and weddings. It was a delight to begin the visits to schools. I was assigned the delightful task of visiting St. Anne Line Infants School where I have spent many a happy morning, with the children and the staff, in classrooms, assemblies and even in the playground. Children love to sing and I dusted off my aging twelve-string guitar and in the classrooms we always included one or two songs which hopefully fitted in with what they were currently studying – albeit that the links were sometimes a little tenuous. At Christmas I received a new guitar and this contributed to us making better music in the spring term!

Life within the team

Among the happiest memories of my year as part of the Basildon Team Ministry will be the tremendous mutual support given by the team members. There was a real level of concern and humour which helped us through some difficult and stressful times. This goes for the "extended team", those who are in a close daily working relationship with the Team and provide help and assistance for the Team to function. These are a veritable army of people who work quietly and efficiently at what they do. They are the backbone of any enterprise and truly the ones who make things happen. I make unreserved thanks to these people for enabling me to carry out my role within the team ministry.

Parishioners too have been superb in this. Without fear of exaggeration, I would say that in the order of 98 per cent have worked in collaboration and encouraged the Team in their efforts at every turn. Those who sadly have appeared to work deliberately against the Team were, I am pleased to say, a very small minority, but even these we had hope to bring on board and help them to understand that the concept of team ministry is new for everybody – particularly those who have been given the mantle to make it work

Looking back

As the time approaches for me to leave Basildon, I wish to put on record how much I appreciate the way that the good citizens of Basildon, including Vange, Pitsea, Laindon and Langdon Hills, took me into their hearts and their homes. I have been incredibly privileged to spend so much time in their company, to share both the highs and the lows, to visit the Isle of Wight with a year six group from St. Anne Line School, to minister to the bereaved, to officiate at baptisms and weddings and to be present at so many social occasions.

A great joy for me has been sharing at the heart of the spiritual life of the parish. Being so much involved in liturgical activity as I have been has meant that I have been able to feel completely involved with the growth and life of all that happens in a spiritual context. For instance, sacramental preparation, whether it be baptism, confirmation or marriage, and not forgetting the RCIA group of 2003-2004 drawn from all three parishes in the Basildon Team Ministry area, with whom we all shared so much.

When I first stood in the pulpit to say how happy I was to be in Basildon I mentioned too that it was only for a short time. As I write, that time now sadly draws to a close. My chief regrets are that I had hoped to spend more time visiting people at home and in the schools, but the realities of parish life soon taught me how much I could plan for and how much I had to respond to the urgent needs of others.

There are a small number of things I would have done differently in my time as Deacon Paul in the Basildon Team Ministry, but not too many. The sense of camaraderie within the Team has helped me immensely and not a day went past when laughter did not ring out in the house. I have felt it a huge privilege to be a part of the setting up of the first Team Ministry and a bit of me is sad that I will not be around to continue the work so earnestly begun. Like others I will have to watch from the sidelines as things develop, but look forward to being invited back from time to time for any big events within the Team.

All I can say is, thank you Basildon, my time with you was quite *fantastic.*

Postscript

As I pen these few words it is early June, and at the end of this month I will once again be invited to make the journey to see Bishop Thomas to see where my first appointment will be. I do not know where he will send me as an assistant priest. I try not to think about it too much. I would probably be as wrong as I was last time if I were to try. All I do know is that I will be delighted to take up the ministry to which he will assign me, to be with God's people where they are, as I did last October when I walked through the door at Basildon.

A text that has helped me to remain focused during my years of priestly formation is a quotation from the prophet Jeremiah which Pope John Paul II has written about on a number of occasions.

I will give you shepherds after my own heart and these shall feed you on knowledge and discretion. Jer. 3:15

The Lord, who promises to be with us until the end of time, tells us that he will send pastors to tend his flock who will ensure that his Word and his Love will reach past the end of time.
Deo Gratias

A. Corringham

If Corringham led the way by holding its first Mass in Herd Lane in 1903 in the church that became St. Francis de Sales, its use as a Catholic church was short-lived. A few years after the creation of Our Lady and Saint Joseph's in Stanford-le-Hope, the small Corringham church was sold to Essex County Council, and the space which had doubled as a one room schoolroom became part of a new primary school. The decision to sell the property was influenced by a measure of parish debt and the declining congregation numbers, so that by 1918/19 there were very few people attending Mass in this little Corringham church. In addition, there was some damage to the windows of the church and the locks also had to be changed. Father Carless stated that the damage had been caused by the munitions workers at Kynochs, who lived in huts close to the church. Father Carless wrote "I trust someone may soon be found for this place".

The negotiations for the sale of the church and its land were quite protracted, dragging on through 1919 and 1920 before the property was sold in 1921. Although Canon Shepherd had advised the diocesan solicitors that the valuation was £2,500, but that the sale price would be £2,000 and that £1,600 would be accepted, the property was finally sold for £1,350. With the original mortgage of £1,530 still in place, the Diocese of Brentwood can hardly have made a profit. Indeed, a valuation

The exterior of Corringham Primary School, showing some of the original brickwork of the church of St. Francis de Salles

had been made in 1920 which suggested that the building itself was worth £4,000 but that there was little prospect of this being obtained as it would be difficult to adapt it for commercial purposes.

Yet the sole party interested in the building and its land was Essex County Council, who wanted it for the expansion of its school places. That the church suited the County Council perfectly well can be seen in the fact that the surviving primary school in Herd Lane still has remnants of the church within its buildings, so that this first Parish Church in the modern era has not entirely disappeared.

A Class at Herd Lane School in 1930 (that radiator is still there)

The Corringham Catholics were now without a Mass centre and had to choose between a journey over to Stanford-le-Hope and one to Vange, each a walk of a few miles in each direction. With no proper bus service on Sundays and few parishioners fortunate enough to own a car, this posed quite a problem for the elderly, the infirm, those with young children and all parishioners in bad weather and wintertime. The parishioners became aware that the Anglican Vicar in Corringham had offered a room attached to the Vicarage where Mass could be said, but that the Diocese had not accepted the offer.

When asked for his comments on this in 1936, Father Snell stated that Mass was already being said in three places in the parish and that a fourth station would necessitate an additional priest. He reminded the Bishop that he has earlier suggested saying Mass in a room in Corringham but had been told by the Bishop to concentrate his efforts on Stanford-le-Hope where the school was. Although the parson was described as "extremely high" and was referred to by his own congregation as "Father", it had been decided not to use Church of England premises. Ecumenism was not yet a power in the land.

In 1943, Father Snell was able to gain approval from the Bishop to say Mass once a month in an alternative venue in Corringham, a billiard room at Woodville Hall. That this was preferred to the earlier offer from the Church of England says much about the attitudes of the times, for one cannot imagine such a response being made today. The monthly Corringham Mass was at the expense of East Tilbury where, as Father Snell stated, "the response is not too good".

Catholics living in Corringham had a long wait for a new Mass centre in their area, but on Sunday, 13th November 1955 Mass was said once more in the town. The British Legion Hall, in Giffords Cross Road, was purchased freehold for the parish. The Hall was served with mains drainage but no provision had been made for gutters or drains for rainwater, and the site was prone to flooding. It was no architectural gem, comprising as it did a Nissan style hut with concrete additions. As well as the main hall, there was a kitchen, two rooms for storage and use by committees and basic toilets. It was accepted by the vendors that the central heating was not satisfactory, as the boiler was too small and often under water. The asking price was £800, but after the Bishop of Brentwood visited the site in person he recommended an offer of just £600. It was finally purchased for £725. Although the Diocese had been prepared to lend the sum of £500 towards the purchase, it finally agreed to advance the total amount, at 2 and a half per cent interest. The capital was to be repaid at not less than £75 per year.

Canon Wilson was asked to draw up the documents and make the necessary arrangements. Although he did so, he was not overly enthusiastic at the prospect. In July 1955, he wrote

> When I first took the diocesan accounts, twenty seven years ago, a bugbear was 'Corringham loan'. It was eventually disposed of and now I see it is to be resurrected.

Whilst this might be an appropriate comment from a financier, it is an unexpected observation from a man of the Church.

Meanwhile, timing was critical, as the parish had been advised of a big new development of council housing in Corringham by the London borough of West Ham. It was to start in early 1956, and would offer additional Catholic families for the parish.

The stage at the new Mass centre was soon fitted with a confessional box, and a moveable altar was placed on the stage for the saying of Mass. Heating was provided by electric radiators suspended on the walls. Regular Masses were said here and the hall provided a venue for social occasions.

One of the first tasks was to give the Mass centre a name. When owned by the British Legion, it had been called Victory Hall. Father Hibbert suggested that a more suitably Catholic name would be Loretto Hall, named after the home of Mary which was rebuilt in Loretto, Italy in the late thirteenth century when a Muslim army invaded Palestine. Our Sisters of Mercy, however, informed Father Hibbert that the name St. Teresa's had been earmarked by Father Snell for any future chapel in Corringham. To be fair, Father Hibbert acknowledged this in a letter to the Bishop, asking him to select the more appropriate name. And so St. Teresa's it was.

By 1960 Father Hibbert was making plans to demolish the Mass centre and have it completely rebuilt. This would have cost substantially more than the original purchase of the hall, but Father Hibbert though that the overall cost of £7,500 would be a worthwhile venture in terms of providing a more suitable venue for Corringham Catholics. The architect for Thurrock Council, Mr. Bannister, was approached to draw up suitable plans for the proposed development. The parish had already been granted a new permanent site in the nearby Corringham Town Centre Development, but this was not scheduled for completion until at least the mid nineteen seventies. It was finally decided not to proceed with the rebuilding of St. Teresa's.

Unfortunately, there was insufficient money to maintain the building adequately, and by 1967 it had become very dilapidated. It was no longer possible to keep the Mass centre open. The Rev. Father Hill, of St. Mary's Church in Corringham, offered shared use of St. John's Church in the new Corringham town centre and this time our parish was happy to accept the temporary arrangement. This 'short term' measure continued until 1977.

Now that St. Teresa's had been abandoned, it was necessary to decide what to do with the site. It was put on the market and early interest was shown by the British heavyweight boxer, "Golden Boy" Billy Walker.

As part of a growing property empire he owned a petrol garage next door to St. Teresa's and wanted to expand the business. With a street frontage of 54 feet St. Teresa's was considered to be a desirable property, even if the building itself was beyond repair. Billy Walker's business interests were handled by his brother, George, another well known boxer who was Billy's boxing manager.

Interestingly, many of the letters were written directly by George Walker, rather than by a solicitor acting on his behalf. The very polite and formal letters from George Walker reveal how keen the brothers were to buy the site, and they made no objection as the price of the site rose steadily during some detailed negotiations. When the figure of five thousand pounds was reached, there was some delay whilst the Walkers tried to obtain the necessary planning permission. In the meantime, a development company put in its own bid at the same price, and Halrod Developments bought the site in the summer of 1971. St. Teresa's was demolished and two private houses were built on the site.

Naturally enough, parishioners were keen to have their own church again in Corringham and they began to raise money to make this possible. In October 1972, they succeeded in buying the plot of land in St. John's Way that had been allocated to them by Thurrock Council as part of the Corringham Town Redevelopment. The detail from some of the early letters reveals that it was originally envisaged that a presbytery would also be built on the site, but this idea appears to have been shelved.

The site was just under an acre and was situated across the road from the town library. It was offered to them at the preferential rate of £11,415 and this made it possible to build a new Mass centre. The foundations, flooring, 'services' and decoration were provided by Greenan Contractors and the building was constructed by S. Wernick and Sons, a company based at Billericay. The new building was to be 64 feet long and 42 feet wide with a pitched roof. Its total cost was just under £21,000.

Our Parish Priest, now Father Taylor, wrote to Canon Grady in June 1976 with details of the proposed building and estimated costs. In asking for a loan from the Diocese, Father Taylor proposed to repay the £21,000 from the income the parish received from its tax covenant scheme. This had raised nearly four thousand pounds in 1976, and it was estimated that the income would be nearly five thousand pounds in 1977. Father Taylor proposed to pay off a loan at the rate of three thousand pounds a year, which would, in his words clear a loan of £21,000 plus interest within 8 years without straining other aspects of parish life and without detracting from other parts of the parish.

As evidence of his financial management skills, Father Taylor referred to the steadily declining debt owed by the parish in its contributions to the Schools Quota. Within six months, he had reduced this from over three thousand pounds to less than a thousand. This was an impressive record, and it certainly impressed the Diocese who gave permission for Father Taylor to borrow more than he had requested. He was authorised by Father Drea, the Diocesan Financial Secretary, to borrow up to twenty four thousand from a bank in Brentwood.

The construction of the first St. Augustine's Church in Corringham : note the sliding doors that divided the building into two

Bishop Patrick Casey formally opened the new church and hall in St. John's Way with the celebration of Mass at 8.00 p.m. on Thursday, 26th May, 1977. The new church was dedicated to St. Augustine. It just so happens that, among other things, St. Augustine is the patron saint of brewers. Internally, the building was divided into two by folding doors, so that social occasions could be held in one part of the building and Masses in the other part. The congregation grew so quickly, however, that the folding doors were soon drawn back to make more room for the increased numbers attending Mass.

These Masses were characterised by some energetic singing, and many parishioners still remember the Christmas Eve carols which took place a good hour before the Midnight Mass itself. Anyone hoping for a seat at the Mass had to be there for the carols beforehand, as the small Mass centre was packed to capacity. In 1980, our curate, Father Neil Tozer, suggested an alternative to the traditional carols which preceded Midnight Mass. He introduced a slide show of pictures suitable for the Christmas period, accompanied by prayers. There was a great deal of controversy over the new format. Whilst some parishioners stated that it did make them think more deeply about the real message of Christmas, others were outspoken in their opposition. Some parishioners stated that they didn't like it, and others went as far as to say that it spoilt their Christmas. The following year, the carol singing was back.

The Parish Youth Club found a home for some years in the 'social' half of St. Augustine's Church. It had begun life in the Methodist hall in Stanford, and had also made use of St. Joseph's Hall. Regular club nights were held in Corringham on Mondays. There were many helpers who shared the work, but two leaders in particular played a vital role in the success of the Youth Club. They were Peter Farrell and Ron Spoors. Fortunately, both Parish Priests and their assistants took a real interest in the Youth Club and actively supported it. At one of the Youth Club's Annual General Meetings, the decision was made to move the Youth Club back to St. Joseph's Hall, where it was later carefully supervised by Susan and Brian Hargis.

Father Gostling visits the site of the second St. Augustine's Church, Corringham

In 1979, just two years after St. Augustine's was built, a development company approached the Council to build a supermarket on the land where the church stood and adjoining land already owned by the company. As part of the proposal, the development company offered to rebuild St. Augustine's on an alternative site that they owned in St. John's Way, opposite St. John's Church.

The plan was agreed, and in 1983 a Somerfield supermarket (now Morrisons) was built, and St. Augustine's Church was relocated. The Brentwood based development company, Dudley Anderson Limited, organised the preparation of the new site for the church and its complete rebuilding. A considerable sum of money was offered to the Diocese of Brentwood as compensation for the inconvenience and as "a contribution towards constructing a new church or for other parish purposes".

Once again, the Rector of the Anglican church of St. Mary's was kind enough to offer the shared use of St. John's whilst the Catholic church was relocated. In the rebuilding, a few changes were made to the internal layout of St. Augustine's. A small oratory for private prayer was introduced for a while, but this was not a success and was eventually removed. The folding doors between the church and the hall were replaced by a lattice work screen, so that the overflow congregation could both see and hear the Mass although they could not access the pews.

St. Augustine's Church : rebuilt where the furniture store now stands

It has to be said that the new church of St. Augustine's was not a great success. It never lost its hall-like atmosphere and, in the words of an earlier writer, Peter Preston, on whose words much of this book is based, "it never took on the serenity of a church". For a while it operated as a Mass centre whilst the new Stanford church was being built, after attempts to hold Masses in St. Joseph's Hall proved to be impractical. All parish Masses were said at St. Augustine's except for the 9.30 Mass, which was said at East Tilbury.

When a decision was made to sell the site to help meet the cost of rebuilding Our Lady and St. Joseph's, St. Augustine's soon fell into disrepair, as frequent vandalism damaged the fabric of the now unoccupied building and broken windows were boarded up with unsightly plywood.

With its demise and the earlier sale of the Sacred Heart Chapel in Horndon on the Hill, our wide ranging parish was now served by just two Mass centres rather than the four it had enjoyed. Of course, many more people have cars, and there continues to be a real shortage of priests, but there are difficulties for some parishioners, and there are frequent requests for help with transport to Mass.

B. Horndon on the Hill

Doctor John Stansfield was an evangelist from Bermondsey in London. In 1897, he founded the Oxford Medical Mission as a part of the Oxford movement. The Oxford movement itself had become part of the debate between Anglicans and Catholics during the middle years of the nineteenth century. Many priests who were influenced by the views of the Oxford movement found it difficult to obtain livings, as their Anglican Bishops were by and large opposed to its teachings, especially the call for closer links between Anglicanism and Catholicism This led many would be priests into social work in the poorer areas of cities and to develop ideas about just wages for working people, safe working conditions in factories and ways to combat the high rate of infant mortality. The influence these people brought to bear on the Anglican Church was to develop into the Anglo-Catholic movement, which was to influence Christian thinking throughout the world.

In 1901, Doctor Stansfield bought 23 acres of land in Horndon on the Hill, for the use of the Oxford Medical Mission. For many years, this area was known as The Priory, and it seems probable that Oxford Road in Horndon is a reference to his foundation.

Doctor Stansfield worked among the poor and sick of Bermondsey, especially the consumptives who were debilitated by tuberculosis. The land in Horndon was to be used as a camping ground for boys in the days before the Boy Scout movement was founded. Doctor Stansfield bought the ruins of a demolished chapel in the Old Kent Road and his friends helped to move this building material by horse drawn cart all the way to Horndon on the Hill. They built a play castle with it, designed by the doctor himself. It had a square, wooden tower topped with battlements, and an upper platform reached by a ladder. The old chapel's vestry door, with its handle still attached, was now to be found halfway up one of the walls of the castle.

The camp proved to be a great success. Doctor Stansfield wrote

> Lads without money continually walk down the 26 miles for the sake of coming, others cycle on 'fifth hand' machines or some arrive with cheap fares by train.

The good doctor and his wife were helped by other members of the Oxford movement, as they cooked vast quantities of food for the boys, using galvanized dustbins over a trench fire. One of their young helpers was Geoffrey Fisher, later to become Archbishop of Canterbury 1945 – 1961. Others included Alec Paterson, later Prison Commissioner, who argued for the rehabilitation of prisoners rather than simply their punishment, and Barclay Baron, a leading figure in the founding of the interdenominational Christian society Toc H, which carried out so many acts of service to the community throughout the twentieth century. All of these men were to be seen at the Horndon camp, helping the charismatic John Stansfield with his work.

Each evening there were camp fires and sing-songs, and in the daytime there were dips in the swimming pool they dug out by hand. Many of the village boys learned to swim in the pool, although they were not supposed to be there. They would break into the Priory grounds from Blackbush Lane, and would run the gauntlet of an elderly man called Mr. Clark, who was both caretaker and groundsman. If he saw them he would chase them out of the grounds. On one occasion he caught them in the pool, and they swam up and down with the old man chasing them from the poolside, until he got out of breath and they were able to escape.

Doctor Stansfield was primarily an evangelist, and he believed in spreading his faith by setting an example for the boys in his care. An adjutant to the doctor wrote the following words:

> Stand one evening at 'quiet time' in the little circle of our tents and when the moon is bright in the sky. You have never felt the world so still. In each tent a ring of boys is kneeling. Some have never

> prayed before and some perhaps may never pray again. The heavens are proclaiming the Glory of God and the earth replies in wonderful accord.

There was a long low hut alongside the play-castle. This was called Wycliffe House, perhaps a reference to the fourteenth century Catholic philosopher who made an early translation of the bible into vernacular English. The doctor later added what he called Oxford College, a quadrangle of open cubicles for his convalescing patients, most of whom would have had tuberculosis.

The Priory : September 1917

There was often quite a crowd of men and boys camping out at the Priory, as can be seen from this extract from the *Langdon Hills Parish Magazine*, dated September 1906.

> Oxford Medical Mission, Lads and Men, Boys Club, Bermondsey S.E. We shall not forget the visit of nearly 200 men and lads from their encampment at Horndon on the Hill, on Sunday 5th August, when a special service was held and they filled our church. The Rector officiated and the address was given by the Rev. H. S. Pelham, BA, their warden and Chaplain. Mr. V. L. Chilman kindly presided at the organ and the singing was such as we have never heard in our church. At the close of the service the men were regaled with light refreshments in the Rectory grounds.

When Doctor Stansfield left the area for Oxford itself, the land was handed over to the Diocese of Southwark. A Catholic social worker in the East End of London, Miss Green, managed to buy the land from the Diocese. One of the boys who had attended the camp in earlier years, Bob Marriot, bought land next to this. Miss Green now set about developing the area. Houses nearby were used by her friends from London and a Catholic community began to form in the village.

In the nineteen twenties, Miss Green worked with Miss Ida Woollard to organise a children's home. It was somewhat vaguely described as 'a kind of children's home for unfortunate children'. Miss Green was a Catholic convert and it was obvious that her faith meant a great deal to her. In all the plans she had for her new project at Horndon, she always contacted the Bishop for advice and permission. The only difficulty was that she seemed to change her mind so often.

In 1924, she was asked by a Father Constantine to help found a Benedictine convent at Horndon and, after a private audience with Pope Pius XI, who gave a special blessing to Horndon Priory, she decided that this was what she must do. Now that the site at Horndon had both a proper road and mains gas, Miss Green decided that 'it is perfect in every way for their work'. The Benedictine combination of the contemplative life, active Mission work and teaching was also, in Miss Green's word, 'perfect'. In her letter to Bishop Doubleday she referred to the retreats for women and children that the Benedictines organised within their Order. There would need to be substantial building, but after everyone involved undertook a week of prayer, Miss Green announced that the answer was yes. Now that God had made his will known, Miss Green felt that she must carry it out, but she asked the Bishop for his blessing in the new venture.

Bishop Doubleday was not encouraging in his response, which was written the following day. He thought that the community at Horndon was 'not suited to a foundation of Benedictine Nuns' and reminded Miss Green that she would need to build a school and a retreat house to accommodate the work that this Order did. The Bishop advised Miss Green that he did not know Father Constantine or the nuns and so would not be able to give his permission 'to let them establish themselves and undertake spiritual duties in this diocese'. Further, he reminded Miss Green that she had already made over the church at Horndon to the Brentwood Diocese and if she carried her plans through 'we shall have to decide what to do with it'.

Priory Church (note the stocks, presumably for fun!)

Miss Green does not appear to have been in any way discouraged by the tone or content of the Bishop's letter. The following day, she wrote back.

October 26th 1924

My Lord,
I cannot tell you how grateful I am, for your most kind letter. I need hardly say that I want to be guided by you in everything, and will do nothing for the present, about giving over this property to the Benedictines, though the Holy Spirit shows me very clearly, that I must be prepared to do so, but I shall await your advice about it, when the time comes. I am very shortly going over to Belgium to see the convent and to be received into the Order as an Oblate. I do value having your blessing in this step.

The Benedictines get all the money for their Order, by the dowries brought in by the nuns. They do not depend on any work for their income. They do not do school work unless it is really needed. The life of prayer, and Retreats for poor people, is I understand, their mission. This place they felt was ideal for Retreats, it is now on such a good bus route from Harwich, Clacton, Colchester and Chelmsford, and also the Southend district and Tilbury. Father Constantine is the architect for the Order, he felt that the grounds (there are 27 acres) would be perfect for their buildings. But I must not weary you with a longer letter.

With renewed thanks for your kindness and forbearance, and asking for your prayers,
Yours sincerely
Alice Green

It is clear that Miss Green was not a woman to be easily dissuaded. It is also clear that, whilst guided and even driven by her faith, she was not a notably practical person. In 1928, a Catholic nurse went to Horndon Priory to help out, at the request of both Miss Green and her associate Miss Woollard. The conditions encountered by the nurse caused her to contact a colleague from the Catholic Nurses' Guild, Mrs. Reidy. After the latter's visit to Horndon Priory, she wrote to Bishop Doubleday. Expressing herself as 'horrified' at the dirty condition of things, she described it as unfit for young children. She commented on the feeding, the state of the beds, the smells, the sanitary arrangements and, most significantly, the safety of the Blessed Sacrament in the chapel. The Bishop asked for a response to these charges from Father Snell.

Our Parish Priest assured Bishop Doubleday that the charges of poor standards of hygiene were misplaced. The bedsheets were washed and changed every week, the children received a weekly bath, Miss Kenny as Head Teacher of St. Joseph's was satisfied with the cleanliness of the children from Horndon Priory, the visiting health officers were satisfied with the sanitary conditions at Horndon and the doctors employed to examine the children carefully saw no cause for concern. Father Snell suggested that the criticisms were made because the nurses had considerable experience of hospital wards, where there were "vast sums of money and supplies" which a small venture such as this could not hope to match.

On the more significant charge of the safekeeping of the Blessed Sacrament in the chapel, Father Snell managed a neat turning of the tables, reminding the Bishop that the very detailed arrangements had received the blessing of the Bishop himself and castigating the complainants who had dared to challenge the Bishop's judgement. Father Snell also refuted the charge that those involved in organising the work of Horndon Priory had done so for personal gain. Referring to the considerable expense of setting up the community and the very great running costs, he stated that the community might eventually aim to become self-sufficient, but that it could never be financially profitable.

The Bishop appears to have been satisfied with the detailed rebuttal prepared by Father Snell, and there was no further criticism of, or challenge to, Miss Green and Miss Woollard's work.

It was becoming clear that both Miss Green and Miss Woollard wanted the parish to take overall responsibility for the chapel at Horndon. It was equally clear that Bishop Doubleday did not want to take on this task.

When Miss Green became ill, it was Miss Woollard who wrote to the Bishop in September and October of 1931 to inform him that they were making arrangements to transfer to the Diocese the property of the little church and the land on which it stood.

Miss Green supplemented these letters with her own, suggesting that the parish should provide a priest to live at Horndon so that Mass could be said there several times a week. She recommended what the new Mass times could be at Laindon and Horndon, offered a bungalow at a rent of eighteen shillings a week, suggested a suitable housekeeper for the priest and offered one hundred pounds a year to support the priest and the chapel.

Father Snell was not anxious to become too closely involved with the work at Horndon Priory. After Miss Green's repeated requests for the parish to provide a regular Mass at the Priory, Bishop Doubleday asked Father Snell to consider the possibility. Father Snell's response was immediate.

> My Lord,
> Will you give me the privilege of driving you on Thursday, Friday or Saturday from Brentwood through Laindon to Horndon so that you may see for yourself what a dangerous, narrow and twisting road it is.
>
> Throughout the whole winter it is a bad road and I am sure when Mass is said on dark mornings and Benediction is given on dark evenings at Horndon, it is going to make things very difficult for the priest who undertakes both Horndon and Laindon.

The chapel and its grounds remained as part of the Horndon Priory, served by priests who were supplied directly through Miss Green's contacts.

In 1936, the chapel received a particularly fine gift. Miss Green was given some beautiful Stations of the Cross, carved in northern Italy in the Tyrolean style. She was given permission to erect them in the Horndon chapel so that they could gain the attendant indulgences, and they were to remain in Horndon until the Sacred Heart Chapel was sold to help pay for the rebuilt church of Our Lady and St. Joseph. Today, these Stations of the Cross are found on the walls of our new Parish Church, and are just as impressive as they must have been in that little chapel just before the Second World War.

The buildings immediately around the Horndon Priory chapel, mostly old wooden huts, were condemned as unsafe in 1936. The Urban Council ordered that they must be demolished. This left just the chapel itself, apart from the more substantial bungalows which formed part of the Horndon Priory community. Miss Green correctly foresaw that it would be only a matter of time before the chapel itself, "a very frail structure", would have to be pulled down. Claiming a lot of local support in the village, and noting the arrival of several Catholic families in Horndon, she asked the Bishop's permission to build a new chapel. She offered the Diocese a better shaped parcel of land fronting Hillcrest Road for the site of the new chapel. It had been measured at 110 feet by 82 feet. She even sketched out a plan of what she thought to be a suitable design for the chapel. In exchange, Miss Green asked for the return of the plot of land that had housed the original chapel, a process that the Bishop agreed to readily enough.

By March 1937, Miss Green, never one to let grass grow under her feet, had seen the plans for the chapel passed by a Council Committee and was ready for action. When she returned from a holiday at the end of May 1937 she expected to see the chapel nearly complete, but there had been no progress. The Diocese had been worried about road charges and so had not pressed ahead until this matter was resolved. Miss Green's legal team judged that road charges would not be necessary, and offered to create suitable road access to the new chapel and pay any road costs directly to the Council in the unlikely event that they were required.

As late as June 1937, the Bishop was on record as uncertain whether he ought to take on the obligation of a public church at Horndon (the chapel had been considered 'semi-private'), citing the road approach to the chapel and the difficulty in finding a priest to say Sunday Mass. In July, he wrote to Miss Green to make his position clear.

> I have put the question of being responsible for a public church on the new site you offer before my Chapter and they advise it is not wise to accept the responsibility.
>
> I have no objection to you building a chapel on this site and I am willing that the priest at Stanford-le-Hope should say Mass in it on Sundays and Holy days of obligation if he finds it convenient and you can make arrangements with him, but it must be understood that it is only a semi public chapel in your ownership and quite temporary.
>
> With the consent of my Chapter too I shall be pleased to convey back to you the ground which you have already given to the Diocese;

> your solicitor holds the deeds for this piece of land and I am willing that you should instruct him to this effect whether you decide to build the new temporary church or not.

By no means discouraged by this response, Alice Green wrote back by return post, thanking the Bishop for his permission to put up the new church and referring to the excitement that this had created in Horndon.

Another letter from Miss Green in October 1937 referred to the community at Horndon Priory and what she hoped to do with the property. Returning to an idea that the Bishop had not welcomed some fourteen years earlier, she now proposed once again making the property over to the Benedictines. Aware of the Bishop's reluctance, Miss Green saw what she believed to be a compromise.

> My Lord,
> Please forgive my worrying you, when I know you are so busy. But I wanted to ask if you would allow me to make a gift of this property to the Benedictine order, who seem to have had such a heavenly inspiration to make a foundation here. If you do not feel that the moment has come for them to start, if the property was theirs, they could begin when you feel that the time has come. It seems so wonderful that God has guided them to this spot, and I naturally long to help in the wonderful work in every way I can. What a glorious thing it would be to have a Retreat House for women and children.
>
> A party of working women from here wanted to make a Retreat last month, and we had to take them to the Conacle Convent at Hampstead, at great expense and trouble. This would be such an easy journey by bus, from Southend, Chelmsford and Colchester districts. I simply long to help in however humble a way, in bringing such a wonderful powerhouse of prayer, into our poor heathen England, also such a glory to the diocese.
>
> The Benedictines have no idea I am writing to you, and I believe are returning to Belgium tomorrow.

In March 1938, Miss Green wrote again to the Bishop, but this time to advise him of a completed project.

> My Lord
> The little church here is now complete and all the furnishings will be ready by Easter. Would you do us the very great honour of coming to say the first Mass in it. If so, would the Sunday after Easter be convenient to you, or of course any Sunday that suits you best, after Easter. We are longing to get into it. I do so very much hope, that now it is all complete, you will be kind enough to accept it as a gift.

The people have been so splendid in helping to collect the money for it, and we have had such wonderful gifts from friends that we have been able to make it more beautiful than I had ever hoped it could be. It has also given the people the keenest interest and joy in it.

The Tyrolean Crucifix installed in the Sacred Heart Chapel in 1938

Parish records indicate that Father Snell played quite a large part both in designing the chapel itself and the interior decoration, including the style of the altar and the interior furnishings of the chapel. A very imposing crucifix from the Austrian Tyrol, an earlier gift that Miss Green had accepted from a friend, now matched the Stations of the Cross.

The interior furnishings of the chapel were in what was then called 'the modern style', with light oak furniture and a light oak altar. In the place of a reredos, a green brocade curtain was placed behind the altar. In front of this was the life size wooden cross and figure of Jesus, which remained in the chapel until the building was sold to help pay for the new church in Stanford-le-Hope. The six oak candlesticks in use in the church were also designed by Father Snell.

The new church building was made of concrete and steel and it had a high, gabled roof. Bishop Doubleday, the Bishop of Brentwood, came to dedicate the chapel. Just a few days before the first Mass, whilst inviting the Bishop to breakfast after the service, Miss Green again expressed the hope that the Bishop would accept the church as a gift, so that it would become both a dedicated church within the diocese and licensed for marriages. Once again, the Bishop declined this offer. Aware that Miss Green had invited the Bishop for breakfast, Father Snell asked the Bishop to breakfast at the presbytery instead. In suggesting this alternative, Father Snell referred to the lack of suitable accommodation at Horndon Priory, with "no washing or decent lavatory there". One is reminded of the stout defence that Father Snell had made of the cleanliness of Horndon Priory when it had been castigated by members of the Catholic Nurses' Guild.

Although the Sacred Heart Chapel was designed to hold up to 200 parishioners, there was not enough space to accommodate the people who came from miles around to support the new venture and attend the inaugural Mass, on Sunday, May 8th, 1938. The choir from Our Lady and St. Joseph's chose to sing 'Ecce Sacerdos' (Behold the great priest, who in his days, pleased God) when the Bishop arrived to celebrate the Mass, together with Father Snell, Father Hopkins and Canon McKenna.

The greater part of the costs of the new chapel was paid by Miss Alice Green, and other members of the parish donated money, so that the new church in Horndon on the Hill was almost free of debt from the outset. A village resident, Mrs. Chambers, offered the Bishop some War Stock shares, the income from which could support the priest and church at Horndon on the Hill. This was to be used as long as "in the opinion of the Bishop" it may be necessary, after which the capital could be put to any use the Bishop might desire.

The Bishop, however, saw a problem. The chapel was still owned by Miss Green, as the Bishop had refused the gift of the building to the Diocese. Accordingly, Miss Green as owner was directly responsible for the upkeep and maintenance of what he persistently termed the 'public oratory' at Horndon. He would accept the gift from Mrs. Chambers only if the interest derived from it helped to maintain the priest who would say Masses in Horndon and was not used to maintain the chapel itself.

Just after the new chapel was blessed, there was a dispute with a neighbour who had been sold the adjacent land by Miss Green. This plot had originally held the earlier chapel, but had now had a bungalow built on it. The boundaries of the chapel site and that of the neighbouring bungalow were not clear and, in the dispute which followed over a very small piece of ground, the new owners of the bungalow denied access to what they considered their property under the law of trespass.

Unfortunately, this land had to be trodden on in order to remove the life-size bronze statue of the Sacred Heart which had stood outside where the original chapel had been. Two letters written to the Bishop in September 1938 relate what happened next. The first is from Dorothy Sandwell, who had recently moved into the adjacent bungalow with her husband.

> My Lord,
> I am not writing this in any spirit of maliciousness, but as a definite protest at the treatment I was subject to on Friday afternoon by our Parish Priest. Father Snell accompanied by a policeman in uniform together with six men came and took away a statue of the Sacred Heart which stood on a concrete foundation in my private grounds. I appealed to Father Snell to take my part and order the men off. He would not meet my eyes and mumbled about removing diocesan property. Since the beginning of this case which we wrote you about in June we have had no satisfaction but a genuine muddle all around. Three men tried to remove the statue on Tuesday and I naturally resented their trespassing and said they must go away and await both Miss Green's and our own solicitor's further instructions. This last action is most questionable as I thought Miss Green and Father Snell would respect the law. We have never ever said we would keep any diocesan property and only wished to await the finish of the case.
>
> I am seven months pregnant and felt the shock acutely.
>
> Whilst not boasting I would like to add we came to Horndon 11 months ago and promptly started weekly Whist Drives, a very nice Boys Club and a Girls Club on three evenings in the week to help the Catholics here. All took place in our rather large sitting room and were greatly appreciated. This was without any consent or aid from our Parish Priest, whom we were told considered Horndon people should go the two and a half miles to Stanford for that kind of thing. We have done all in our power to foster the Catholic spirit here.
>
> Verification of these facts could be given by Miss Green and Father Hopkins. We only gave up in May on account of my health. I do consider I deserve better treatment than I have been subject to this week and would hope your Lordship will look into this affair.

Not surprisingly, Father Snell was asked by the Diocese for his own version of events. This is his reply, written on September 10th.

> Thank you for your letter of September 6th, re Mrs. Sandwell etc. The facts concerning the incident I append.
>
> 1. A large lifestyle bronze statue of the Sacred Heart six or seven years ago was given by the late Father Higley of Limehouse to the Catholics of the Horndon district to stand outside the church.
> 2. When the new church was erected, it was proposed to mount it on a concrete base and to put it outside the new church.
> 3. Apparently there is some dispute as to the present ownership of the land, upon which this statue stood. It belongs to either Miss Green, the Diocesan Trustees or to the Sandwells, but it is an understood thing that the Statue was not sold to anyone but is the property of the Trustees.
> 4. The Sandwells themselves made suggestions as to the new site, but recently quarrelled with Miss Green and forbad anyone to step on to a piece of grass unfenced and four or five feet from the public path to remove it on the ground of trespassing.
> 5. The Statue weighs half a ton and requires six men to lift it, it was desirable to move it before the wet weather sets in, to rebronze it and set it up on a new basis made of concrete before the new church. In order to prevent a breach of the peace, I asked a policeman to go with the removers.
> 6. If Mrs. Sandwell received a shock, she brought it on herself, she could have remained inside the house.
> 7. It is true, I never gave my consent to a boys club or a girls club to be run by these new comers in their private house. I know nothing about them. There is a club here in the school every Wednesday evening. With regard to the whist drives, there is one here in the school every Friday. Horndon is not two and a half miles away. Mr. and Mrs, Sandwell do not go to Mass, their children also go (to) the Church of England School at Horndon although a 'bus is provided to carry them to Stanford.
>
> ……

In the total failure of either side to see the other person's point of view, the close attention to trivial detail, events running out of control and the rapid decline into farce, one is tempted to see this whole episode as an early script of *Dad's Army*.

The bronze statue of the Sacred Heart at Horndon on the Hill

During the Second World War, the statue made quite an impression on German prisoners of war who were working on nearby farms, and they repainted the statue as well as taking part in the regular Masses in the chapel. Ironically, when the chapel was sold in 1991 no-one wanted the statue and a local parishioner agreed to look after it. The family still has it today.

In 1941, a German landmine fell near to Horndon Chapel. The acting priest, Father Michael Hopkins, alerted the Diocese and removed the sacred vessels to Stanford-le-Hope for safekeeping. Whilst approving of this move, the Bishop reminded Father Hopkins that the chapel at Horndon was not diocesan property and that if there was any damage to the chapel parochial funds should not be spent on its repair. Fortunately, naval personnel removed the detonator, making the landmine safe, and took away the casing. (*See the account by Mrs. Lilian Webb in Parish Voices later in this book.*)

The Interior of Sacred Heart Chapel

After the Second World War, Miss Green was at last able to transfer the title of Horndon Chapel and the land on which it stood to the Diocese of Brentwood. In December 1949, the property was made over to the Diocese for the sum of five shillings. If it was now diocesan property, another aspect of the building which the Bishop had acknowledged, its temporary nature, was soon recognised by Thurrock Urban District Council, who required the Bishop to apply for a licence for the temporary building under the Public Health Act 1936. This annual renewal for the temporary structure was continued for forty years, until Sacred Heart Chapel was finally sold in 1991.

The only other concern for Horndon was the Tithe Redemption Committee, who had the task of commuting ancient tithes in return for an annual fee paid to the state under the 1936 Tithe Act. This applied to the plot of land on which the Sacred Heart Chapel stood. In 1952, an initial flurry of anxiety subsided when the land was assessed at one shilling per year.

For many years, the chapel was looked after by Dave Arnold, who was so involved with the welfare and care of the building that he was nicknamed the Bishop of Horndon.

The Two Bishops : Bishop Thomas McMahon and Dave Arnold, 'The Bishop of Horndon'

After the chapel was sold in 1991, local members of the parish looked after the statues both inside and outside the church to ensure that they did not deteriorate or become mislaid. The last organist in the chapel, Jane Wheatly, agreed to look after the organ.

Many Horndon on the Hill villagers retain fond memories of The Sacred Heart Chapel or, as it was sometimes called, the Blessed Sacrament Chapel. They remember some of its quirks, such as the very cold starts on winter mornings, before the industrial sized blowers took the chill off the air as they roared away. Others recall the annual Midnight Mass at Christmas which would begin as early as 8.00 p.m. We all liked the little organ which accompanied the singing and which never seemed likely to drown out the voices of the congregation.

The Sacred Heart Chapel at Horndon on the Hill

C. East Tilbury and its Neighbourhood

In the East Tilbury, Mucking and Linford areas, the first Masses said in modern times were in private homes. Later, permission was given to hold regular Masses in the ballroom of the Bata Hotel in East Tilbury. It was described by some early parishioners as quite imposing and dignified. Eventually the hotel was converted into flats, with shops now occupying the space where the ballroom once stood.

After the Bata Hotel was sold off, the Social Centre in East Tilbury was used for regular Masses, usually at 9.30 a.m. on Sundays. It had once been a theatre and a cinema. For a while, music for the Mass was provided by the visiting choir from St. Augustine's, or the school children singing to the guitar of Sister Barbara. These arrangements continued while there was still a St. Augustine's choir and before Sister Barbara moved on to new work. Peter Preston led a music group which often played there.

The East Tilbury Social Hall, as its name implies, has many uses. The 9.30 Mass was followed by a 10.30 Martial Arts Club. This meant that there was just one hour to assemble the Altar and chairs, say the Mass and pack away all the furniture before the Martial Arts group started.

And you certainly wouldn't want to get on the wrong side of people with those skills.

Land was bought in Gloucester Avenue near to the Social Centre and next to the library at East Tilbury. One parishioner remembers that they argued long and hard to agree a price with the vendor, but then our diocesan religious went in to have a chat and reduced the price substantially. The intention was to build a small chapel to serve local parishioners. Unfortunately, the land bought was on the wrong side of the railway line, and the town planners created many objections to the development, commenting on problems of access, car parking and safety. Eventually the plans were put on hold whilst attention focused on the rebuilding of Our Lady and St. Joseph's.

In 1998, the East Tilbury Village Hall was closed for a while so that it could be redecorated and repaired, and the local Catholics were again without a home of their own. There followed a remarkable turn of events, as the *Brentwood News* of July 2000 reported.

Methodist Mass forges friendship

Believed to be the first of its kind in the diocese

Under special agreement believed to be the first of its kind in the diocese, Mass is being celebrated on Sundays in the Methodist church at Linford. The time of the Mass, 9.00 am, is even billed prominently on the church noticeboard. The need for an alternative Mass centre came about when East Tilbury Village Hall was closed for refurbishment in 1998. Linford Methodists came to the rescue at the last moment and with the grateful thanks of Fr. Martin Nott, Parish Priest of St. Joseph's, Stanford-le-Hope, in whose parish the Methodist church is located.

The original temporary arrangement worked so well that Bishop Thomas, in the spirit of ecumenism, gave his blessing to the change and both congregations entered into a formal contract for the shared use of the Methodist church.

Linford Methodist Church

"We are greatly indebted to our Methodist friends for letting us use their church," said parishioner Maureen Walsh who has led the support for the new venture.

"It is a wonderful example of fellow Christians coming together in a spirit of love and respect for each other's traditions."

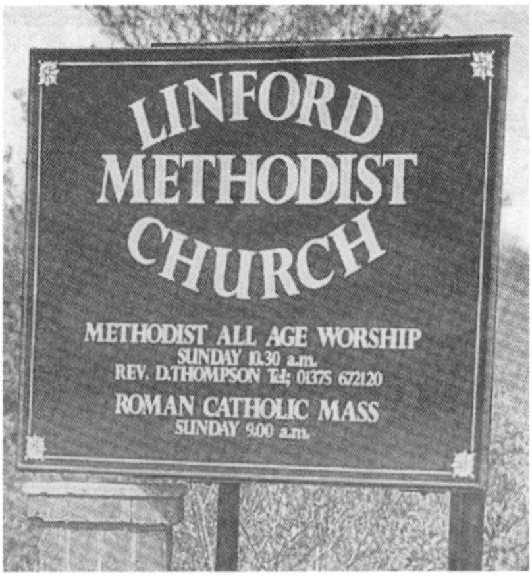

A sign of the times

Over the years, outlying areas of the parish have been served by Stanford-le-Hope, and there have been attempts to set up Mass centres to cater for the Catholic people who live there. Some of these arrangements have been short-lived and some parts of the parish have been subsumed by adjoining parishes.

D. Vange and Pitsea

In the later part of the nineteenth century, the few Catholics living in the area had a choice between a Mass at Westcliff to the east, or Grays and Tilbury parishes to the west. The choice was effectively made for them as Grays and Tilbury were served by a very poor train service. On Sundays, the first Southend bound train stopping at both Pitsea and Westcliff was 10.15 in the morning, allowing travellers the chance to attend the 11.00 o'clock Mass at St. Helen's, Westcliff. Unfortunately, the return train to Pitsea was not until 2.15 p.m. and so these hardy people would not have returned home before 3.00 p.m. Later on, bicycles became more prevalent and the decision as to which direction to go to Mass might have been helped by the wind direction on that day.

When the parish of Stanford-le-Hope was set up, the Catholic residents of Pitsea and Vange had the opportunity to attend Mass at Our Lady and St. Joseph's, but this too was quite a journey. One day Father Snell made a visit to a sick parishioner living in Northlands Drive, Pitsea and discovered that there were many more Catholics living in the immediate area than he had realised. Recognising this, in October 1923 Father Snell began saying Mass once a month in Pitsea, in the garage at the home of Mr. and Mrs. Bishop. As the accommodation was less than adequate, Confessions were heard in the ditch outside.

The names of those families who helped out with the early Masses are still remembered. Amongst the family names are Ahrens, Barclay, Baron, Bishop, Campbell, Carter, Casey, Cook, Hall, Jarman, Jenkinson, Kenway, McDade, Ranner, Thomas, Trickett and Wilson. Many of the children walked to Stanford-le-Hope each day to attend St. Joseph's School, and they received instruction in the catechism on a Saturday morning.

Fund raising began in the nineteen twenties for a new chapel in Pitsea and Vange. There were whist drives at the homes of Mesdames Bishop, Campbell and Thomas. Many parishioners recalled dances held at Sunnydene Hall and later at Market Hall and the church hall. The success of these ventures enabled Father Snell to buy a plot of ground on London Road in 1924.

There was dancing on the lawn at Mrs. Barclay's house in Timberlog Lane and a concert party from Bow Catholic Church helped to swell the funds. The Bishop of Brentwood, Bishop Doubleday, opened a fete for the church funds in a field near Mrs. Bishop's house. By 1925, when the sum of £500 was donated by Miss Barnescone, the new chapel was built. As the church was timber framed, it was necessary to apply to the Billericay District Council to license the building as a temporary structure. The trustees of the Diocese of Brentwood undertook to remove the building if the Council ever required them to do so, as its design breached Council bye-laws for a permanent building.

The new church was dedicated to The Sacred Heart. Miss Barnescone provided money for the statues of The Sacred Heart and Our Lady. The Bishop was present to celebrate Mass at the opening of the little church in 1925.

Before long a Mass was said there every Sunday, which meant that there could be only one Mass at Our Lady and St. Joseph's. Some of the Stanford parishioners objected to this but the arrangement at Vange continued, with the Pitsea and Vange parishioners taking great pride in their church. Whatever was needed by the Parish Priest for the upkeep of the chapel and grounds the local people managed to provide it. The Catholic Women's League obtained paint and other materials to renovate the church from time to time, the labour being provided by their husbands and sons. Later on the entire church was pebble-dashed to preserve the asbestos sheeting. Water and gas services were laid on through the good offices of the redoubtable Catholic Women's League, who continued paying the water rates until the church became part of the parish of St. Basil the Great, in the new town of Basildon.

The existence of the new church at Vange meant that the parish boundaries could be extended eastwards, and Father Snell was recommending this to the Bishop as early as August 1924. The parish of Stanford-le-Hope was becoming quite extensive, which created organisational problems for the regular provision of Masses and the lengthy journeys of some of the parishioners. Father Snell arranged with his Bishop to do all that he could for his congregation, even to the extent of carrying out all Holy Week ceremonies at Stanford-le-Hope and Vange.

Originally, the Sacred Heart Church was intended as a temporary structure, and there was to be a fine new church built on nearby land. Father Snell had postcards made of what the new church would look like, but unfortunately the postcards were the nearest the parishioners came to their new church. There simply wasn't enough money in the area to carry out such an ambitious project. When three plots of adjoining land came up for sale in 1936 at a total price of £400, it was not possible to purchase the additional land and the prospect of a more permanent church on a larger site was lost.

A partner in a firm of solicitors based in Gravesend, Francis Tolhurst, saw the potential of the land for the little Catholic community and arranged to buy the land himself, and to hold it for the parish until they were ready to buy it directly from him. He asked only that interest on the loan needed to buy the land was paid by the parish in the interim. Unfortunately, the interest was not paid and Father Snell later stated that he had no recollection of such an arrangement. When Francis Tolhurst offered the land at cost to the Diocese of Brentwood in 1939, the offer was not taken up. A judgement seems to have been made that the Catholic community at Vange would not be able to support such a costly venture.

In 1939, the Diocese of Brentwood commissioned a structural survey of the church of the Sacred Heart. It was carried out by Thomas H.B. Scott, a chartered architect and surveyor to the Diocesan Trustees. He found that the temporary building was on a subsoil of shifting clay, but that the foundations were sound and would continue to prevent the building from sliding down towards the lower marshlands. Similarly, the concrete raft that formed the base of the chapel was considered to be in good condition. On the exterior of the chapel, a wire-mesh netting had been nailed to the timber frame and a rough-cut cement rendering had been floated onto it. This was judged to have been well done, with a few insignificant hair line cracks due to the contraction of the cement when drying out. One fracture was discovered on the angle quoin in the south west corner of the church, where the prevailing winds and occasional gales hit the side of the building, causing the wooden superstructure to rock on its base. This was considered unsightly and not reparable, but it was not considered to be in any way dangerous. Sacred Heart Church was considered to be very sound structurally and decoratively, and in a good state of repair and maintenance, with periodical attention and painting. It is obvious that the initial enthusiasm of the Catholic Women's League and the preparedness of the local men to rally round had not diminished since the church was completed in 1925.

By 1952, the plans for the development of Basildon New Town were well advanced, and the Bishop of Brentwood wrote to Father Watson in Stanford-le-Hope about what provision could be made for the Catholics in Basildon. The little church at Vange had survived the war years, although the steady advance of a new parish on its doorstep was to have far greater impact. In 1954, a Parish Priest was appointed for the Basildon and Vange area. This new priest, Father T. Barrett, was required to make a detailed examination of church property in his parish and had found it difficult to ascertain the precise boundaries of the chapel site at Vange. The Urban District Council was itself unsure of the detail, although this was necessary for the planned expansion of house building in the area. There was also some uncertainty about the ownership of land adjoining the church, possibly the plots that had been offered by Francis Tolhurst before the Second World War. The Urban District Council of Basildon wished to purchase the land so that a Doctor Robertson could build a surgery there.

For a while, it was thought that the land had been owned by our Parish Priest, Father Snell, based on "an old man who said he had seen Father Snell showing people the property in 1926". There was further confusion when it was thought that Father Snell had been the beneficiary of the estate of a Miss Wetham, in the form of her house in Rashleigh Drive, although whether this was personally or on behalf of the Diocese was also unclear. It later transpired that Miss Wetham had intended to leave Father Snell her home, but he persuaded her to leave it to her own family instead. As for the recollection of 1926, it seems that Father Snell was trying to help a parishioner to sell the land, in which he had no interest personally. If such confusions can occur over a mere thirty years, I hope the reader will excuse any inaccuracies noticed in this account of the past hundred.

With the growth of Basildon and the increased number of people living in the Vange area, it was soon apparent that the church of the Sacred Heart was too small to accommodate a steadily increasing population. The main Parish Church of St. Basil the Great was to be opened in October 1956, but in June of that year Father Barrett asked the Bishop of Brentwood for permission to engage an architect to draw up plans to enlarge the church at Vange. The Diocesan Finance Board approved the move and a Mr. Newton was appointed as architect. An early concern seems to have been the provision of adequate car parking on the site, not an issue that had troubled the planners back in the nineteen twenties, when car ownership had been quite rare.

For over ten years, the question of whether to extend the Vange church was not settled. In January 1967, as Father Barrett was leaving the Basildon Parish, a company of chartered accountants wrote to Canon Goldingay at the Parish Priest's request, in an attempt to resolve the matter. The land needed for the extension, about half an acre, had been offered by Basildon Development Corporation, which was to occupy the adjoining site, at a very advantageous rate, and it was prepared to offer further land if it was required.

As an indication of the growing numbers of people in the immediate area of the church, the population was forecast to increase by three and a half thousand as a result of an additional eleven hundred homes. By 1970, the numbers were predicted to increase by a further three thousand. The church of the Sacred Heart was right in the middle of this huge development. Although the Diocese took an option on the land offered by the development corporation, they did not invest in an enlargement of the church itself, and the vacant land fell into some disrepair. Even as late as May 1974 there was the prospect of an extension to the church, based on an anticipated increase of at least fifty people at Sunday Mass, but the Diocese remained reluctant to press ahead.

In October 1976, the Basildon Development Corporation was still pressing the parish of St. Basil the Great to commit itself to the new development of what was called Vange 60, a housing development of flats for one and two persons and some dwellings for old people, which was to surround the church of the Sacred Heart. Despite discussions on details such as fencing, drains and landscaping of grounds, the Parish and the Diocese appear to have decided not to proceed with an extension of the original church. By 1977, the arguments put forward were that to extend the little church would spoil the basic design of the original, and that in any case the church was too close to St. Basil's to warrant such enlargement.

By June of the following year, the writing was on the wall. The Parish Priest of Basildon wrote to the Bishop of Brentwood, Bishop Casey.

> I am writing to ask your advice about the future of the Sacred Heart Church, Vange. At the moment, it stands in need of extensive repairs. It is only used for one Mass per week – 12 noon on Sundays. The average congregation is 100 people, on Holy Days at 9.00 only 12. The church is only 1.1 miles from St. Basil's, where our 10.45 Mass is getting more crowded as people move into the expanding Chalvedon area.
>
> I am considering the possibility of transferring the midday Mass to St. Basil's and am inclined to suggest the closure of the Sacred Heart Church, which is a little isolated and has been broken into about a year ago. It is simply a Mass centre, and if it was not there I would not be inclined to open a Mass centre in that location, especially as St. Basil's Church is really underused.

There was some opposition to the proposed closure from parishioners who had attended the church for many years, and the plans to close Sacred Heart were shelved for a decade. But in 1986, the new Parish

Priest at Basildon, Father Brian O'Shea, wrote to Bishop Thomas McMahon.

> …. SACRED HEART VANGE : The future. Now that I have been here for nearly a year I feel that, in facing the future we must be honest about Vange. Whilst appealing to you for a while on personnel, I know the future must be faced. Although Sacred Heart is the 'mother' church of the area it is four minutes drive from St. Basil's. It is used for Mass at 12 noon on Sundays and holydays.
>
> There is now no actual community there – people use it because of the convenient Mass time. Most people drive there. The few who walk could easily be catered for by our mini-bus service – door to door to St. Basil's.
>
> Because there is no real sense of belonging there, it is difficult to get the people who attend Mass there to take on real responsibility for the building – for the liturgy and for the cleaning.
>
> What I would like to do in a very positive and tactful way is to have a parish meeting in the autumn, to put to the people the situation. I do think it is an opportune time to look at Vange I promise that we will handle things in a sensitive way.
>
> I would be happy to have your opinion on this, and your permission to have a meeting with a view to closing Vange, if you agree.
>
> The matter was last raised in 1978, and didn't come to anything. Most of the older parishioners who used the church out of sentimental value have died since then. ….

After the Bishop agreed that the matter ought to be considered, Father O'Shea decided to write an open letter to his parishioners in St. Basil's weekly news sheet, 26th October 1986.

> Dear Friends,
> At last Sunday's parish pastoral assembly I mentioned a matter which has been on my mind for some time – the future of Sacred Heart Church, Vange. I have discussed it with Fr. Martin, Rev. Keith and the Sisters. Obviously the next place to mention it was at the parish assembly, the official place of parish consultation, and then to let you know the situation as I see it, after a lot of prayer and thought.
>
> With the Bishop's and Vicar General's permission I think we must look into the possibility of closing down the church in Vange. I know that it is the mother church of the area and has meant a lot to people. However, there is no church in the diocese with a Mass centre a mere 1.1 miles away from the Parish Church. Eight years

ago the situation was discussed at great length, but the recommendation to close Sacred Heart didn't come to anything,

Things have changed radically in eight years. Most importantly we have an acute shortage of priests. Six parishes – many with larger Mass attendances than ours – have had their assistant priests moved this autumn, and the Bishop is unable to replace them.

Stanford-le-Hope often used to help us out when one of your priests was away or sick – but they can't now as they only have one priest. The Bishop has been very kind to us – Basildon definitely needs its quota of priests and you know that we really love being here – learning and serving together. But we must plan for the future, and use our energies wisely. I'm sure that eventually there will be only one priest at St. Basil's. To be quite honest one priest cannot cope with what would seem to be an unnecessary Mass centre.

We have been carefully watching the attendance at Sacred Heart. Most people seem to attend there because they find it a convenient time. There is no real sense of community there and it is difficult to get people to look after the church. I think it says something, that for the last two months there has been 2 ft. graffiti on the outside wall and no-one has volunteered to clean it off! As transport could be a problem for a few people, particularly the elderly, you can be assured that anyone requiring a lift – especially the elderly – can be brought to and from St. Basil's.

Obviously, all your views will be taken on board, and I shall give them to the Bishop, with my own recommendations, after a Parish Meeting to be held at Sacred Heart Vange on Thursday, November 6th, at 7.30 p.m. Please feel free to write to me as well.

No people are more realistic as yourselves. Please ponder on what I've said. I'm not saddened by the shortage of priests. I'm sure that the Holy Spirit is teaching us that the laity must take a greater part in parish life. May our partnership continue to grow. But remember, we really believe that we're here for you.
Father Brian

The response of the Sacred Heart congregation was not long in coming. A typical letter was dated 2nd November, 1986.

Dear Father Brian,
I am writing to you with regard to your proposed closure of the Sacred Heart Church in Vange. I have attended this church for 34 years and I hold it in great affection, as do many other people, so you will realise that I cannot support your proposal.

> You spoke last week of the imminent shortage of an assistant priest and I do appreciate this will mean a considerable increase in duties for the remaining priest, but the Sacred Heart is used for only one Mass per week, with additional services a rarity. I was very surprised by your belief that the church is used by many because of the convenient time; I have always thought 12 noon a most inconvenient time and I suspect other parishioners are of the same opinion, but for one reason or another they prefer that particular church – surely a compromise is possible. Perhaps the noon Mass could be discontinued, with one of the three St. Basil's times being transferred to Vange, or maybe the 6 p.m. service is unnecessary – I imagine that most of us usually know if we are likely to be away from home on a Sunday, in which case the Saturday evening Mass would be chosen.
>
> I have searched my conscience on this issue and can say that I don't think it is just pure selfishness to want to keep the church open. I feel very strongly that while the building is sound enough and while people express the wish to keep the Sacred Heart Church in use, then every possible effort should be made to resolve the problem – it would be a far happier and more welcome conclusion to this sad episode.
>
> I do hope and pray that we can continue to enjoy one of the few remaining 'roots' of Vange/Basildon – it is my view that we can ill afford the loss.

The parish meeting duly took place on Thursday, November 6th, 1986. Father Brian, Father Martin, Sister Rose and the Reverend Keith were present, together with 25 parishioners. The meeting was summarised in terms of points made against the closure and points made in favour of the closure.

Points Against the Closure

- Masses had already been cut to allow for the fact that there was only one priest in the parish. Father O'Gormon had been the Parish Priest without an assistant.
- Other parishes had Mass centres within one mile of each other, including St. Ann's and St. Margaret's in Canning Town.
- There was a feeling that Lourdes Hall, where the Parish Club met, was being protected for purely mercenary reasons, whilst the church which served spiritual needs was to be sacrificed.
- There was no public transport from Vange to St. Basil's in Basildon, and so couples with young children would find the journey very difficult.
- The problem could be overcome if Sacred Heart held the evening weekend Mass on a Saturday, leaving St. Basil's with two Masses

on the Sunday. Alternatively, Mass could be said at Sacred Heart only once a month.

- Sacred Heart had been the recipient of 'cast-offs' from St. Basil's rather than new input, and it received no encouragement from the parish.
- Many people had a real affection for the Sacred Heart Church.
- The physical care of the building, such as the graffiti which had been quoted by the Parish Priest, was not important, but the positive atmosphere inside the church was important.
- It was not fair to say that Sacred Heart Mass was attended only because it was at a convenient time, as all Masses were attended at a time convenient to the individual.

Points For the Closure

- The services at St. Basil's were more enjoyable.
- The poor 'turn-out' at the meeting (25 parishioners) showed a lack of 'caring'.
- The Mass was more important than where it was celebrated.
- It had to be remembered that clergy needed more time for other duties.
- There should be agreement that the parish should take the priest's advice as the spiritual leader.
- The future situation made Sacred Heart Church unrealistic as a Mass centre.

Ten days later, on November 16th, Father Brian reported on the Parish Meeting at Vange in the parish newsletter, *St. Basil's Weekly News*. Points in favour of the closure were included in the report, but no points against. All the views and comments of the parishioners would be forwarded to the Bishop, together with the Parish Priest's recommendation for closure. The same day one of his parishioners wrote to Father Brian.

> Dear Father Brian,
> Further to my brief conversation with you on Tuesday 11th November regarding the Sacred Heart Church, I feel I must write to you even though, as I told you at the time, I do not feel part of the parish.
>
> I am very sad at the prospect of the Diocese closing the little chapel; the reasons given are unacceptable to me.
>
> The possibility of a one priest parish was discussed at the last attempt to close the church, so the times of the Masses were altered

to allow for one priest to say Mass on Sunday at all three churches. This, I feel, is not too much to ask of any man; your predecessor had to manage on his own for quite some months and the relief priest who came while he was on holiday did not find it so inconvenient.

The idea of the mini-bus picking up people to ferry them to Mass at St. Basil's is ludicrous to me. Surely it is better for one man (priest) to travel to Mass for 100 than have 100 plus people travel to the priest!

The Sacred Heart Church costs nothing to run, all the collection money is given to St. Basil's. It is, therefore, unfair to blame the parishioners of Vange for their lack of support for the church. St. Basil's has a church cleaner who is paid to clean the church. Flowers and plants are provided to enhance and beautify the church. Nothing is provided for the Sacred Heart Church.

You mention lack of community spirit, but every community must have a leader. What have you done to foster community spirit in Vange? The shepherd leads the sheep, the sheep do not lead the shepherd.

With regard to the graffiti on the outside wall of the church, I spoke to you about this weeks ago and told you where to find the paint to paint it off; you said you would ask the Knights (of St. Columba) to paint it. Did you do this? Yet you complained that no-one cares for the church. In my opinion the church was neglected so that the parishioners could be blamed for its closure.

The Diocese has been trying for years to close the church. It was given to the people of Vange and Basildon for their benefit, so one would understand if it was said that a Mass centre or Social Club was to be rebuilt on the site, or that the Diocese has to sell the church in order to pay off the debt of x amount of pounds of the covenant scheme, because of the dishonesty of some people not giving what they pledged, the rest of the money going to the third world.

One might not like these alternatives, but one may accept them better than your reasons.

A copy of this letter will be sent to the Bishop.

God Bless,
Yours sincerely,

Father Brian may well have promised the Bishop that his approach would be positive, tactful and sensitive, but it doesn't seem to have had quite the effect he had anticipated. Nevertheless, Father Brian wrote to Bishop Thomas a week later with his own recommendations.

> Hard as I do find it to perhaps be slightly 'unpopular' in a parish – as someone said "The man who shot Liberty Valance" - I feel that in the future it (the Sacred Heart Church) will be an unnecessary burden on the parish. Martin, Keith, Sister Rose (the Convent Superior) and myself are in agreement. I didn't think it fair to examine too closely what we'd do with the building. We can discuss this with you later. For the moment I would recommend closing the church before Easter . . . I feel in <u>my</u> heart this is the right step for the future, and I know we must be people of faith, and that the issue must be faced, but I also feel that we must take very special care of the few people who will be deeply hurt by this. And I <u>promise</u> to do <u>that</u>.

At the end of the month, the same parishioner wrote again, this time to Bishop Thomas, about her concerns over the proposed closure of the Sacred Heart Church. The Bishop's thoughtful reply illustrates the quandary that Catholicism faced when trying to meet the needs of its congregation in an ever more secular world.

> 3rd December 1986
>
> Thank you for your letter of November 28th and for the trouble you have taken in writing to me.
>
> I quite understand the sadness you must feel at the proposed closure of the Sacred Heart Church, Vange.
>
> As you know, we have considerably less priests now than we used to have when many places like Vange church were started. In a number of parishes, priests are rushing around from one Mass centre to another and this is gravely affecting their health, apart from other considerations.
>
> As you will understand, I have to look at the overall situation in the diocese. I cannot simply react when an emergency occurs, such as when a priest falls ill, or dies, but I must look ahead and consult about the future. That is precisely what I am doing now in looking ahead and considering the whole situation of the parish of St. Basil's, which, of course, includes your church.
>
> I feel sure that I can count on your prayers that I may be guided by the Lord in making such important and very often difficult decisions, whatever they may be.
>
> With my blessing,
> Yours sincerely,
> Thomas McMahon
> Bishop of Brentwood

The Bishop's decision was that the last Mass to be said at Sacred Heart Church, Vange would be on Easter Sunday, 1987. In a message to his Vange parishioners Father Brian's message asked them to sympathise with the Bishop's plight and to be realistic about the situation they were all facing. Expressing concern for any hurt caused to his parishioners, Father Brian stated "I'd rather not be closing a church, but in my heart, in this situation I really believe we are being realistic and honest – about now, and the future".

E. Orsett

The link with Orsett hospital, which had begun in 1921, was revitalised in 1953 with the regular saying of Mass in the nurses' recreation room. Both staff and patients were able to attend, and they were soon joined by Catholics who lived nearby in the village. A multi-denominational chapel was built in the grounds of the hospital, and Mass was then said there every Sunday. Either the Parish Priest or his curate would be appointed as Chaplain to the hospital. In 1955, Father Hibbert managed to obtain the services of the Verona Fathers in Bayswater so that a regular priest could say Mass for the villagers and hospital staff at Orsett, where average attendance was about 40. Following parish boundary changes, both Orsett and Chadwell St. Mary were reassigned to the parish of Tilbury.

The small, black barn that had hosted the first public Mass in Stanford-le-Hope since the English Reformation was opened as a Mass centre and school in June 1910. It was called the School of Saint Mary and initially had just eight pupils. The school did well but it soon outgrew the limited accommodation it had.

In 1914, a new school was built next to the recently completed church. It was built of brick, it had two classrooms and was known as Saint Joseph's High School. A playground was also laid. There was room for one hundred pupils, so an estimate can be made about anticipated class sizes at that time. One classroom was used for teaching the juniors and the other for teaching the 'seniors', who had to leave to join the adult world at the age of 14.

However, the school did not thrive in its early years. There were few pupils and the buildings were not maintained sufficiently and fell into a state of disrepair. Father Snell was concerned about the school when he arrived as the new Parish Priest. There were no qualified teachers, and the education being offered seemed haphazard. In a letter to the Bishop, dated March 1921, Father Snell stated that the school 'is a great worry'. The main difficulty was a schoolmaster, Mr. John, described as being 'of Hindoo extraction'. He was judged to be 'a good fellow, but not good enough'. Mr. John's ability to speak English was poor, although he had somewhat unexpectedly expressed a willingness and ability to teach <u>any</u> language. Father Snell's decision to get rid of him was hampered by the fact that he was a lodger in Mr. John's house.

The Bishop was asked if he knew of "any woman who would accept the position at £120 per annum, with the chance of doubling it the second year". There was no reference to suitable qualifications or experience. In the meantime, Father Snell felt anxious about dismissing Mr. John "because I might get somebody much worse". One is reminded of Hilaire Belloc's lines

> And always keep a-hold of Nurse
> For fear of finding something worse.

The school closed for a short time and reopened at the start of the academic year in September 1921. There were then 45 children, and the Headmistress was Miss B. J. Kenny, who was not a qualified teacher.

Father Snell was having a hard time of it persuading the Bishop of Brentwood to persevere with the independent parish of Stanford-le-Hope, and the school's future looked equally precarious. Father Snell informed his Bishop of the state of the school at the start of his tenure as Parish Priest.

> The school has 70 pupils, of these 21 are Catholic. The school is carried on entirely for the benefit of the Catholic children – this can be done inadequately enough but can be done because the non-Catholics pay varying sums weekly from three shillings and six pence downwards according to age and circumstances. The school building is in an extremely bad state of repair and I am informed on good authority has been neglected during the last 3 or 4 years.
>
> The water comes in through the roof in many places and has softened the walls inside so that the plaster is coming away from the walls. Every door in the school requires attention. £100 could easily be spent in putting the school into a good state of repair.

Catholic School
Stanford-le-Hope

Expenses, including salaries of Two Teachers, Gas, Water, Oil, Repairs etc. from Nov 12 – March 4 1921 i.e. 4 months	£68 – 3 – 7
Total Income derived from a small fee for charges to non-Catholics	£58 – 3 – 9
Debit Balance	£9 – 19 – 10

The goal was to persuade the Local Education Authority to take over the school, but this was unlikely as there were some 200 vacancies at the Council's own school. Father Snell hoped for a government grant of some kind to improve the viability of the school. He admitted that the salaries of the two teachers at the school were 'appallingly low' and this had affected the quality of the teachers, whose educational attainments were 'not high'. The parish was able to make a small contribution to the running costs of the school, but the whole venture was based on the possibility of future expansion and success rather than what was happening in the here and now. The plan was to hold on and hope for the best. As Father Snell wrote to the Bishop of Brentwood, Bishop Doubleday:

> It is to be feared that the Catholic parents would not at the moment demand a Catholic school, so that the only thing to be done is to wait and carry on as well as possible.

A pupil at the school from 1924 to 1930, Kitty Price, recalled her years there.

> Teachers at the school included two sisters, Miss Murkin and Mrs. Phillips (who was addressed by the pupils as Miss Phillips) and a Miss Cook. Miss Kenny, the Headmistress, taught the older children – Miss Murkin and Miss Phillips jointly taught the second class and Miss Cook the babies.
>
> The classrooms were very big and there were paintings on the wall. However, as the classrooms were so big this meant that they were often very cold in the winter as the heaters were not able to heat such large rooms. Each child had his or her own desk with lift up tops and an inkwell. Inside their desks the children kept their exercise books, pencil and nib-pen. The children had squared books for maths and lined books for English. They also studied R.E., history and geography. They also did P.E. in their classroom – in the form of exercises. The girls played netball as well.
>
> The children went straight into their classroom when they arrived at school and said prayers at the beginning of each day. They were not allowed to speak in class and had to listen and do exactly what the school teacher told them to do.
>
> There was a uniform even in those early days – white blouses, red ties and blue slips for the girls. However, it was still obvious which children came from better off families as these girls often had pleats in their skirts – something which I really wanted!

Designated as a private school, St. Joseph's charged fees of one guinea per term, but some of the families were quite unable to pay anything at all. Nevertheless, their children were allowed to attend school without any money changing hands. The school hours were 9.00 until 4.00. As the school did not have canteen facilities for the children, they either went home for lunch or took sandwiches. Miss Kenny sorted out any problems to do with the girls. Misbehaving boys were seen by Father Snell.

Stanford-le-Hope was in the process of considerable change. It was no longer a rural village, and was becoming a suburban area, with many new houses built to accommodate those who worked in London and commuted daily by train. The Shell Haven Oil Refinery was opened in

1916 and the employees were encouraged by the company to live in the immediate area.

By 1927, the school had 123 pupils on roll, 72 of them Catholic. The school building was simply not large enough to accommodate these children comfortably. School fees for the year brought in £228, but the teachers' salaries alone amounted to £273. On top of this, money had to be found for equipment, heating (such as it was), lighting, and repairs to the school premises.

The school received a boost in its numbers after the closure of what had been a "kind of home for children and unfortunate children" over at Horndon on the Hill. This 'broken down building of concrete and wood' had been used by two philanthropic ladies, Miss Green and Miss Woollard for children in need from the slums of London. The project ran for some years, building on earlier charitable work organised by Doctor John Stansfield of the Oxford Movement. When the home closed in about 1930, the 40 children were transferred to Saint Joseph's in Stanford-le-Hope. A temporary classroom was added to cater for the extra numbers of children, and plans were drawn up for the construction of a larger school, but these plans were not put into effect.

One of the parish's main benefactors, Mr. Burgess, had been approached for help in raising funds for school building, but he felt that Father Snell's ambitions to educate the local Catholic children needed more focus. In July 1929, he wrote to the Parish Priest.

> I have no doubt that you are right in your desire to build – that is enlarge, your present schools, and prepare for keeping your 11+ children, but you are in this matter, of course, taking what I should call a diocesan view rather than a local view.
>
> Your present schools and ground would, no doubt, be sufficient for your own parish children for some time to come, but, when it goes beyond a parochial matter, I think that the first step should be to enlist the support of the Bishop and the diocesan authorities; and, if you can do this and they will lend you the money, I have no possible objection, and I will endeavour to do my little bit in helping you to reduce the debt.
>
> You will, no doubt, realise why I think this course is necessary: you are, at present, catering for more than your own parish and, as I understand, you have 40 children from Horndon, who come to Horndon from the slums of London.

> Horndon is by no means a sure thing: it may be closed down at any time, and it is of no use to saddle the parish with the responsibility, that cannot be placed upon it, except at the desire of the authorities.
>
> Another thing that appeals to me is this: you cannot possibly put up a £2,000 school or new classrooms on your present ground, and if you are requiring that amount of money to be spent, surely it would pay you to acquire some ground close at hand – right opposite your present school, or at the back, if possible!
>
> You say, if the new building be not recognised by the Board of Education, it will be maintained as a private school.
>
> I think it is easier to maintain lesser premises than greater, and the only reason that I suggest to you that the Bishop should be first consulted is because of your broadness of view in going afield to cater for the needs of other parishes and for the East End of London children, who are, temporarily, at Horndon.
>
> I am entirely sympathetic with you, but my view, I repeat, is that it is, primarily, a diocesan matter to find the money, because the finding of the money also entails moral and other support from the authorities, which you cannot do without in matters of this kind.

Yet Father Snell was not discouraged by this response. He was advised by one of the school managers, Mr. Angilogoff, who also served on various education committees in the area. This was a time of major reorganisation, when new schools were springing up in communities that had been built or enlarged since the Great War, and the Board of Education was stretched to the limit in the work it had to do to assess and recognise schools which it wished to bring under national control. Father Snell was certain that the time had come to act. In late July 1929, in a letter to Bishop Doubleday, he wrote:

> … I wish to assure you that I have considered our position from every point of view and I want to emphasise that whatever happens in the next few months, and whatever the upshot of the enquiry may be (the Board of Education's recognition of the school) one thing remains clear and that is that I must build and build now. If I do not, I shall have 40 children in the streets within six months.

Father Snell's concern was exacerbated by the fear that if St. Joseph's School were recognised, this would prohibit further building adjacent to the school building, so he wished to have new buildings in place prior to the recognition. In the event, it was made clear that further extensions to a newly recognised school would be permitted, so the parish adopted a plan to rearrange and reorganise existing accommodation in the school, pending a larger rebuilding when the state of the finances made this viable.

The school now flourished, helped by Father Snell's particular interest in education. He acted as a Diocesan Schools Inspector and was in the forefront of collecting money for the Brentwood Ecclesiastical Education Fund.

In December 1929, Father Snell was able to write to his Bishop with welcome news.

> My Lord.
> The Sisters at Wanstead have written to me this morning informing me that they decided to take over the education in this parish, subject to your Lordship and to the school being recognised, we hope next year.

The Sisters are now so well known to many of us, that we should perhaps take a step back to look at the organisation they have served with such distinction over the years.

Catherine McAuley was born in Dublin towards the end of the eighteenth century. Her family were wealthy tradespeople but Catherine saw the desperate poverty of working people at close hand, and she was moved by the dreadful conditions they had to endure, both at home and at work. Catherine's parents died when she was still young and she now had to look after her younger brother and sister. With little money surviving the death of her parents, Catherine found work as a companion to an elderly lady and her husband. The Callaghans were a Quaker family and they were suspicious of Catholics and their faith. Yet they were impressed by Catherine's steadfast determination to help the poor in whatever way she could. After Mrs. Callaghan and, shortly afterwards, Mr. Callaghan died, Catherine found herself the sole heir to a considerable fortune. Her employers had realised that Catherine could be trusted to put their money to good use.

Despite family objections, Catherine built a House of Mercy in a very fashionable part of Dublin. This took place before the Catholic Emancipation Act was passed, when Catholics still found it difficult to gain acceptance in society. There was some objection to the work that Catherine and her supporters began, partly because such charity had traditionally been performed by nuns in cloistered settings, and partly because some of the poor of Dublin were now near neighbours of the rich and privileged.

This first building encapsulated the aims of the new religious Congregation. It contained a school for the poor, an Orphanage, a Hostel and Training Centre for young women in service in the fashionable houses of Dublin, and accommodation for the ladies who carried out these charitable works. They were soon challenged by the cholera infested slums of Dublin, but their numbers grew with their determination. The ladies were originally volunteers but, as they began to realise that God was calling them to do this work, they founded a non-cloistered order, dedicated to works of mercy. Along with their vows of poverty, chastity and obedience, they added a fourth, to serve the sick, poor and ignorant.

In the remaining ten years of her life, Catherine opened twelve new convents dedicated to this work, ten in Ireland and two in England. When she died in 1841, there were already plans for convents in Liverpool, Pittsburgh, and Newfoundland, indications of an international involvement that are still in place today.

A Convent of Mercy was set up in the Commercial Road in London's East End, typically among the poor and needy of the great capital. From this base, St. Joseph's Convent of Mercy was established in Wanstead. When the Archdiocese of Westminster was reorganised in 1917, and part of it became the new Diocese of Brentwood, the Wanstead Convent became independent of the Commercial Road Convent.

When Father Snell approached the convent with a plea for help in his parish and particularly the school, the Sisters considered the request very carefully and with many prayers. They were eventually guided to take up the challenge, and in 1930 they bought a small house near to the church in Scratton Road, to serve as their convent.

Reverend Mother Anthony, and Sisters Mary Joseph, Philomena and Bernadette opened the convent on April 24th, 1930. After a few days, they were joined by Sisters Mary Columba and Therese. Sister Mary Joseph was put in charge of the House, and Sister Mary Philomena acted as Headmistress of the elementary school until Sister M. Bernadette was released from her teaching duties in Colchester and arrived to take charge. She was to remain in post until 1953.

As the previous incumbent, Miss Kenny, was not a qualified teacher, she was not accepted by the Board of Education and she left the school to live in Scotland. She died there in February, 1949.

On the same date that the Sisters of Mercy took over St. Joseph's School, 28th April 1930, it was formally recognised as a public elementary school for junior pupils. Its future was now assured. There was, however, a condition attached to this recognition. As the school buildings were judged to be inadequate, the Managers of the school had to arrange to build a new school within the space of four years.

The school opened for the first time in April 1930, with 120 children. The total accommodation comprised three classrooms and a small office. In 1937, a school hall was added and central heating was installed. If their parents shivered in the church in the winter months, at least the children were kept warm in the adjoining school. Or they would have been if the system had only worked properly.

Times were hard for our Sisters of Mercy. Their little house had no curtains, lighting was by gas, and with no chapel in the convent they gathered in the front room to pray. Every opportunity was found to save money, with Reverend Mother Anthony bringing money over from Wanstead when funds were low. One teacher, Sister Columba, was paid as an unqualified teacher despite her qualifications, simply to save money. Two days a week, the Sisters had to travel over to Horndon on the Hill to attend Mass.

Sister Bernadette was a very organised and practical person. A brilliant needlewoman, she worked tirelessly for the Annual Bazaar, where the target was to beat the total raised the previous year. She was also a keen gardener, and grew flowers, fruit and vegetables.

In those early days, life in school was fairly leisurely and, unlike modern times, there was little pressure or interference from the Inspectorate. Most of the pressure came from the cramped accommodation. The small school hall had to serve as a dining room, classroom, gymnasium and, in the evening, as the Parish Hall. This meant that everything had to be packed away daily, and then brought out again the next morning. Sadly, the premises were not always treated with the respect required.

Sister Bernadette was assisted by Sister Columba O'Dea, who taught all the Infants, and Sister Joseph Powell, who taught the lower and middle Junior pupils. The Headmistress taught the older pupils.

The first Superior in charge of the convent was Mother Vincent O'Neill. She had earlier opened a house in Wanstead, together with a small group of Sisters from Commercial Road in London. When Brentwood Diocese became independent from Westminster, the Sisters had to decide whether to return to Commercial Road or to become independent. They chose the latter. Mother Vincent O'Neill was the aunt of Sister Aidan, who was later to become the Head Teacher of St. Joseph's.

Mother Vincent was gentle, shy, unassuming and dearly loved by all who knew her. People loved to call at the convent and chat, and left feeling all the better after unburdening their troubles to a woman with a real mother's heart.

Mother Vincent loved shopping, especially if she found a bargain. She often confided that she forgot an item on purpose so that she would go back again to the shops. But there was a genuine reason for her action: she loved people and would meet many parishioners on her shopping trips and so keep in contact with them and their affairs.

When the number of schoolchildren increased, Sister Aquinas O'Connor joined the staff. There was a considerable age gap between this well established staff and herself and, being possessed of a good sense of humour, she referred to her new home as "Stranded-no-Hope". However, within a short space of time, more youthful members came to the convent in Scratton Road, including Sister Francis Grace and Sister Dolores Doherty, who taught the Infants.

For a while there was something of an overlap from the previous arrangements that had allowed children as old as 14 to be educated at the school. Father Snell considered an earlier proposal by Bishop Doubleday to build a shed in the convent garden so that these older children could be taught there, but the Local Education Authority would not hear of such a thing, and a room was built over the Sacristy to accommodate these children until they were 14. Permission for this £300 addition was given both by the Diocese and the Local Education Authority. The money for the adaptation came from the proceeds of the 'Grand Christmas Bazaar' and a number of large donations from parishioners. This Senior School remained private and the children were taught by Sister Benignus in what became known as the Upper Room. Sister Joseph offered after-school lessons in Pitman's shorthand and typing, at a cost of 6 pence per lesson.

Space was at a premium with the cramped accommodation available. The school was closed for two days that first December in 1930 so that arrangements could be made for the first annual Parish Bazaar, the proceeds of which would help the School Building Fund.

Things did not always go smoothly: the records show that Sister Columba, the teacher of the infants, fell ill on 3rd February 1931, and a lay teacher was provided as a temporary replacement. Unfortunately, the replacement herself fell ill the following day. Later that same year, the 36 children from Horndon Priory were unable to attend the school as they had been in contact with Scarlet Fever, a quite serious condition in the days before antibiotics such as penicillin. Other closures that year included a day to prepare for a concert in St. Margaret's Hall in October, and the return of the Christmas Bazaar in December.

By 1932, St. Joseph's Public Elementary School was growing strongly. The number on roll of the Junior and Senior School was now 155, of whom 125 were Catholic children. Just as the parents were likely to shiver in the winter Masses, so their children often shivered in their classrooms. On 29th February 1932 there was a strong north wind blowing and the recorded temperatures in the school at 2.20 p.m. were 50 degrees Fahrenheit in the Infants and just 41 degrees Fahrenheit in the Juniors. It was the day of an H.M.I. inspection. Let us hope that the government inspector had a good overcoat, although few of the children would have been that lucky. By April 1932 there was an outbreak of whooping cough in the school, followed by chickenpox.

Many of the organisational problems of the early school related to the largely inadequate buildings. By April 1933, there was a proposal to erect permanent buildings to cater for 175 children, but the stumbling block was the Essex County Council. They had pointed out the previous year that there were many vacancies at the nearby Council school and so they saw no point in making any improvements or enlargements to St. Joseph's while the other school was undersubscribed.

Fortunately, the Essex Education Committee reversed this decision, and agreed to substantial changes to St. Joseph's School so that it could accommodate 144 pupils. When these plans were passed up the line to Whitehall, the government's response was that an entirely new school should be built on the site, a proposal that had been recommended locally a good three years earlier. Father Snell hoped for a new site altogether, where there would not be such a shortage of space, and he hoped that the London and Thames Haven Oil Wharves Company, which owned a lot of land in the area, might be prevailed upon to offer a new site.

A couple of inspections of the existing school brought a little breathing space. The initial deadline of four years for a new school was extended, partly because the inspectors had a more favourable view of the condition of the buildings and partly because the national recession was putting a brake on all economic activity in the country. The Board of Education wrote in March 1934:

> The Board's Architect has visited the school and it appears from his report that the premises and site, though not so convenient or commodious as we should like, are not so bad as to make it necessary for us to consider the immediate termination of their recognition. We recognise the Managers' difficulties and will be ready to meet them by continuing our temporary recognition of the premises for a further period of two years from the present date without imposing any conditions regarding alterations or extensions. If, however, recognition is to be continued after 31st March, 1936, the Managers will have to take definite steps to improve the school.

Meanwhile, minor building work in and around the school continued, and records show that a new concrete playground was constructed and railings erected to keep the children safe. This cost £165.

Eventually an English compromise was agreed. The school's present site would be utilised, and the school would be renovated and extended rather than being purpose built. The additional accommodation was sorely needed, as in October 1936 the Bishop had already instructed the Headmistress to make more room for Catholic children by insisting that 'Protestant children should not be admitted but sent to the Council schools'.

In January 1937, Father Snell wrote to the Bishop of Brentwood about the new building works at the school. As the person responsible for giving consent for the building and any loans that were needed, the Bishop was to decide on the builder.

> My Lord,
> I now enclose the new and reduced prices for the proposed alterations and extensions to the School here.
> Messrs Sullings and Son. Stanford-le-Hope. £2,815
> Messrs Fowler and Hewitt. Chelmsford. £2,760
>
> The local builder Sullings of Stanford is £50 dearer, but both Mr. Scott (architect) and myself recommend the local man. He has already done much work here and will not cease to take an interest in the work after it has been completed.
>
> To give the contract to a local man also promotes good-will in this small place and I am going to get support in Catholic efforts to raise

> funds by making choice of a builder from the village, whereas I feel that if a builder from another town does the work, it will create unpleasantness and I feel that I shall not get that help and support in raising funds which otherwise would accrue.
>
> The moral value of employing a local man is worth far more to me than the extra sum involved.
>
> I hope, My Lord, that you will see your way clear to use this Messrs Sullings and Son of Stanford.
>
> I am, My Lord,
> Yours very obediently …..

Bishop Doubleday chose the company from Chelmsford.

Somewhat unexpectedly, permission for the arrangement of a building loan had to be given by the Holy See, after the Bishop of Brentwood, the Chapter and the Council of Administration had given their assent. Accordingly, the Bishop of Brentwood wrote to Pope Pius XI in March 1937. The letter is a curious mixture of the business and religious worlds of the nineteen thirties.

> Most Holy Father,
> The parochial school at Stanford-le-Hope in this Diocese of Brentwood is in danger of being closed unless it is extended in accordance with the requirements of the Board of Education. The cost of the extension will be £3,000 and arrangements have been made to repay this amount by annual instalments of £200, covering capital and interest. The rate of interest will most likely be 4%.
>
> The Parish Priest of Stanford-le-Hope humbly prostrate at the feet of Your Holiness asks that he may be permitted to contract this loan.
>
> We recommend this petition and we have consulted with our Chapter and Council of Temporal Administration and they approve of the loan.
>
> Bishop of Brentwood

In today's world 'humbly prostrate at the feet of Your Holiness' may seem a little excessive, although those of us who applied for a High Street Bank loan in the nineteen sixties will remember the position.

Whilst Father Snell assured the Bishop that he would be able to meet the payments of £200 per year, the Bishop wished to be quite certain. Recognising that the Sisters of Mercy paid £100 per year to the parish for the services of Father Snell as their chaplain, the Bishop organised that this money was paid directly to the Diocese. The charitable Gillow Trust made a donation of £100 to the parish of Stanford-le-Hope, and the Bishop ensured that this money was diverted to the diocesan account. This left the parish to pay £99 - 11s - 8d at the end of June and the end of December each year until the sum of £3,000 was repaid.

A new hall was added to the existing school and some heating was installed, an improvement that must have been welcomed by all. During the construction, the state of the existing school roof caused some concern. Mr. Scott, the architect, confirmed that the flat roof was in a very bad condition. The asphalt surface was perished, cracked and blistered, and the skirting on the parapet had come away from the brickwork, which allowed the weather to penetrate the walls of the school. As the asphalt contractors were already on site applying the roofing protection to the new extension, Mr. Scott recommended that the additional asphalt work on the old building was carried out, to avoid serious damage to both the old and new parts of the building. The cost was £56-3-0.

The Bishop had no objection to the emergency repair, adding that the work might be started 'if Father Snell can undertake to pay for it but the Bishop is not prepared to meet the cost'.

St. Joseph's High School, with some additional building on the same site, was opened as a 'new' school on October 22nd, 1937 by the Bishop of Brentwood.

In 1938, it was possible for the Sisters to buy another house in Scratton Road, as the accommodation in the little convent had become very cramped. A chapel was at last constructed in the convent so that daily Mass could be offered, and Father Snell and his curate, Father Hopkins, celebrated the first Mass. Reverend Mother Anthony came over to live at the Stanford Convent, as it was thought that two Sisters should remain in the convent during the hours of the school day.

In early 1939, Father Snell announced a donation of £1,000 towards the cost of the new school. It was the gift of a parishioner, Mrs. Chambers. In return, Father Snell asked that half of the annual £100 paid by the Sisters of Mercy might now be returned to the parish, as it was difficult for the parish to manage without this income. The Bishop gratefully accepted the £1,000 donation to reduce the loan, but stated that the other arrangements must stay in place. All that he could offer was that the loan would be paid off that much more quickly by the payment of the donation, and Father Snell would then receive full payment from the Sisters of Mercy at an earlier date.

At the start of the Second World War, the school closed for a while. After two months, the education department decided to reopen the school on a shift basis. For reasons of safety, there were to be no more than 48 children in the building in any one session (morning or afternoon) and no infant age children at all. However, after considerable pressure from parents, the education department decided to allow infants to attend school. No children from the school were evacuated to the countryside by order of the government.

On 10th September 1940, it was agreed that if the all clear siren had not sounded until after midnight, the school would not open in the morning until 10 o'clock. There were many air raids during this time, and the school was often closed until 10 a.m. or for the entire day.

At about this time, Father Snell's ill health resulted in a period of convalescence, and Father Michael Hopkins took charge of the parish. The upheaval of the war created some difficulties for the school. Apart from the absence of Father Snell, the four School Managers had been reduced to two. Father Hopkins managed to find a third Manager, from Stanford-le-Hope, to complement those from Tilbury and Orsett.

During the war years, the school began to serve a meal for the children in the middle of the day. The Head Teacher, Sister Mary Bernadette, gave up her small office so that it could be used as a kitchenette to prepare the meals. She moved her desk into the main hall and, although she had many administrative duties, she used the same space to teach Years 3 and 4. After school each day, Sister M. Bernadette set to work on her administrative tasks. With no secretary to provide support, this was a considerable responsibility. It was not until 1947 that the increased numbers of pupils made it possible to employ an additional teacher, Sister Aquinas, and Sister Mary Bernadette was released from teaching duties to continue her managerial role.

In 1942, there was some sign of military activity when a sandbagged rifle post was installed on the balcony of the school building. Two dozen sandbags were placed on the asphalt floor next to the stone parapet. The parish school was ready for invasion.

In June 1943 the telephone finally arrived at the school. Parents, officials and double glazing reps could now ring Stanford 306. Although the school suffered little damage during the war, an air raid shelter was built in the playground. On 4th August 1944 the school's daily routine was disturbed by the aerial attacks of Hitler's new weapon, the flying bomb. In May 1945, the school was closed again, but this time for a much happier reason – the VE celebrations which marked the end of the war in Europe.

After the war, as families were once again reunited and new families moved to the area, the roll of St. Joseph's School increased steadily.

September 1945	96 pupils
September 1947	115 pupils
September 1951	130 pupils
September 1952	152 pupils
September 1953	182 pupils
September 1954	198 pupils
September 1955	227 pupils

In 1946, the Divisional Education Officer recommended that

> a plot of land facing the school be purchased for the erection of a canteen and school hall and approximately one acre of land behind this plot be purchased for a school playing field.

A decision to buy the land was made in November 1946, although the land's owner did not want to sell and a compulsory purchase order was applied. The lower part of the land, where a gravel pit had been, was not filled in but levelled off to provide a playing field on a lower tier.

From 1944 onwards it became compulsory for all local authorities to provide a midday school meal. The School Meals Service brought the meals to St. Joseph's and the children began their love of jam sponge and custard and their fear of sago. One aspect of the diet at St. Joseph's, the meatless Fridays, caused considerable difficulty. The School Meals Service offered to save up the cheese salads from the week to give to the children on Friday. Perhaps the prospect of a four day old cheese salad put a bit of a damper on Friday. The arrangements did not work too well, however, and lunches containing meat would regularly arrive on Friday. Eventually the Bishop himself had to intervene and liaise with the authorities to create a more satisfactory Friday school dinner.

The school continued to serve Stanford-le-Hope, Corringham, Horndon on the Hill, Vange, Pitsea, Langdon, Shell Haven and East Tilbury. As the school grew in numbers, an additional teacher was needed for the Infant classes. In 1949, Sister Francis came to the school and relieved Sister Columba of the admissions class. Sister Columba had to teach all the other Infants! After the death of Sister Columba in June 1953, Sister Dolores joined the school in September that year.

The story of the development of the school followed the same theme: too many children in too confined a space. The school was now very crowded. Sister Monica described it as 'bursting at the seams'. The school still mainly consisted of two halls, the larger of which was divided by a partition to form two separate classrooms. Both of these classrooms were also used in the evenings by the parish, for cubs, scouts and socials etc., so everything had to put away at the end of each day and brought out again in the morning. Fortunately, in November 1951 the school became recognised by the Ministry of Education as an aided school, under the terms of the 1944 Education Act. This meant that half the cost of all future repairs and alterations to the school would be paid by the government, as long as the work had been initiated by the School Managers and approved by the Education Minister.

The highlight for many in the early fifties was the annual School Concert. It was very popular amongst the children and their families, and it helped to raise much needed funds for the parish. We shall never know the full details of the unexpected talent that first saw the light of day in the school hall.

Economic conditions in Britain remained bleak in the decade after the Second World War. Although huge advances had been made in the fields of public health, education and social welfare, money was very tight and additional economies were required. In 1952, the school was faced with a change in the teaching staff quota, with a ruling that the number of full time teachers, or their equivalent, was to be reduced. This was to take effect in September 1952, a mere three months ahead. Father Watson wrote to Bishop Beck in some alarm.

> My Lord,
> I have received an instruction from Mr. Frost (an education officer working for the council) that the assistant staff of our school must be reduced from four to three for the year 1952/1953. We are already crowded, and in fact have more children on the register than when the Committee authorised an extra teacher. At the end of this term 12 children will be leaving, but at least 25 are already seeking

admission. If a teacher is taken away, the position will be impossible, and new admissions will have to be drastically curtailed.

Acting upon Canon O'Donnell's advice, I am protesting to Mr. Frost pointing out the difficulties as this is the only Catholic school to serve a large and ever increasing demand for Catholic education. I would be grateful for Your Lordship's comments.

The Bishop shared Father Watson's concern, as his reply the following day demonstrates.

My dear Father Watson,
Thank you for your letter of June 22nd, and for the information which you give me about your staff problems. You are acting quite correctly in protesting to Mr. Frost, and you should be able to justify the need for your fourth teacher by the numbers in the school and seeking admission next term.

I think the Essex Education Committee have reduced their staffing ratio in order to effect some economies, but we shall certainly resist this attempt to reduce the staff in your school. I shall be glad to hear what reply you get from Mr. Frost, and shall be ready to take the matter further if necessary.

In July 1952, a letter from a parent brings this problem to a more personal level. A particularly eloquent plea to the Bishop was to create a dialogue between the Diocese and Essex Education Committee that would eventually see additional accommodation at St. Joseph's. This is the letter.

My Lord,
For some time now I have been trying to register my daughter's name at a Catholic school, so that she might start school when she is five years old, on January 24th, 1953. The parish school of St. Joseph's, Stanford-le-Hope, have flatly refused to accept Joan, my daughter, before September 1953. As there is no other Catholic school within easy travelling distance for such a young child, I shall be very grateful if you will give me permission to send my daughter to a non-Catholic school.

At the same time I must stress that I am anxious for my child to attend a Catholic school, and I would much prefer it if you could help me to arrange this. I have seen my Parish Priest, Fr. Watson, and also the Headmistress, Sister M. Bernadette. They inform me that the school is full. At the same time they tell me that there are five Protestants at the school. In view of the heavy financial burden we are being asked to bear to support our Catholic schools, it seems to me very unfair to turn away Catholic children and yet to accept non-Catholics.

Actually, removing these five non-Catholics would not help me since Sister Bernadette informs me she has turned away thirteen children before refusing to accept my child.

In the matter of classroom accommodation, the older parishioners tell me that over the sacristy is a room which was formerly used as a classroom. Fr. Watson says that this could still be used if a new staircase were put in. For the sake of these fourteen children being turned away, could not a new class be started in this classroom?

Surely it would cost much less than the £375 which this parish contributes annually to the School fund.

My Lord, I am very anxious for Joan to attend the Catholic school and I am distressed that it should be necessary to send her to a Council school. I am aware that this will gain her less than a year's schooling but this is a lot in view of the examination at eleven years of age for the secondary school.

For myself, and for all the other Catholic parents in a similar situation, I do beg you to assist us in this difficulty.

The Bishop wrote to Father Watson in August 1952 about the possibility of making use of the room over the sacristy that the parent had mentioned, and the following week addressed a letter to the Education Committee at Grays.

Dear Mr. Frost,

Stanford-le-Hope, St. Joseph's School

I understand that the accommodation problem in the school is growing acute and is likely to get worse as Catholic families begin to come to Basildon New Town. I wonder whether your Committee would help with temporary accommodation should that prove necessary.

I also understand that more than a year ago the Committee asked the Headmistress to give up her room in order to provide kitchen facilities. Apparently this was agreed to by the Managers but the Headmistress has now no room of her own and is obliged to carry out her work in a corridor of the school. I visited the school yesterday, and was shown a room over the sacristy which could easily serve as the Headmistress's room if a new staircase could be installed and minor alterations made to the windows. I understand that your Committee have already given approval, in principle, to

> this arrangement, but that the matter has been held up by the Ministry of Education since July 1951.
>
> I have asked Father Watson to estimate the cost of the suggested alterations, and I shall be grateful if you will urge the Ministry to give approval to this quite minor project which will involve the expenditure of about £200. It seems to me entirely unfitting that the Headmistress should be asked to conduct her work in a corridor of the school.

At first sight this might be seen as a change of direction, but Bishop Beck had realised that there was likely to be more success in refurbishing the room as a Headmistress's office, and then to arrange for the Headmistress to take additional children into her room which would serve as a temporary classroom. For the moment, any plan at all was blocked by a restriction on capital expenditure imposed by the government in a time of economic stringency.

In a note to Father Watson in October 1952, the Bishop's strategy became clear.

> I have ... asked (Mr. Frost) for the formal approval of for the conversion of the room over the sacristy into a Headmistress's room. I decided, however, not to send Mr. Bannister's (architect) plan to him as the plan shows the new room as a "proposed new classroom" for 20 pupils. While the alteration would be approved in order to provide a room for the Headmistress, I do not think it would be approved for the purpose of providing a substandard classroom, although I believe it is the Headmistress's purpose to have a certain number of children in the room. It would be wiser to have the plan amended by Mr. Bannister so as to show the room as a "proposed Headmistress's room", and I shall be grateful if you will get him to do this on the plan, which I am now returning, or on a new copy.

The Bishop's pressure on the Education Committee proved successful, and in December 1952 permission was given to proceed with the alterations to the room. The Council had found a way through the bureaucratic minefield. Whilst capital projects were blocked by the government, Mr. Frost had realised that the Headmistress had originally lost her office in order to provide kitchen facilities for the children. The provision of a new room for the Headmistress could therefore be authorised under Minor Capital School Meals Projects, a fund that was not hampered by government restrictions.

Of course, even this strategy would create only a few additional school places, and the Parish and the Bishop were only too well aware that the proposed growth of Basildon New Town would place additional pressure on St. Joseph's School until Basildon had its own Catholic primary school. Bishop Beck suggested that temporary accommodation could be erected on a site opposite the existing school, where it was already proposed to build a canteen and kitchen for the school.

Yet again, the world of practical politics created its own difficulties. There was no denying the overcrowded state of St. Joseph's School and, equally, the influx of new Catholic children from the families moving into Basildon was entirely predictable, but the Council had to be all things to all men. A proposed extension to the Corringham primary school, although urgently required, had been rejected on grounds of cost and the overspill children had been offered accommodation in the old practical block at Hassenbrook Secondary School. The argument given had been that the need for new expenditure was greater in other areas of the local authority. A Council spokesman gave his unofficial view that the authority was now wary of agreeing to even temporary classrooms being erected at St. Joseph's to accommodate schoolchildren from Basildon. This action, he judged, would cause 'a tremendous outcry'. Such was the community frustration at the shortage of school places, he was almost certainly correct in his judgement.

However, by 1953 it was recognised that the interest shown by the London County Council in building large public housing estates in the area was an indication of a rapid increase in population in both Stanford and Corringham. Such pressure would inevitably lead to a growth in pupil numbers, and both Corringham and Stanford would see large extensions to their school buildings. At this time, St. Joseph's was listed simply as a 4 class school of 100 pupils, and moves were soon under way to reclassify it as a full one form entry primary school. Bishop Beck thought that this was the most sensible way forward, and had even earmarked a site for a proposed new school. In his words

> In view of … the future development of Stanford, I think it is likely that we shall require a full one form entry primary school … I think this would probably mean the transfer of the school to a new site, and the one across the road…would, of course be very suitable.

In the meantime, there were major changes in the staffing of the school. In June 1953, the month of the coronation of Queen Elizabeth II, Sister M. Columba O'Dea died. She had been one of the first teachers in St. Joseph's School. She was replaced by Sister M. Dolores Doherty. In the same year, Sister M. Bernadette Orton retired as Head Teacher after twenty-three years in post. She was elected as Superior of the Mother House at Wanstead and Sister M. Aidan O'Neill became the new Head of the school.

By October 1953, St. Joseph's had 186 children on roll, in a school designed to accommodate 100. Whilst new buildings were required, and perhaps an entirely new school, the more immediate need was to house the additional pupils. There was no plan to build a Catholic Primary School in Basildon before 1955, and so pressure on St. Joseph's intake continued to grow. The proposed 'Basildon Vange Roman Catholic Junior and Infants School' was listed on the Essex Education Committee's reserve programme for 1955-1956, at a time when even the main programme was likely to be affected by economic stringency.

Sister Mary Aidan had the reputation of being a very strict disciplinarian. She was highly conscientious and hard-working and she expected everyone else to follow suit. Sister Aidan was regarded as a serious person who could not tolerate disobedience. Beneath the guise of being 'tough' was a kind, understanding and sympathetic person.

During her time as Head Teacher, from 1953 to 1975, two classrooms were heated by an anthracite coal boiler, which required to be stoked up a few times daily. The colder the weather, the more often the boiler needed to be 'fed'. There was no male caretaker to sort out blocked sinks, drains, leaks etc., so DIY tools were readily available for the next crisis.

At Easter 1954, Sister Gertrude Horrigan, a gifted musician, came to teach in the school, and in August 1954 Sister Monica Cremin joined the staff, sharing with another Sister the teaching of 75 children in one room.

At the start of the new academic year, the Bishop of Brentwood wrote to Father Hibbert to advise him of the pressures that would be placed on the St. Joseph's School's numbers by the delay in building a school in Basildon, and indicated that a move to a one form entry school would be an inevitable consequence. The Bishop asked Father Hibbert to discuss the matter with the Sisters of Mercy, as additional teachers would be needed for the rapidly growing school.

It was proving to be very difficult to find suitably qualified teachers at this time, and most of the teachers at the school were Sisters of Mercy. Amidst all the turmoil they provided a very stable and calm environment, and all were qualified teachers in their own right. The convent was now too small, so the house at the end of the garden was bought in 1954. Three years later a new chapel was added to the convent. It was solemnly blessed in November 1957 by Father Hibbert, in the presence of a group that included Reverend Mother Superior and Sisters Aloysius, Bernadette, Ignatius and Catherine.

Later on, in January 1958, the Stations of the Cross were erected in the new chapel and they were blessed by Rev. T. Stoneham, O.F.M. The old chapel was then adapted to become the dining room for the Sisters of Mercy.

Extra-curricular activities offered at the school included Music taught by Sister Gertrude and Irish Dancing taught by Joan Conway. A couple of men from the parish helped with P.E., but the facilities available were very poor. In addition, there was no caretaker at this time and so a maintenance man or cleaner sometimes lit the boiler to heat the school very early in the morning. Sister Aidan would check the boiler at 6.30 a.m. and then go to Mass. At about 8.00 a.m. she would return to the school. She did a lot of teaching, including needlework to the older juniors. Her secretarial work had to be done each day after the school closed.

Whilst moves were afoot to provide new, if temporary, classrooms for the school, the old school building needed attention. In September 1954, Father Hibbert informed Bishop Beck that

> It will also be necessary for the Managers to carry out repairs to parts of the roof of the school. There are quite a number of leaks where the water enters the classrooms. It may be necessary to have the whole of the flat roof, which covers that part of the school built in 1913, renewed.

In the meantime, there was a desperate need for additional accommodation. The Co-op Hall in King Street was hired in September 1954 a cost of £3 per week. It was open from 9.00 to 12 noon from Mondays to Fridays and from 1.30 to 3.30 on Mondays, Tuesdays and Thursdays. It served as a base for teaching some of the junior school children, until two new classrooms were built on the other side of Scratton Road, where the gravel pit had once been. Four more classrooms were added later. Bishop Beck now lobbied the Council's Education Committee, Divisional Education Officer Mr. Frost, The Chief Education Officer, Dr. Lawrence, and the government's own Ministry of Education to build up a momentum that saw the temporary classrooms, known as Medway huts, erected on the new site opposite the existing school. These were to house two classrooms for older pupils. Not for the first time, the term 'temporary' was something of a misnomer, as the later story of the school will reveal. Indeed, for a while the Bishop considered whether it would be feasible to build the entire new school in this temporary format.

The day after the Co-op Hall first came into use as classrooms for St. Joseph's, September 10th 1954, the Development Plan for Roman Catholic Schools included a proposal for our school.

> The revised proposal is to enlarge this school to a one form entry primary school (juniors and infants) for 280 pupils. At present 200 pupils are in attendance and the buildings are totally inadequate. The Executive of the Education Committee recently approved the temporary hire of an adjacent hall to provide some relief, but additional accommodation is required urgently. Many of the children (about 80 at present) come from the new town of Basildon and pressure from this area will continue as the proposed new R.C. primary school there is not likely to be completed for some years.

The Divisional Education Officer confirmed the earlier proposal to enlarge the school, when he wrote on 10th October 1954 that

> … this school be enlarged to a one form entry school for approximately 280 junior and infant pupils. The Schools Committee recommend that no objection be raised to the proposal of the Managers to erect a temporary building to provide two classrooms for use in January 1955, and possibly two further classrooms for the beginning of the school year 1955-56.

However, the hydra headed division of powers between local and central government made it possible for the Minister of Education to reject the expansion, as notices had not been published about the proposed classrooms and 'the enlargement is considered to be such as would amount to the establishment of a new school'.

Thus a finely judged legal interpretation of the rules was allowed to stand in the way of what was an urgent need for more classrooms. In the meantime, the temporary accommodation was built. An indication of the urgency of the situation can be gathered from the fact that planning approval was gained in early October and the two classrooms were completed just four months later. A tender of just under six thousand pounds was accepted from Bell and Edmonds. This was for the two Medway Mark IV classroom units, together with cloakroom, lavatory units, mains services and drainage. The site itself, part of a larger plot of land purchased by the Council under a Compulsory Purchase Order, provided the school and playground with 1.375 acres (the minimum allowed under law) and 1.5 acres for playing fields.

Meanwhile, the Basildon children continued to be bussed in to attend St. Joseph's. The bus service was not very reliable, as both the new Parish Priest in Basildon, Father Barrett, and the Bishop acknowledged. There was a new primary school on the Fryerns estate, and there was the possibility that parents would be tempted to send their children to this local non-Catholic school rather than have them hanging around in the rain waiting for unreliable transport. The Bishop put pressure on Thurrock Council to organise a more efficient coach service with designated stopping places so that the children could be 'conveyed to Stanford-le-Hope with the minimum of difficulty'.

As late as 30th December 1954, Essex Education Committee was predicting 'considerable delay' in bringing the additional classrooms into use, as proper legal processes had to be followed under the 1944 Education Act, but the Bishop was prepared to go ahead with the classrooms and await the anticipated approval later. His strategy was proved correct.

On January 17th 1955, Standard 1, with 37 children, and Standard 2, with 40 children, moved into their new home. The school now consisted of four classrooms in the main building and two Medway classrooms on the other side of Scratton Road. These six classrooms housed the 220 pupils on roll. The Sisters of Mercy, true to their name, provided break-time tea for the teaching staff, carrying the drinks over from the convent.

In July 1955, approval was given for the building of two more classrooms on land next to the Medway huts. These, however, would be built of brick, and would effectively be the first part of what was to be a new school on the new site. At the same time, the issue of accommodation for teaching staff and cleaning staff was considered. The Bishop considered what was known as Spooner buildings for the new extension, an economical form of construction that would provide pupil spaces at about one quarter of the normal cost, but was advised against this by the architects Burles and Newton, who regarded the general standard of finish as 'severely economical'. Fortunately, these light timber framed structures with their corrugated asbestos roofing were rejected. It was agreed to build the new classrooms on a principle similar to the original Medway Huts, with the exterior and interior walls built of brick. A quotation of £7,792. 7. 10 from Bell and Edmonds was accepted for the additional classrooms and staff accommodation. The builders were finally able to deliver the work at £659 below the tender, an experience that is even rarer today than it was then.

On March 1st 1956, the first of these classrooms was ready for use, and on the same date another event occurred – the arrival of the school's first male teacher, Mr. Fisher. Gas heaters were installed in the classrooms whilst a new heating system and boiler house were constructed.

As the school continued its steady expansion, permission was at last granted for the Head Teacher to employ a part-time secretary to assist with administrative work. The staff were given a new staff room in June 1956, and the school cleaners were also given a room of their own.

Sporting facilities began to improve for the pupils with the first school swimming lessons being provided at the open air swimming baths owned by the Shell Club. The Head Teacher decided not to accept an offer to share the nearby Hassenbrook School's playing fields for outdoor sport, preferring to use St. Joseph's own field, where a parent had offered to take the boys of the 'top class' for a weekly football session.

On November 22nd 1956, just 177 children turned up for school, relieving the pressure of pupil numbers, if for one day only, because of a bus strike in the Basildon area. The following April, there was a more significant easing of numbers when the new St. Teresa's School opened in Basildon. 118 children transferred to the Basildon school, which left just 156 children to start the summer term at St. Joseph's.

At the start of the new academic year in September 1957 the school roll was down to 143 and the teaching staff consisted of four assistant mistresses. All of the infants were taught by one teacher and the two infant classrooms were made into one big room by drawing back the glass partition that separated the two rooms. There were 51 children in this class, ranging from admission infants to 6+. The Head Teacher helped Sister Francis Grace, the infant mistress, as often as she could.

After the temporary reduction in the school population, the nearby London overspill estates began to provide a new influx of children:

September 1958	152 pupils
September 1959	197 pupils
September 1960	234 pupils
September 1962	295 pupils

Once again, St. Joseph's School was crying out for another classroom. It was thought that this would cost about six thousand pounds, but the money would have to be provided by the parish. The Local Authority was unwilling to provide funding, either for the building of new classrooms or for the general refurbishment of the existing buildings. The latter problem was solved by the introduction of volunteers to redecorate the interior of the school, a practice that continued for the next thirty years.

The Sisters of Mercy found that they had ever increasing responsibilities as the years passed by. Whilst there were so many more schools opening up in the Wanstead area, the main centre for our Sisters of Mercy, our school of St. Joseph's continued to grow. Eventually a decision had to be made to employ secular teachers to work alongside the Sisters. The first such teacher was Monica Gurney who, as Monica Allen, had once been a pupil at St. Joseph's School.

Sister Emmanuel joined the staff as a newly qualified teacher on December 8th, 1958, just one week after the first School Assistant, Mrs. Hill, was appointed. In June 1959, the School log records that a shed containing P.E. equipment was broken into by some boys and a football was stolen. It was later recovered from the prefabs across the road. Through the haze of time, it all seems so innocent now.

Many Sisters of Mercy taught at the school during the nineteen fifties, sixties, seventies and eighties. They included Sister Dolores Doherty (1953-1958), Sister Gertrude Horrigan (1953-1958), Sister Veronica Kenny (1955-1956), Sister Monica Cremin (1954-1968 and 1975-1986) Sister Assumpta Casey (1956), Sister Finbar Doherty (1960-1962), Sister Gerard McCarthy (1962-1963), Sister Carmel McEnery (1963-?), Sister Patricia Stanton (1976-?), Sister Michael Doherty (1976-1980), Sister Dominic Kennedy (1979-1980), Sister Campion Furness (1980-1986), Sister Agnes Williams (1986), Sister Barbara Jeffery (1984-1990) and Sister Perpetua Ennis (1989-1990).

As time moved on, however, there were signs of change. An entry in the School log states that it was decided 'as a matter of policy that the post of first senior assistant would in future be held by a male'.

In 1962 our Parish Priest, Father Hibbert, was instructed by the Diocese to study the setting up of a one form entry primary school in Corringham. The school, however, did not materialise. The pressure of numbers at St.

Joseph's continued, leading to an HMI stating in April 1962 that an additional classroom was now necessary. There were 280 children in the school and between 20 and 30 were to be admitted after Easter. Each of the three infant classes contained over 40 pupils.

In October 1962, the Divisional Education Officer wrote a letter about St. Joseph's, recommending a change that had been considered for nearly ten years.

> Educational development plan proposes that this school should become a one-form entry school for junior and infant children which would require accommodation comprising hall and eight classrooms, together with the usual ancillary facilities.

At the time, there were three classes taught on the old school site, and they had still had the dreaded 'outside toilets'. On the new site were four classrooms and a staff room. In April 1963, an estimate of £4,100 was accepted for the provision of an additional classroom. The school was now divided into two sites, separated by Scratton Road. This new classroom and a cloakroom were built on the new site and opened in January 1964. The following September, after 39 children transferred to the new Blessed Anne Line Catholic Primary School in Basildon, there were 254 children on roll at St. Joseph's. The two infant classes now numbered 44 and 46 children.

As the focus of the school began to move towards the new site, the problem of what to do with the old school buildings had to be considered. The parish wished to use the space to house the work of the expanding church, and there was an alternative proposal to utilise the space as a school dining room and kitchen. In return the County Council would be asked to build two additional classrooms on the new site. At the same time, the provision of an assembly hall for the school was discussed. It was agreed that the best option would be to integrate a new assembly hall with the newly built classrooms on the other side of Scratton Road.

In January 1965, the team of chartered architects who advised the parish and the diocese about St. Joseph's School summed up the development plan for the school.

> The development plan for the school has been approved both by the Department of Education and Science and the Essex County Council Education Committee. At present there are five classrooms and staff accommodation. The accommodation to complete the school consists of two additional Infants' classrooms, Assembly Hall, Head

> Teacher's and Secretary's rooms, school kitchen and heating chamber and paved play area.

St. Joseph's would be a seven class school built to accommodate 280 pupils, which Father Hibbert confidently predicted would be too small until there was a Catholic school in Corringham.

When the proposal for the new classrooms was finally accepted by the authorities, there was a stated condition that one of the classrooms on the old site be taken out of commission. In addition, it was required that the old premises be 'completely discontinued' once the one form entry school was completed. The Chief Education Officer's response showed his concern at this proposal, when he wrote in December 1965 that

> St. Joseph's R.C. Primary School itself has only seven classrooms and there were already 269 children on roll in September 1965, and an estimated enrolment of 300 in the Summer term 1966.

This concern was echoed by the Head Teacher, Sister Aidan, when she wrote to the Chief Education Officer, Mr. Rodhouse, on March 18th 1966.

> I am very worried about what to do with the children who have applied for admission after Easter. I have the names of 19 children who will be already 5 before the term begins, and I have no accommodation for them. I have a third infant class of 43 using the hall all this term and in the other two infant classes there are 44 and 36 children.

In another letter to the CEO the following month, Sister Aidan referred to primary school classrooms furnished for 46 pupils each.

The next new classroom was finally in place on February 15th 1967. The Ministry of Education paid 75% of the cost of the new build, leaving Father Hibbert to pay off the remaining £1,200, at the rate of £80 per year plus interest. Our Parish Priest was more than ready to take on this new expenditure, having just paid off the parish's remaining diocesan debt of £360.

At the start of the academic year, in September 1967, Sister Aidan decided that the Infants would be taught in the two 'Medway' classrooms and the Juniors in the four brick built classrooms. There were already 274 children on roll, and by January this increased to 297. This set a pattern for the next decade, a September roll of about 270, rising to a January roll of about 300.

In July 1970 a formal request was made to change the address of the school from Southend Road to Scratton Road, thereby acknowledging the primacy of the new buildings that had been established on the new site.

A First Communion Breakfast in 1971 – how happy they all look!

The final phase of the school completion on its new site was to include one more classroom, an assembly hall, a staff room and administration office, a kitchen, a new boiler powered heating system, stores and changing rooms, a playground and a car park. This was costed at just over £41,000 in February 1968, but a visit by the Diocesan Secretary for Education, Mr. D.K. L'Estrange shows how little of this had been achieved by September 1971.

> I called on Sister Aidan and had a look at the school. Next to the church there are two buildings dating from about 1914, consisting of two small classrooms and a very small hall (which only holds about 100), on to which has been built, more recently, a small scullery. Dinners are brought in cooked, and served in two sittings in the hall. There are one or two toilets and cupboards attached, and upstairs over the front of the building is an Office which serves the Headmistress, her secretary and also as a staff room. Adjacent to these buildings is a hard surface play-ground.
>
> Over the other side of Scratton Road is a site which Sister informed me was adequate for a one form entry primary school. On it there

are two temporary classrooms built in 1955 and attached to one is a small permanent structure which was intended as a staff room, but is used as a library and store room. The temporary classrooms are in quite good condition, are adequate in size and equipped with water and toilets. The small permanent structure was intended to be part of a permanent enlargement of the school, and subsequently – about 1965 - 4 classrooms have been built in permanent construction, but not contiguous with the small "staff room".

What is needed now, therefore, is a hall, a kitchen, an administrative block and at least one more classroom to complete the one form entry school.

Mr. Rodhouse (Dirict Education Officer) whom I saw subsequently said that he felt sure that if we were prepared to do a minor work consisting of a hall and administrative block, the County would provide a kitchen. The other classrooms could follow later.

Father Collings, whom I saw just before I left, said that he thought the parish were very anxious to keep the old school buildings for parochial use.

I told Sister Aidan there were many pressing needs in the diocese, but that I would bring this to the notice of the Commission and we would see what could be done in due course. There is no doubt that although the children have roofs over their heads almost every other facility which the school should have is lacking.

Both Father Collings and Sister Aidan thought that the completion of the school was more important than a new school at Corringham, where, they said, there is not great pressure.

D.K. L'Estrange

As for the 'temporary' Medway huts installed in 1955, a request was made at the end of 1972 to have them examined to ascertain 'the condition and life expectancy' of this accommodation. They were to remain as classrooms for another twenty years before a decision was made – to refurbish them with external cladding so that they then became a permanent part of the school buildings!

The lack of a proper playing field for the pupils of St. Joseph's was considered once again in February 1973. It was realised that it would be very expensive to purchase a large area of land for this purpose. An offer from neighbouring Hassenbrook School to share their playing fields, originally rejected back in 1956, was now accepted and the children at last had access to a substantial playing field for their outdoor sports.

First Communion : believed to be 1973

Nursery provision at the school was considered at this time, when it was thought that such a facility might be included in the 'remodelling of the School'. Not that such remodelling was without its set-backs. In November 1974, the School Managers tried to reorganise the 'new' site of the school, which had seen various additions and temporary arrangements for the best part of twenty years. They asked the Local Education Authority to include in their minor works programme for 1975/76 the provision of a proper hall, kitchen and boilerhouse. The request was turned down.

On 31st August 1975, Sister Aidan's time as Head Teacher of St. Joseph's School came to an end. She had agreed to go to Kenya for a period of Mission work. Initially, she did not wish to go off to Kenya, but later she enjoyed the experience. After a few years there, she was assigned administrative work in Canvey Island and Wath Convents. She later returned to Scratton Road, but this was not a wise decision as she had lost contact with old friends and life had moved on. Sister Aidan retired to the Convent of Mercy in Wanstead, where she spent her remaining years prayerfully and happily.

The day following Sister Aidan's departure as Head Teacher of the school, an old friend of the parish, Sister Monica Cremin, became the new Head Teacher. In October 1975, Father John Timmins and Sister Etheldreda of the Brentwood Religious Education Service paid a visit to the school. They summarised their impressions of the school in the following words:

> Because of the change in headship, and a virtually new staff, there is little to say, except that the whole syllabus, and approach to worship in the school is undergoing reappraisal by what appears to be the makings of a fine staff, under good leadership from the Head, and encouragement and support from the priests of the parish. The prospect looks good.

One of the Sisters of Mercy, Sister Philippa Kohlbecker, wrote a short account of the school at that time.

> The school still occupied the old building between the church and the convent, where there was the 'Upper Room' – head and secretary shared this office, two Infant rooms, a small hall plus a scullery. On the opposite side of Scratton Road were the two wooden Medway huts and four permanent classrooms, separated by a disused gravel pit. The children (280 approx.) had to cross the road daily for playground and dinners. Sister Monica worked very hard, with the full support of P.T.A. and Governors, to get the school built on one side of the road.
>
> Even as late as 1975, there was still no caretaker for the school and the Head Teacher had to open the classrooms and light each gas radiator which the teachers extinguished at the end of the school day. By the Summer term 1976, the school roll was 298. At this time again, there was a very stable staff.
>
> Curriculum wise there was very little detailed planning and no real syllabus to follow. Teachers almost had the opportunity to teach what they pleased. It was a time of learning through play and learning when ready. 'Officially' the children didn't have to learn tables or spellings but formal teaching did also take place. Sometime in the 1970s, the 'Mass Attendance' roll was dropped. Most of the teachers were still religious and it was generally accepted that they had a very positive influence on the school. Sister Monica's extra-curricular activities included netball and games as well as visiting parents with problems, sickness or bereavement.

On 30th October 1975, St. Joseph's School's Parent Teacher Association decided to try another tack in pressing for the completion of the school on the new site. The PTA chairman, C. Butters, wrote to the Member of Parliament for Thurrock, Hugh Delargy, a prominent spokesman for Catholic issues at Westminster.

Dear Sir,
May I draw to your attention to a situation which exists at St. Joseph's R.C. Primary School, Scratton Road, Stanford-le-Hope, Essex.

The original building attached to the church was built in approximately 1927. This houses a tiny hall which is used for assembly and for dining also. There are no facilities for Physical Education in the way of climbing bars etc., so during the cold weather the children cannot have P.E.

The Headmistress and Secretary share a small room, which is an attic borrowed from the church, and which is reached by climbing a steep flight of stone stairs – a hazard for young children.

This same building also contains the two infant classrooms, which at present house 39 children in each, in very cramped conditions. These classrooms have high ceilings and high windows, which makes it impossible for anybody to see outside – an extremely depressing environment for young children.

A long corridor with double doors at each end serves as access to these two classrooms and the Headmistress's office. This corridor makes it very difficult to maintain sufficient heating to the whole building, due to heat loss when these doors at either end are used.

The toilet facilities for these young children take some believing; they are out in a corner of the playground, and of course in the winter they freeze up making them inoperative.

This summer we applied for a licence for alcohol for a family social evening, which was refused "due to lack of proper toilet facilities". It seems that they are not good enough for one evening's drinking, but are quite good enough for children the whole year round.

The main part of the school is situated on the opposite side of a busy road, necessitating children crossing several times daily.

This school takes children from surrounding areas of up to approximately four miles radius. In Stanford-le-Hope and Corringham alone there are five new modern junior schools with <u>every</u> facility at hand.

Are Catholic children in this area becoming second-class citizens to those of other denominations?

As a practising Catholic your comments and help to get a completion of the proposed building would be appreciated.

The following month, the School Managers of St. Joseph's School wrote to the Diocese in "distress and indignation" that the improvements to the school had been removed from the County's Minor Works list. They referred to the continuing problems with inadequate buildings and the split site on either side of a busy road. The diocesan reply hardly helped matters. The minor project for St. Joseph's had not been removed from the list, as it had not been on the list in the first place. There was the hope that it could be included in the 1976/77 programme, but this would be determined by the Essex County Council.

Mr. L'Estrange followed up the problem on December 6th, when he wrote to the Assistant County Education Officer, Mr. Howarth, about St. Joseph's School. He made reference to the involvement of M.P. Hugh Delargy, who had passed the case to the Department of Education. With the involvement of these authorities already known, Mr. L'Estrange expressed the hope that

> some room for a project of up to £50,000 will be found in the minor capital programme for 1976/77.

Mr. Howarth made a visit to the school immediately, and reported that he had "discovered" that classes at St. Joseph's were exceeding 35 pupils per class and that this could lead to "dire trouble" with the main teaching union, the National Union of Teachers. He suggested the immediate provision of a relocatable classroom. However Mr. Howarth's view, which he expressed to his committee, was that the school was "in no worse situation than plenty of other schools" and so there was no justification for spending a lot of money. Whilst the toilet provision was recognised to be poor, Essex County Council had over 100 schools with outside toilets, a dreadful indictment of the standards the Council was willing to accept for the children in its care and which few, if any, working adults would have had to experience.

The proposed improvements at St. Joseph's would be a large project, and Mr. Howarth could not see such a programme being included in the 1976/77 budget. The solution was to divide the work into two separate projects, of which the first would be two classrooms, toilets for the infants and a playground. The second phase would include an Assembly Hall and kitchens.

Of more immediate significance was that the school simply did not have sufficient spaces in which to teach the children. The decision was made to install a further 'temporary' classroom on the new site, together with a playground on the new site and some alterations to improve road safety. Details of these were still being discussed in June, with the need for the classroom and the traffic barriers to be in place by early September. At the beginning of the academic year 1976, the school consisted of 4 Infant classes and 5 Junior classes. Unfortunately there were only eight classrooms, so one 4th Year Junior class had to work in the hall until the 'temporary' classroom could be installed.

The Head Teacher now had an office of her own, with the added luxury of a telephone. There was a new Deputy Head Teacher, Peter Hall, who had arrived at the start of the Summer term, and the Head of Infants was Joan Taborda. As a first indication of more modern times, there were now problems with cars parking outside the school at the start and end of school sessions, and two road safety officers came to the school to give advice. Alternative transport in the shape of the school bus had its own problems – secondary school children were smoking on the bus!

One of the long running problems at St. Joseph's School was the provision of adequate playing fields for the pupils. An area of land had been set aside by Essex County Council, to be shared with Hassenbrook Comprehensive School. One part of the land was for the primary school and one part for the secondary. A letter from Essex County Council in July 1976 illustrates the complexities which developed as a consequence. It was addressed to the Head Teacher, Sister Monica Cremin.

> Dear Miss Cremin,
>
> Playing Field Deficiency
>
> It is proposed to provide an all weather pitch at the Hassenbrook Comprehensive School to go towards overcoming the present playing field deficiency at that school.
>
> As the playing field of your own school is also agreed to be deficient and because of past agreement that a section of the Hassenbrook playing field would be available for your purposes, it has been suggested to Mr. Williams, as a possible alternative proposal for your consideration, that the availability of the four pitches on the top field would enable Hassenbrook to avoid using the two pitches on the lower field – whenever all but the largest P.E. Blocks are timetabled – which would then each be available for half a week giving the same total time as one pitch for a whole week.
>
> Please advise me if you consider this proposal acceptable for your purposes.

Confused? You should be. Incidentally, a recent discussion with a former St. Joseph's Head Teacher highlighted the fact that the problems with shared access to the playing fields rumbled on for many years, with countless letters and telephone calls failing to provide a permanent and clear solution.

The teaching staff at this time included Miss Sue Corrie, Sister Philippa, Miss Keogh, Mrs. Mary Drury, Sister Patricia, Mrs. Elsie Mason, Miss Wilkinson, Miss Tessa O'Leary, and Sister Michael. As the numbers of professed religious began to decline, the lay staff were becoming more prominent in the life of the school, a process that would continue until the last Sister of Mercy at St. Joseph's, Sister Philippa, resigned on August 31st 1992.

The Staff of St. Joseph's School in the nineteen seventies
Front Row : Honor Timmins, Stella Webb, Gwen Riley, Pauline Hill, Louise Weddell, Lilian Webb, Joan Taborda
Middle Row : Sister Michael Doherty, Anne Harrod, Mary Drury, Susan (Corrie) Russell, Sister Benignus Lehane, Elsie Mason, Peter Hall, Masie Hobson, Sister Philippa Kohlbecker
Back Row : Maria Martin, Elaine Wilkinson, Tessa Duggan, Breda Baker, Beryl Reeves, Pauline Steer, Teresa Tobin, Sister Monica Cremin, Father John Taylor

By the end of 1976, it was agreed to revise the total size of St. Joseph's School upwards from 280 pupils to 320/330. The entirely predictable increase in the school population had indeed taken place and the school could scarcely accommodate its pupils. There was a pressure on the school intake, leading to difficult decisions for the Head Teacher when parents applied to an already over-subscribed school.

The times of the school day were altered in June 1977, when the Juniors were given permission to finish at 3.30 rather than 3.45. During the Summer term, Mrs. Pauline Hill retired as school secretary after 27 years at St. Joseph's. Mrs. Betty Farrell became the new Clerical Assistant and Mrs. Teresa Tobin started at St. Joseph's as its new welfare assistant. They were both to remain at the school for a considerable time.

As late as 21st July, 1977, the Assistant County Education Officer commented on the proposed building improvements at St. Joseph's School in bleak terms. In a letter to Mr. F. J. Murphy, the Assistant Secretary of the Brentwood Diocesan Commission for Education, he stated:

> … I must repeat the misgivings I personally have expressed over the last year or two about the priority to be attached to this project. I keep on coming across examples of school buildings which in my opinion are demonstrably worse than those of St. Joseph's School, and which have no immediate prospect of inclusion in a Building Programme. The present position is that St. Joseph's is one of a long list of projects to be considered by members of the Education Committee for 1978/79. It is not unlikely that a number of them will have to be deferred.

In August 1977, a Games Store was completed at the school, and it looked as though that was all the school could expect in the way of building improvements for the foreseeable future. Yet in September the Diocese and the school were to receive exciting news. Mr. Howarth wrote to outline the new situation.

> I think you are aware that the Department of Education and Science has notified the Authority of an additional allocation for minor projects for the financial year 1977/78.
>
> I now confirm that approval has been given on behalf of the Authority for £75,000 of this allocation to be taken up for extensions at Stanford-le-Hope. The Department of Education and Science is being informed accordingly. This approval is given on the understanding that no part of the building work to be carried out in 1977/78 will involve the Authority in capital liability. It is anticipated that such elements of the building project as are the Authority's capital liability, including furniture, equipment and fees, will form a second, continuation project which will form part of the

> Capital Programme for 1978/79 and be set against the Authority's building allocation for that year.
>
> If this project is to start by the end of the financial year 1977/78 it is obviously important for briefing to take place and design work to proceed without delay.

By October 1977, a team of chartered quantity surveyors based in Southend had drawn up estimates for the new buildings to be completed in the first phase and the projected buildings to be constructed in the second phase. The first phase would comprise the much anticipated school hall, a store room, a 'quiet' room, an audio/visual room, an administration area, half of a corridor and a boiler room. Externally, there would be paths and one third of the car park. Although the boiler room was to be installed, the consequent upgrade of the heating system on the classrooms was not to be included. An additional series of buildings to house the school kitchen was separately costed.

The second phase was to be two new classrooms, a second 'quiet' room, a cloakroom, the other half of the corridor, adaptations to toilets, further paths, the completion of the car park and landscaping.

In December 1977, it was confirmed by Essex County Council that all of the work would be carried out under the allocation for the adjoining financial years of 1977/8 and 1978/9. A total cost of £131,635 was agreed. This was on the understanding that the old school buildings attached to the church would no longer be maintained by the Council, but would become the responsibility of the Church authorities.

In the meantime, building contracts had to be signed by the end of the financial year in order to qualify for the grant. Five companies submitted tenders for the work, and Clark and Kemp Limited were awarded the contract. It was estimated that the buildings would take a year to complete.

In the summer term 1978, the admissions class was taught in the school hall because (you guessed it!) there weren't enough classrooms. That Christmas, the P.T.A. entertained the children with two performances of a special pantomime, *CinderAlfred.*

At about this time, there were some concerns about the foundations of the school because of 'the nature of the soil'. Apparently, building on the site of a disused gravel pit was not the best idea. Improvements to the school fabric were also required, as Sister Monica noted in 1979.

> The teaching and cleaning staff have shown a great deal of patience and good humoured tolerance under very trying conditions this term. The climax was reached on 9th March when rain poured through the roof in 3 classrooms. Builders, staff and children armed with brushes, mops and cloths kept the flood at bay.

There was also a mention made of a considerable sagging in the roof of rooms 4 and 5. But later that year, Sister Philippa was able to write

> An administrative area, kitchen, hall, two new classrooms, and extensive alterations to the existing ones, meant that at long last, we were all in one joined-up building.

This completion of buildings on one site meant that at last the original building between the church and the convent could be vacated. St. Joseph's School log contains the momentous news that

> Tuesday, 19th June marked a great day in the history of St. Joseph's School, when formal permission was given to occupy our new school.

After only 24 years from the construction of the first Medway Huts on the new site on Scratton Road, the building of the new St. Joseph's School was completed. Some areas remained unfinished: there was no money to landscape the grounds or even to clear away the weeds, there was an urgent need to paint the exterior of the school and decisions still had to be made about the longevity of the Medway Huts. The School Governors accepted the share of the costs of the new buildings, and arranged a loan of £18,700 over a period of 30 years.

The numbers of pupils at the school continued to increase and in 1979 the school roll reached its highest ever figure – 315. It was decided the same year that the Infants and Juniors could share the same playground so it was no longer necessary for the children to cross over to the other side of Scratton Road. In the Autumn term of 1979, the times of the school day changed again, with the end of the day now at 3.15 p.m. 'in order to comply with a request to economise'. Presumably some faceless bureaucrat, ignoring what might be called the quality of the education provided, saw St. Joseph's as a building that needed heat and light and taking fifteen minutes off each school day would save money.

1980 marked the Golden Jubilee of the school. It was also the Golden Jubilee of the Sisters of Mercy at St. Joseph's, as Father McWilliams's letter to the Bishop of Brentwood reveals.

My Dear Lord Bishop,
Thank you for accepting the invitation to celebrate Mass in this parish at 8 p.m. on Friday, 25th April, to mark the Golden Jubilee of the Sisters of Mercy at Stanford-le-Hope. Sister Bernadette who is now 88 years old and a member of the community here was one of the foundresses of the school 50 years ago.

Sister Monica, the present Headmistress of the parish school, tells me my Lord that the school has never been officially opened or blessed by the Bishops of Brentwood. Therefore My Lord, the Sisters would be most grateful if you could give a simple blessing of the school after the Mass in the church. It so happens My Lord, that the arrival of the Sisters in Stanford took place at almost the same time as the opening of the school which has always had as its Head Teacher a Sister of Mercy.

Hoping that these arrangements will be suitable My Lord,
Yours sincerely in Christ,
Bernard McWilliams

The school's Golden Jubilee followed in July. House matches took place with the P.T.A. providing the refreshments. There was also a special School Concert. Trees and shrubs were planted to mark the event and the school received a statue of St. Joseph, as a gift from the parish.

In 1981 the Infants were given a playground of their own and our Parish Priest, Father McWilliams blessed the new area. On July 6th the playground became so hot that the new tar melted. At about this time, the school planted some Leylandi conifers to protect the school grounds from penetrating east winds.

In a meeting of the St. Joseph's School Foundation Governors at the presbytery on Thursday, 18th February, 1981, the basis for admission to the school was stated, as required by the 1980 Education Act. There were four statements.

1. Catholic pupils only will be admitted.
2. Entry numbers will be based on the staffing of the school, up to a maximum of 40 pupils.
3. Pupils will be drawn from Horndon, Corringham, Stanford-le-Hope and East Tilbury areas.
4. Catholic children from other areas will be admitted only under exceptional circumstances, and providing that parents accept the responsibility for transport.

There was a sad occasion in October 1981, when the Vice-Chairman of the School Governors died. Mr. W. O'Donoghue had been a loyal servant to the school and had personally done a great deal to unify the school of St. Joseph's on one site. So it was fitting that everyone at St. Joseph's School stood outside as a mark of respect when the funeral cortege passed by.

There was better news for the school the following month when it was announced on Essex Radio that St. Joseph's had won their Carol Competition. The children were invited to Chelmsford to record their carol at Essex Radio's studio, and the recording was then broadcast over the Essex Radio airwaves.

The school records reveal that there were a number of minor burglaries over these years, when relatively insignificant items were stolen. Some of the items sound like the odd things often left behind on buses and trains. Amongst the swag were some plastic balls, three cassette recorders, eighteen tapes, two violins and a Father Christmas outfit. In October 1982, a three foot tall plaster statue of Our Lady of Lourdes was stolen. The police were baffled. There was a more serious theft when intruders broke in through a skylight, found the safe keys and ransacked the contents.

By March 1982 there were over three hundred children on roll at the school. John Flitcroft, who served the school so well over subsequent years, first became a member of the School Governors. Some improvements were made to the school site at this time. The P.T.A. raised money to have wooden seating placed in the school playground and the following year the school had a modern alarm system fitted. In one purchase, the significance of which no-one could possibly have foreseen, the school bought its first computer, an Acorn. The rest, as they say, is history. And yet who can forget the 1977 prediction of Ken Olsen, the president, chairman and founder of a huge American computer company, 'There is no reason for any individual to have a computer in his home'.

In January 1984, Father Gerald Gostling informed the Thurrock Education Office of the level of pupil numbers at St. Joseph's School.

> The composition of classes at St. Joseph's School is as follows:

JUNIORS	BOYS & GIRLS
4th Year	36

4th & 3rd Year	30
3rd Year	23
2nd Year	32
2nd and 1st Year	30
1st Year	30
INFANTS	
Top Infants	31
Middle and Top Infants	26
Part Reception	26
Reception	24

> There are a further 21 Catholic pupils from the parish catchment area whose 5th birthdays will occur before 31st August 1984 but the majority of whom cannot be admitted because of staffing allocation. As Chairman of the Governors I wish to draw attention to the concern of those parents whose children will not be admitted to St. Joseph's until September 1984 and who are mentally and physically ready for full time education. Unfortunately there is not a Nursery attached to this school and furthermore few parents in this area can afford to take their children to a Play Group more than once or twice weekly and a few not at all. Children of average or low intelligence will be affected by this privation and in the present economic climate this school is not the recipient of extra remedial assistance.
>
> We, the Governors, would be grateful for the assistance of a temporary Teacher for the Summer Term 1984.

Father Gostling's request was turned down.

In 1984, after considerable discussion, a new statement was included in the school's views on the school curriculum, namely

> To express the opinion that the role of the family is of great importance in instilling respect for religious and moral values, not only the teaching profession.

Of course, the statement has more than one facet. It affirms the significance and influence of the family in the creation and fostering of moral and religious values, but it is also a disclaimer that states 'it is not solely the task of the school to develop such attitudes'. This deceptively simple statement enjoined the modern debate on the social responsibility for moral behaviour – particularly in the context of its perceived decline. It has now been a talking point in our country for over a generation.

Bishop Thomas McMahon talks to the children of St. Joseph's School

Sister Barbara first started teaching at the school in 1984, taking over the teaching of the fourth year Juniors. Most of the teachers were now lay staff. In the nineteen eighties and nineties they included Mrs. Phil Young, Miss Catherine Nutbourne, Mrs. Catherine Dixon, Mrs. Geraldine Franklin, Mrs. Elaine Varley, Mrs. Maria Davey, Miss Sue McGuiggan, Mrs. Karin Gillett, Miss Sue Ferry, Miss Mary Pollard, Mr. Mark Dunbavand, Miss Marie Cox, Mr. Bill O'Donnell, Miss Angela Sludden, Mrs. Una Murrells, Mrs. Jenny Radford, Mrs. Imelda Fadden, Miss Michelle Turley, Mrs. Tricia Barbour-Bourne, Miss Kathy Amos, Mrs. Linda Price and Mr. Jeremy Jackson.

Towards the end of 1984, the School Governors inspected the school site, its buildings and immediate surroundings, to gain an impression of the state of the fabric of St. Joseph's School. The report they wrote was sent to the Diocesan Commission for Education for their advice. Amongst other things, the report gives a good understanding of the responsibilities of those who try to run and maintain a school. The author remembers an elderly Head Teacher many years ago who once said "Ah yes, Education, very important. You'll see it in the Council entry in the phone book, next to Drains."

The report highlighted many niggling problems that had escalated when there was insufficient money to carry out running repairs on the school. These included preservation of timber cladding, the need for extensive spot painting, rotten facia panels, damp carpets, faulty window seals, loose and dangerous wire fencing, inadequate school gates, unsound asphalt surfaces, dangerous manhole covers, leaking roofs, damaged felting, broken drainpipes, inadequate heating in toilets, broken and missing floor tiles, lack of air inlet for gas heaters, cracks in walls and ceilings, broken electrical sockets, 'unpleasant' smell in toilets, cracked urinals, rain water leaks around roof lights, and potential hazards from paint containing lead.

The more experienced DIY enthusiasts among you will recognise that many of these problems were not major, but the sheer number of them attests to a climate where there was simply insufficient money to ensure that the school was adequately maintained. Leaking roofs, unpleasant smells, freezing toilets, shabby paintwork, uneven floors, damp carpets and rotting woodpanels combine to give an impression that despite the best efforts of those who tried to make the school a congenial environment, an air of neglect was apparent and additional financial support was sorely needed.

On 29th September 1985, the Diocesan Education Commission was asked to give a decision on a plot of land that had been reserved by Essex County Council as the site for a proposed Catholic primary school in Corringham. The site was situated in the detached playing field of Gable Hall School. As Corringham was not expected to grow substantially beyond its current population, the Council believed that it had the right number of primary and secondary schools. When the Commission agreed to this deletion, the hopes for a Corringham Catholic school were at an end.

In the Autumn term of 1985, Sister Monica became very ill and had to go into hospital for an operation, leaving Peter Hall as acting Head Teacher in her place. It was no longer possible to reassign a 'spare' Sister to cover any teaching vacancies and when, in the Spring term of 1986, a post of temporary reception teacher was advertised, there were literally no applicants.

Sister Monica decided that her health would not permit her to continue as Head Teacher, and when she resigned in 1986 it was Sister Philippa who was appointed. There had been no fewer than eleven suitably qualified candidates. Although it was not realised at the time, Sister Philippa was to be the last Sister of Mercy to work at St. Joseph's School.

Of all the Sisters of Mercy who have played an active role in the life of our parish, no-one has made a greater contribution than Sister Monica Cremin. In the course of compiling this book, Sister Monica was asked to pen a few words about her life. It is entirely typical of this gentle and modest woman that she chose to write about herself in the third person.

> Despite being born in turbulent times in her beloved Ireland, at a time of the Civil War and the economic war, Sister Monica enjoyed a happy childhood. She was the only surviving girl among four brothers, three older and one younger. When she was about ten years of age, she saw two nuns and confided to her friend Mary that she would like to become a nun to which her friend replied that she too would follow suit if only they would wear pretty clothes!
>
> A brother who was two years older became a Religious Brother, and a younger brother followed his priestly vocation.
>
> In 1942, an invitation to join the Sisters at the Mercy Convent in Wanstead, London, when there was a brief lull in the Second World War, seemed a definite call from God. Parents were heartbroken but willingly gave their consent. She and a friend sailed from Dublin to Holyhead and travelled onward to Euston, where she parted from her friend who was joining the Little Company of Mary, a Nursing Order.
>
> A great welcome awaited her in Wanstead, and for supper a boiled egg. From a very early age she had detested the smell of a boiled egg. That 15th October was a quiet night, but for the next nine Adolf Hitler decided that she needed testing by fire. As soon as the air raid siren sounded, it was a quick dash for the shelter. The Church ruling was fasting from midnight, so occasionally Mr. Hitler sent out his planes before 12.00 a.m. which meant that light refreshments were allowed, and weren't they welcome! Rationing was in force so tea, sugar etc. were in short supply.
>
> Fear, regret, second thoughts about her vocation never entered her head. Religious Orders had many young Novices and testing time was very strict. On completion of six months Postulancy there was the Ceremony of Reception. The young ladies were dressed as brides before donning what was then the heavy Religious Habit and receiving a white veil and also a new Religious name.
>
> Those two years are very special – prayerful – instruction on the Rule and Constitution – in short, preparation for the serious commitment about to be made. During a ceremony known as Religious Profession she pronounced her vows of Poverty, Chastity, Obedience and the

observance of the Rule and Constitution for three years. On the expiration of that date she was free to leave the convent or make a commitment for life, known as Perpetual Vows, which she willingly did.

After Teacher Training in London, Sister Monica was assigned to Canvey Island. The new convent was opened the day she left College. It was formerly owned by an Anglican Community and later occupied by the Army before becoming a hotel. Sister Monica and Sisters, as well as the Parish Priest, Father Manning, and willing parishioners, had a busy time getting the place in order, to start a private school for Catholic children from the Island, Benfleet and surrounding areas.

At the beginning, numbers were fairly low and there were only three classes, Sister Monica teaching the middle group. There was no spare cash to provide all the amenities which schools enjoy today. The Sisters were teachers, cleaners, caretakers, gardeners and Sacristans, over and above Religious Duties, Visitation and cooking.

February 1st 1953 will stand out for ever in Sister Monica's mind. On that morning she and her five companions were wakened by a Warden at 3.00 a.m. saying that Canvey was under flood and that the local people were to take refuge on the balcony surrounding the convent.

At the front of the house the water was deep, but the higher ground at the rear remained dry. Fortunately, no water got into the building. Phone lines were down, and it was a very worrying time as the Sisters could not communicate with the outside world. Sadly, a number of people lost their lives, among whom were some known to the Sisters.

After two days the Council decided that the Community should be evacuated as they feared the water may be contaminated. A little boat was moored and sadly they left for Wanstead, where they stayed for two weeks. What a joy to return to Canvey Island, which went from strength to strength. Within a fairly short time it was possible to have a new primary school, thanks to the financial help from the Wanstead Community which generously took it on.

Once again Sister Monica was uprooted from Canvey Island and assigned to Stanford-le-Hope. For a very brief period she shared a classroom with Sister Joseph. This was unsatisfactory and Sister Joseph moved to the Co-op Hall for a while until two Medway Huts arrived. They were erected on the east side of Scratton Road, known as The Sandpits. These huts were guaranteed a life span of twenty years, but after half a century are as good as ever – something to be said for good care. It was lovely to have a large, comfortable classroom, but the 'hub' of the school was across a busy road – the playground, hall for lunch/activities etc., and it was necessary to bring coats and blazers during the cold weather. A few more classrooms were erected on the new site and it had the luxury of a Staffroom.

Fourteen years flew by and once again the call came to return to Wanstead and teach in Chadwell Heath. Having recently learned to drive, she bravely battled with traffic along Eastern Avenue and busy Gants Hill with her three companions.

Four years later her life was again disrupted and she and Sister Agnes were asked to go to Kenya for a few years. The Mill Hill Mission was one hundred and eighty miles north of Nairobi and forty miles from the nearest town of Kisumu, on the shores of Lake Victoria. It was four thousand five hundred feet above sea level, making it a pleasant climate despite it being only six miles from the Equator.

Father Joe Geoghegan was the priest-in-charge, assisted by Brother John Veresen from Holland. The compound contained a modern presbytery and a large, airy church with a concrete floor which could be washed frequently. Close beside it was a comfortable, four bedroom convent, a small Clinic, a number of African thatched houses and a school!

The sight of her classroom, when she first saw it, left Sister Monica speechless: walls of mud, wattle and daub, holes for door and windows and a corrugated iron roof. When it rained, the noise was deafening. Equipment consisted of one small blackboard hanging from a large nail in the mud wall, and four primitive desks which normally seated two bodies were the classroom furniture.

For the first couple of weeks Sister Monica had a large class of pupils, ranging from 12 years to 18 plus. Three or four would manage to squeeze onto the two-seater desks while the rest each brought a large stone from the compound. Pupils were eager to learn and it was a joy to impart knowledge to the best of her ability. A few weeks after the start of the term, Mr. Aduogo, the Headmaster, announced that school fees had to be paid in by the end of the week. The next day, and for the remainder of the term, only a handful of pupils attended school. Families could not afford the modest fee. (That was 1971 and times have changed.)

She has many happy memories of that beautiful country. Sugar cane was the main cash crop in the area and there was a sugar factory in the parish. The tea plantations at Kericho were close at hand. A Missionary priest friend, who taught at Kericho Training College, was free at weekends. He lived for many years in Kenya and knew the area well. He loved to introduce the Sisters to some of the Tribes in their Native Reserves to get a flavour of their way of life, customs and food. There were also trips to the Masai Mara game reserve, and many others.

A great bond existed between all the Missionaries. It was no surprise for people to call, uninvited, just to give support and perhaps to stay overnight. One such visitor was a Kiltegan priest, Father Gerry Roche, who would call when on Safari to part of his Mission. He was a wonderful Missioner, full of fun, loved by his people. He was murdered a few years ago in his presbytery, in a burglary that went wrong.

Sister Agnes and Sister Monica shared a special interest in gardening. A generous Missioner gave them a large selection of plants etc. Sister Monica dug out a large, circular bed and planted a selection of rose trees. The soil and climate were ideal, and Sister Monica went to bed and dreamt of her 'Show Piece'. Alas! When she went out in the morning there wasn't a single leaf left – the Buck had come in the night and had a wonderful feast.

She loved her sojourn in Kenya but the area where she lived was 'home' to the malarial carrying mosquito, and unfortunately she was a favourite target on a number of occasions, despite the fact that she never failed to take her tablets

Back in England in 1975 – a brief holiday with family. Those in authority felt that Sister M. Aidan could benefit from a complete change, so she was asked to go to Kenya, which she did not fancy at first, but later enjoyed.

Eight years after she left her beloved Stanford-le-Hope, Sister Monica was asked to apply for the vacant post at St. Joseph's School. A daunting task awaited her. During her absence a number of classrooms had been built, but it was a disjointed complex on two sites. She inherited a dedicated, hard-working Staff, a lively, enthusiastic P.T.A. who had a vested interest in all aspects of school life, and an experienced, devoted Board of Governors who met regularly to discuss the needs of the school.

Letters were written, meetings attended – no opportunity missed in order to influence the Authority to look kindly on St. Joseph's many hardships, including young children forced to use outside toilets in all weathers and the need to cross a busy road for meals, play etc. It was unacceptable in this day and age.

It was a hard struggle but eventually plans were drawn up (modified and reduced on many occasions in order to cut costs!) for the completion of the school on one site. Even then, it was a trying time for Staff and pupils, who had to endure noise, dust and all sorts of inconveniences during the school day – but there was an end in sight!

A recent visit to St. Joseph's brought memories of those distant mid nineteen fifties, when two Medway huts arrived and planning permission was received to build a Staff room and facilities adjoining

> the classrooms – the P.T.A. planted Leylandi around the playground etc. What a joy to walk around the school today. So many people have worked tirelessly over the years – since 1930 – to make it the beautiful school it is today. May they be rewarded for their generosity for the sacrifices they made, which may often pass unnoticed or unappreciated.

In his capacity as Chairman of Governors, Father Gostling wrote in December 1986 to the Diocesan Education Commission about the urgent need for additional accommodation at the school.

> According to the Local Education Authority our school is described as an 8 base with an amenity area, room enough for 227 children. With the relocatable providing for 27 places the total comes to 254.
>
> As far as we understand, by 1990 it is a requirement to have at least a 40 square metre amenity area. What the Authority has done is to presume that the small room which is used as an infant classroom (18 children) is not a classroom but an amenity area. We may also well anticipate that by 1990 4 year olds will be officially accepted into school. There is even talk of that becoming the statutory age.
>
> At the moment on roll we have 251 children. Expected admissions up to 31.8.1987 are 25, the total then being 276.

The Brentwood Diocesan Education Commission responded by advising the school to tailor its intake to match the accommodation available. It saw little prospect of additional classrooms, and recommended that the school accepted the temporary mobile classroom as a permanent fixture.

Whilst every school focuses on the education it provides, that is never the whole picture. The Head Teacher's report to the Governors in March 1987 lists some of the activities that the school had recently organised.

> Mrs. Duggan's class entered the Mobil/Evening Echo Industry Year Competition and one pupil received a Highly Commended award from Paul Channon, Secretary of State for Education.
>
> Twenty Infants have received awards in the Nazareth house "Splash" painting competition.
>
> Ten children have gained their Cycling Proficiency Award and Mrs. Abbott now intends to undertake a small Road Safety Project with the Reception Class.
>
> Concerts were held on the 9th, 11th and 15th December, the proceeds being divided between the Catholic Children's Society and the Barkorwa Mission.

Most classes have visited the local library this term.

Detective Constable King (Parent) spent a morning with the fourth year Juniors, telling them of his work.

St. Joseph's boys are Thurrock six-a-side finalists and will be representing the borough in the County Finals on Saturday 28th March.

The fourth year Juniors attended the Snowdon Club for the Handicapped and provided entertainment for their Christmas party.

Patricia Dollard (Palmers Sixth Form College), Mark Hammond (Hassenbrook) and Ian McCarthy (St. Anselm's) have done or are still involved in Community Service in the school.

The playgroup children attended concert rehearsals and will be visiting the school prior to their admission at Easter.

Fire drill was carried out under the supervision of Tilbury Fire Service and the premises inspected.

Most people who remember the Autumn of 1987 will vividly recall the storm which raged through the United Kingdom on the night of October 15th. With many homes and other buildings damaged or even destroyed, it was no surprise that St. Joseph's School was hit by the high winds. The felt roofing on the Medway huts was torn away, exposing the buildings to the elements. Whilst temporary repairs were organised by a builder who just happened to be a parishioner, the rains that followed caused water to flood through to the classrooms below. A more permanent solution was needed urgently, and Father Gostling arranged for the work to be done.

Inevitably, this fell foul of the usual tendering processes dictated by the Department of Education and for a while it seemed as though this would invalidate any compensation from the government. Fortunately common sense prevailed when even Whitehall recognised that Father Gostling had done the best thing in the circumstances.

The greater transparency in the administration of schools which the 1988 Education Reform Act had brought in encouraged more dialogue between schools and the communities they served. A good example of this is a letter written by a concerned parent to the Bishop of Brentwood, on an issue that has caused controversy over the past half century, sex education.

July 10th 1988

To : Right Reverend Thomas McMahon
Bishop of Brentwood

Your Lordship,
It was with great sadness that I learned at the Annual Parent/Governors meeting of our local Catholic primary school (St. Joseph's) that the Church is altering its policy on sex education.

As I understand it, the long-standing policy of the Church Schools on this matter was that sex education was the "Privilege and Responsibility of the Parents". Now, it would seem, sex education is to be included in the syllabus of the primary school.

I was reassured by the Headmistress that this would not be "Sex Education" in an explicit, biological sense, but more within the context of loving relationships. However, it would seem that there has been a fundamental shift of the Catholic primary schools on this matter, and both my husband and myself, as the concerned parents of two little girls, would like to ask why we were not consulted before a policy change on such a delicate and sensitive issue was taken.

In August, Bishop Thomas replied with his customary courtesy and concern.

Thank you for your letter of July 10th which I have just received. I am very sorry you have been upset by the news that education in personal relationships, and specifically sex education, is part of the curriculum in our primary schools.

I am enclosing a document called "Laying the Foundations for Education in Personal Relationships" produced by the Bishops of England and Wales about a year ago. You will see that it is still the Church's view that parents are responsible for this area of a child's development; but the document calls on schools, parishes and other bodies to do all they can to assist parents in what has become a very difficult task, and to see that our young people are given "positive guidance and a true appreciation of all their human gifts" by appropriate teaching in schools.

Do be assured that diocesan schools will take this responsibility very seriously and that they will want to work with parents at every step.

Wishing you and your family every blessing,

Yours sincerely,

In July 1988, St. Joseph's School changed its admissions policy, as required by law. It now added children of other Christian denominations and other children of parents who wanted a Christian Education for their children. In consultation with Essex County Council, it was agreed that such children should not exceed a cap of 20% of the intake of each year, so that the Catholic character of the school could be maintained.

The involvement of the parents in the life of the school continued just as strongly as in the past. The P.T.A. Fair in 1988 raised over £1,600, and the following year a group of parents redecorated the school entrance and corridor, using paint provided by the Council. Further work was completed at weekends and during the school holidays.

It was fortunate that there was such a band of helpers, for the school was finding it difficult to recruit full time teachers to the school as vacancies arose. The autumn term of 1989 was the first term for three years when every class in the school had a full time teacher, but by the spring term two of these teachers had left. Supply teachers could not be found, and when a new incentive allowance was introduced to the school all the experienced teachers already had an allowance and no-one could be found amongst the other, inexperienced staff.

Among the bright spots in the Governors' meeting of December 1989 was the selection of Mary Pollard as one of only six Essex teachers to take part in an Open University Pilot Course on Science for Primary Teachers. At the same meeting, one of our Foundation Governors, John Flitcroft, was elected as Chairman of the Governing Body, a position he held with distinction for over twenty years.

With the arrival of the new National Curriculum, which included a compulsory section on Science and Technology, as part of the 10 Core and Foundation Subjects, it was recognised that the existing 'temporary' classroom, then in place for 15 years, was no longer suitable. It had no sink, water or toilets. The Governors decided to purchase a new relocatable classroom with toilets and the running water needed for Science lessons.

Planning approval was duly given and the classroom was delivered and erected in June 1990, the Emmaus Province of the Sisters of Mercy donating ten thousand pounds towards its cost. A subsequent gift of five thousand pounds was made by the Sisters of Mercy in order to relieve the parish debt.

During these years, the school buildings were well cared for by Dave Arnold and, later, Bob Ives. Amongst those who helped them in this task were Mrs. Harrod, Mrs. Margaret Mitchell and Mrs. Joan West.

The Sisters of Mercy continued with parish work outside the school, including parenting courses, religious discussion groups for adults, religious education with young children, working with a youth club for 16-18 year olds, parish visiting, counselling, visiting old people's homes and taking Holy Communion to those unable to leave their home.

The pace of educational change began to accelerate. The new National Curriculum was introduced and, predictably, revised, the school now had its own mission statement and a school development plan, and the Local Management of Schools was in place. The rush to computerisation was also to the fore.

Meanwhile, in the background, a far more significant change was quietly taking place. The number of Sisters employed in the school declined until the last teaching Sister, Sister Barbara, resigned in August 1989 and the Head Teacher, Sister Philippa resigned on August 31st 1992. After continuous service of over 60 years, the Sisters of Mercy withdrew from the teaching and management of St. Joseph's School. When they had first accepted the challenge to come to Stanford-le-Hope in 1930, the school was barely viable and its future was at best uncertain.

Over the period of six decades, St. Joseph's School had grown and prospered. A new set of buildings in Scratton Road is a tribute to their determination to improve the quality of education for the children placed in their care, their refusal to be diverted by educational bureaucracy, and their endless patience and fortitude in ensuring that the school achieved its deserved success. The popularity of St. Joseph's School amongst both children and parents is a comment on the dedication and sheer hard work of the teaching Sisters.

In 2004, Mary Pollard, the former Head Teacher of St. Joseph's School, published some research into the school as part of an M.A. dissertation. She considered the legacy of the Sisters of Mercy at the school. It was discovered that the nuns had taught, on average, over ten years each at the school. This must have brought much needed stability to St. Joseph's School. The Sisters were questioned about the modern relevance of the ideals of the founder of their order, Catherine McAuley. The original aims of instructing the poor in their faith, alleviating poverty, educating the poor, and fostering community values were seen to be as real to today's Sisters as when these ideals were first framed.

The parishioners were asked about the influence of the Sisters in the development of St. Joseph's School. One paragraph in the dissertation summed up this influence.

The Sisters provided a caring and secure atmosphere in which children could grow both spiritually and academically. They were perceived as excellent role models providing a strong link between education and religion. As well as teaching, they fulfilled a pastoral role for parents and pupils alike. They brought stability and continuity to the development of the school and many taught two or three generations of the same family whom they knew personally and helped when necessary. Through living in the community, the Sisters established close links between home, school and parish. There was a high level of parish involvement encouraged by regular visits from the parish clergy and school attendance at parish events. They had a common reason to be there and, with a strong faith in God, developed the ethos of the school with lives dedicated to educating children.

Mary Pollard's research then turned to the challenges that the Sisters faced in their work.

The challenges that the Sisters faced were numerous. In the earlier days a serious challenge was the constant use of the school buildings by the parish on almost every evening with the Sisters often left to make sure the classrooms were ready for teaching and learning the next day. The diverse backgrounds of the pupils and their parents were mentioned. At one time many new families moved into the area and much work was needed to establish community. The Sisters had a responsibility to keep the faith alive and thriving in the face of consumerism and materialism as well as keeping the faith relevant to the times.

Another challenge faced was the poor pay conditions for teachers in the early days of their work at St. Joseph's. The poverty of many of the parishioners was commented upon, with the Sisters supportive of all families but especially those where there was real need and unemployment. A lack of resources was mentioned which was exacerbated by this lack of money. A further challenge resulted from the decline in the number of practising Catholic families.

Mary Pollard asked research respondents to consider the effect on change at the school with the gradual withdrawal of the Sisters from their teaching.

One suggestion made was that the lay school leaders turned more towards the pressures and demands of the secularised educational system and part of the inner calm and serenity of the Sisters was lost. It was generally thought that today the links between the school, the parish and families are on a more formal and somewhat reduced level but it was noted too that the governors of St. Joseph's had established a specific pastoral role within the teaching complement to try to re-establish this link.

Some felt that due to the gradual withdrawal of the Sisters from teaching, the challenges were not felt as keenly as they might otherwise have been.

Mention was made that since the Sisters' withdrawal there has been a greater link with other churches, a dedicated room used as a school chapel developed and more involvement with other local schools. However the Sisters' withdrawal did mean that their presence and availability were no longer and a certain serenity was lost forever.

The final question Mary Pollard asked was whether the influence of the Sisters was still in evidence at St. Joseph's School.

One former Sister commented "Yes, I always feel most welcome to visit at any time. It has some of the same ethos and seems to be continuing in the same way with much parental involvement." The physical elements within the school – the altars, statues and plants – were mentioned. There were also comments about the foundations that the Sisters laid down and how these continue to have a subtle influence within the school today.

Another comment made suggested that it is not so much the influence of 'The Sisters' but something beyond them that remains in evidence – that the Sisters themselves were instruments of Christ and of necessity they integrated faith and life. This resulted in all that was good so based as to continue after their departure. However it was also commented that whether this influence will continue when there are no longer staff members who 'served' with the Sisters remains to be seen.

It would be an understandable assumption that this marks the end of the story of St. Joseph's School, so integral were the Sisters of Mercy to its foundation and development. But over twenty years have now passed since the Sisters relinquished their teaching and management duties at the school, and yet the school continues steadily with its work and progress.

The first task was to find a new Head Teacher after Sister Philippa resigned. Unexpectedly, there were few suitable applicants for the position and the Deputy Head Teacher, Miss Mary Pollard, was asked to take on the role of Acting Head. Six months later, Miss Pollard was appointed as the new Head Teacher, the first lay Head Teacher since the school was established as a Public Elementary School in 1930.

This was a period of fairly rapid educational change and St. Joseph's was obliged to implement the many new features of educational policy imposed by national government. The whole area of teacher appraisal had to be implemented at short notice, and short, medium and long term planning became part of everyday discussion and action. The school still found it difficult to recruit suitable teaching staff and more building work was necessary to improve the structure of the school. The 'temporary' Medway Huts were finally given external cladding and were now reclassified as permanent structures, a triumph of hope over experience.

The whole school was then given a new roof and the school's windows and doors were renewed.

In the 1990s there was a fire in the P.T.A. shed after a break in. Despite the billowing smoke that could be seen as far away as the railway station, the quick action of the Sisters of Mercy at the convent and the immediacy of the local fire brigade's response prevented serious damage to the school. The new roof received some slight damage and smoke damaged two of the classrooms, although this was again only slight. One of the firemen, who was a member of our P.T.A., complained about the fire in the shed with the words 'That's my bar going up in flames".

That first Acorn computer, purchased almost twenty years earlier, had been augmented by many others over time. As they say, 'Mighty oaks from little acorns grow'. Our mighty oak was a new I.C.T. Suite which, combined with new library facilities, was opened in the Autumn term 2000 by Father George Stokes, the Director of Education for the Diocese of Brentwood. It has proved a real boon to pupils, teachers, governors and parents.

No less significant in the daily life of the school was the installation of new toilet facilities across the school, including the provision of the strangely named 'disabled toilet'.

Since the nineteen eighties, there had been talk of creating a purpose built school entrance. Whilst this was an eminently sensible idea, there were insufficient funds to carry out the project. The plans that were eventually drawn up were a little too ambitious, but after some simplification the building work began in late 2002. In early 2003, the School at long last had a new Reception and Office area, and the entrance to the school was then officially Scratton Road!

Since the departure of the Sisters of Mercy, the School has appointed a number of new teachers. These included Mr. John Peoples, Mrs. Stephanie Lakin, Miss Kim Russell, Mrs. Joyce Kelly, Mrs. Gill Worrall, Miss Annabelle Norris, Mrs. Sandra Clancy, Mrs. Janice Hills, Mrs. Catherine McLaughlin, Miss Claire Worthington and Miss Michelle Cosgrove. Miss Pollard took a sabbatical year in 2001-02, and then chose to change the direction of her career, becoming Assistant Head Teacher with pastoral responsibility. Mr. John Peoples had been Acting Head Teacher during Miss Pollard's absence, and he was now appointed Head Teacher.

During this time, the School began to employ teaching assistants, who are now seen to be a valuable addition to the life and work of the School. These have included Mrs. Sharon Brown, Mrs. Dawn Lloyd, Mrs. Mandy McDonald, Mrs. Sonia Brown, Mrs. Lorraine Cattaneo, Mrs. Paula Gannon, Mrs. Lesley Jolin, Mrs. Jackie Trigg, Mrs. Sue Sweet, Mrs. Claire Kay and Mrs. Anne Ramsey.

There were changes in office personnel as well. Mrs. Teresa Cotgrove was Office Assistant, primary first aider and sometimes teaching assistant all rolled into one. Mrs. Sharon Jackson became the Financial Administrative Officer. Clerical assistants included Mrs. Anna Nuttall and Mrs. Sue Sweet.

There was an important date for the school on July 14th 2001 when Sean Parsons was ordained to the priesthood in Our Lady and St. Joseph's Church, with a reception held at St. Joseph's. Father Sean Parsons had been a pupil at the school in the 1960s.

Additional changes to the internal structure of the school followed in quick succession. A new school chapel was built in what had been the Head Teacher's room, the old resources room was transformed into a spacious staff room and two other areas became a dedicated resources area and a special needs room. Agreement was finally reached with the local Council to fence in the school land on the Hardie Road side of the school, and in 2005 a brick built classroom replaced the 'new' demountable classroom, that had been on site for fifteen years.

The new site manager was now Will Dollard who, with his team, worked very hard to ensure that the school was both clean and safe. Of course, many people have worked at St. Joseph's School over the years, some for a short period of time and others, such as many of the kitchen staff and dinner ladies, have been with the school for what seems like forever. Our thanks are due to the School Managers who gave of their time and energy to decide on the future direction of the early St. Joseph's School and the School Governors of today, some of whom have served our school for many years. That is not to overlook the contribution of so many parents down the years. These voluntary helpers have listened to children read, helped at swimming, coached and supported sports such as football and netball, and given of their expertise in areas as diverse as gardening, cooking, art and craft and administration.

The contribution and generosity of so many over the years have helped to make St. Joseph's the school it is today.

Our Sisters of Mercy at the last Mass to be said at the convent before its closure in April 2005

On 28th April, 2005, the seventy-fifth anniversary of the first arrival of the Sisters of Mercy at St. Joseph's, an invitation was issued to the Sisters to return to the school. At the ensuing celebrations there was opportunity both for the school to thank the Sisters for what had they had done over the years and for many of the Sisters to meet again with past pupils, old friends and colleagues.

Mr. Peoples continued as Head Teacher of the school until 2009, when the current Head Teacher, Mrs. Lakin was appointed.

<u>A Guided Tour of St. Joseph's R.C. Primary School : May 2012</u>

The first impression of the school as one enters the site is how much things have changed since the early days when the very future of the parish school was in doubt. At the front of the school, behind well-designed security fences, some young children are playing in an area full of purpose built equipment. On arrival, I am given a friendly welcome by the school's Head Teacher, Mrs. Lakin, and the equally friendly office staff. The office itself, with its CCTV monitor screens, computerised data system and high tech facilities speaks clearly of the twenty first century and of continuing investment in the school and its future.

Rather than sitting in a single office, Mrs. Lakin takes me on a full tour of the school, so that we can see St. Joseph's School in action. It proves to be a stimulating journey, as we visit all of the classrooms to see the pupils at their work and the many teaching and learning facilities that have been provided in recent years.

Every classroom has an interactive whiteboard, and these are linked to a bank of computer facilities that enable access to a huge range of resources. Even the very youngest children make use of an interactive whiteboard, to help them with their phonics. The first room we visit, the Library and ICT suite, benefits from nineteen computer screens provided by an active P.T.A. in the past few years. Overall, they have bought twenty eight computers for the school. There were computers before this, but they inevitably became outdated and needed replacement. The school system is screened so that unsuitable material can be avoided. The school is about to extend its concern in this area by arranging special training courses for parents so that computer systems in the home can be equally safeguarded. All of the teachers are provided with their own laptop for their professional work. The children in the room are each compiling a School Leaver's Handbook which they will take with them as a memento when they move to secondary school in the autumn.

Whilst the school is constantly adapting to new technologies, the baby is not thrown out with the bathwater. Mrs. Lakin states that many of the original resources, for example on VHS tapes, are still in use and old-style video players and televisions still provide useful teaching and learning materials. The classrooms are fitted with vertical blinds that are used to darken the classrooms slightly when the interactive whiteboards are in use. There are simply no blackboards anymore. There are computer screens dotted around the classroom for pupil access.

We see a French lesson for eight and nine year olds conducted by a teacher from Grays Convent School, who visits the school once a week. There is rapt attention from the children. Although the school has the responsibility of teaching the national curriculum, it does not confine itself to areas examined by government testing.

As we walk through into the next classroom, it becomes apparent that the school has been designed so that the classrooms run easily from one room to the next with interconnecting doors, and there appear to be toilet and washroom facilities adjacent to the classrooms. Children are seen completing practice papers in preparation for their SATs, which the government is still requiring in primary and secondary schools. This testing system has come in for a lot of criticism from many quarters, but the teachers are too professional to do anything but their best for their own pupils while the current testing regime remains in place.

An example of some of the children's artwork

Just outside this classroom, where a small group is being tested on their phonics, there is an impressive electric kiln that is used to fire the various clay designs created by the children in their classrooms. The kiln is very securely locked behind a grill screen.

Walking around the school we meet many children moving from one classroom to another. Mrs. Lakin greets them all by name. The school has the capacity to take two hundred and eighty children, and it is very close to that number. This is obviously a popular school. It is very important for the school to adhere strictly to its admissions criteria, agreed with the Local Education Authority under the guidance of the Diocese. When a school is so close to its maximum intake, there is the possibility that prospective pupils might be denied access, simply because there isn't enough room. When this happens, any appeal will automatically refer back to these criteria. The school must be able to demonstrate that it has done everything absolutely to the letter. There is some relaxation in the pressure of numbers in that the school is situated in an area where there is an increasingly aging population, and 'overspill' pupils from areas with insufficient school places are soon to be offered places in their own area.

The school places a high priority on its relationship with local residents. One bone of contention is parking and, of course, the school run. The school has introduced a 'park and stride' scheme, whereby parents are given stickers provided by the Council to park their cars in the King Street Car Park in the early morning and then walk their children down to the school. Does this community relationship work? Serious damage to the school was avoided when neighbours alerted the fire brigade to a fire in the Leylandi hedging on the school perimeter. "We are a community," says Mrs. Lakin, "and it is important to maintain a positive relationship with our neighbours."

The school has a number of strategically placed giant umbrellas to create shade for the children when they are outside on sunny days. And yes, those children I saw playing outside earlier were all wearing sun hats. At the rear of the school there is a pergola which provides additional shade, both for the children at playtimes and for parents when they come to collect their children at the end of the day. Close to this is an environmental area, which includes bird tables and a pond where the children go pond-dipping. Fortunately, there is a grandfather who tends the area and prevents it from becoming too overgrown. Future plans include an extension to this area so that it sweeps round to meet with a new community orchard that is to be planted at the front of the school. There are also plans for allotment areas to encourage the children to grow things. There is already a gardening club, run for the children by interested parents. The children are very keen and often come up with ideas of their own.

Half-way across the playground is a reminder of the original site of the school, when there was once a gravel pit. The ground in the 'lower' playground is being monitored by engineers as it is prone to subsidence. Whilst not in any way hazardous, it is equally beyond remedy, as the land will continue to sink where the gravel workings once stood. Much of this area is to be redesigned in the next few years, to remove much of the hard standing and create softer areas where the children can sit and walk during their breaks. The children will be asked for their own ideas when the design is created. The shared use of the fields with Hassenbrook School is working well, with St. Joseph's making use of the facility on a daily basis, and bringing their children closer to their own school when the secondary pupils are on the fields.

Mrs. Lakin has been at the school for quite a few years. When Miss Pollard was the Head Teacher, Mrs. Lakin was a Senior Teacher. She became Acting Deputy Head when John Peoples became Acting Head, and she has been Head Teacher now for over three years. She describes the job as "very rewarding", although the instincts of a classroom teacher are still there. Fortunately, Mrs. Lakin enjoys direct contact with the children in Monday's whole school assembly, Tuesday's Infant assembly and Wednesday's Junior assembly.

Mrs. Lakin has successfully applied for funding from the LCVAP (Local Education Authority Co-Ordinated Voluntary Aided Programme) to install new lighting and alarms, and to help with the reorganisation of the school site so that the younger children are now at the front of the building and the older children are at the back of the school. The children helped to choose the colours for the new area for older pupils at the back of the school, fortunately changing their minds about the use of red and selecting more neutral tones. New toilets have been installed here and better storage facilities are being organised. The area is evolving into something more suitable for older pupils.

We enter a classroom where an interactive whiteboard is in use. The text on the whiteboard has been heavily amended by the pupils themselves, and there is evidence of real engagement. The teacher shows us some of the Maths programmes and these are simply stunning. The difference between this software and the wobbly blackboard writing of a generation ago could hardly be more obvious.

In a quiet little courtyard there is a memorial garden to the memory of a past pupil who died. The garden has now been in the school for about three years, originally tended by the child's grandparents and now by a team of parents. The children come to water the plants every day. The area is sometimes used for meetings and the children occasionally work out here in the calm surroundings. It is clear that gardening is a popular activity and the school is looking for additional areas to cultivate, which is one of the reasons for the planned allotment area. Mrs. Lakin pays tribute to the ever willing band of parents who are so keen to help the school.

The school is quick to celebrate events that are part of our national culture. There is evidence of work and displays related to the Queen's Diamond Jubilee, and the children have been encouraged to define their own ambitions within the framework of the 2012 Olympic Games.

There is certainly plenty of imagination in the child who wishes to become the best ever basketball scientist.

There is a music room where the children are given instrumental lessons in guitar, violin, keyboard, drumming and piano, and there are clarinet lessons for year six students. Two years ago, St. Joseph's was one of eighteen schools in the country invited to perform at a national music festival in Nottingham, a wonderful experience for the children. When the government withdrew the money for this initiative, the children wrote to the Secretary of State asking that it be continued as they did not want to lose the opportunity. They even offered to give up the money for their pencils, if only the support could continue. The government did not respond positively but the parents did, and the music tuition is now paid for from the funds raised by the P.T.A.

In the little school chapel the children's promises for Lent are still displayed on the wall on paper plates. There is quite a range of promises, but if the main one was kept the local sweet shops must have felt the pinch. There is a chapel club composed of children who wish to use the chapel as a place of prayer, and they are allowed to take responsibility for this.

There is a well equipped Special Needs room for children with specific learning difficulties. A member of staff has been appointed as the SENCO (Special Needs Co-Ordinator) and she has two days each week exclusively for this work.

Mrs. Lakin is keen to make use of every available space. The grass at the front of the school is divided into two by the footpath to the school entrance. What was once no more than an ornamental lawn is the well-stocked activity area for the school's younger children. Nearer to the school building, a specially designed curved roof keeps the sun off the children. It works. The day of the tour was particularly hot, and we were cool under the protection of the new roof. On the other side of the footpath, there are plans for the community orchard and the allotments to be installed.

Throughout the tour of the school, the children we met were relaxed and happy and confident. I was as impressed by their natural good manners as I was by their involvement in the work they were doing in all the classrooms we visited.

I left the school confident in the view that the good work of the Sisters of Mercy in establishing and building St. Joseph's School has been continued by a team of dedicated and caring professionals, who will always put the interests of the children first.

Chapter Nine : Tilbury

(Written by Mary Pollard)

A. The Parish of Our Lady Star of the Sea, Tilbury

The arrival of Fr. Paul Dynan as the new Parish Priest of the two parishes of Our Lady Star of the Sea, Tilbury and of Our Lady and St. Joseph, Stanford-le-Hope was the beginning of a new era in the lives of the parishioners of both areas. However things were not that different from the way they were at the dawn of these parishes.

There is evidence of Roman, Saxon and Norman settlements in the area. In the earliest days of Christianity in Essex, St. Chad (although in reality it was probably his eldest brother Cedd) is thought to have blessed a well at the foot of Chadwell Hill hence, some think, the name Chadwell. However the origins of Chadwell probably come from the existence of a 'Cold Well'. It is known that St. Cedd founded a monastery at East Tilbury, then known as Great Tilbury, around 654AD. In the Norman era, there was a church, that of St. Mary, at the top of Chadwell Hill and Tilbury itself was noted in the Domesday Book as a good place for grazing sheep!

The first known construction here was that of Tilbury Fort, built on the banks of the River Thames in the sixteenth century. Those stationed there were served by the Rector of St. Mary's Church, Chadwell, and Tilbury remained part of this parish until 1903. With the Reformation and a very small population, Catholicism must have been at a low ebb in this part of Essex. However, with the Act of Emancipation in 1850, it was possible that things could change and in the year that Tilbury Docks were opened the Tilbury Mission was founded.

Tilbury itself was of little importance 130 years ago. There was Tilbury Fort, the World's End Inn, a railway station near the ferry and railway cottages and settlements in East and West Tilbury, but the area that we today call Tilbury was just flat, badly drained marshland. There was however a railway line built in 1852, linking London with Southend, and this passed through Tilbury. With the building of the docks, the town of Tilbury began to develop. By 1885, a block of tenements, known as 'The Dwelling' was erected by the contracting firm, to accommodate its workers.

In 1885 Cardinal Manning secured a site in Tilbury and in the 1886 directory there is an entry: 'Tilbury. Site for church, schools & presbytery'. The same notice appears in 1887, but by 1888 it states that a church was built in Dock Road, although in effect it was part of a room in the school. The directory for that year lists: 'Tilbury, Our Lady Star of the Sea, served from Grays. Sundays, Holidays, Mass : 10-30am. Confessions before Mass'.

Our parish, which originated as the Tilbury Mission, was served from the parish of St. Thomas of Canterbury, Grays. The parish itself was founded in 1887 when Canon Keens, a priest from Grays who had already begun to build a church and school there was also asked to care for the people of Tilbury. He had been asked to build a Mission there

> in view of the establishment of the vast line of docks which must inevitably lead to the transformation of this portion of the desolate Essex shore into a busy mart of commerce and centre of industry, and the expansion of the Faith here.
> (*The Universe,* 17th September 1887).

The Tablet reported on Saturday 28th May 1887, that

> The first stone of the new school - chapel of Our Lady Star of the Sea, by special permission of the Cardinal Archbishop, was laid on Tuesday by the Very Rev. Canon Keens.

Canon Keens proceeded to give an address on education which showed how much Christian education had done and was still doing, which purely secular education could never succeed in doing.

The recently opened docks in Tilbury had resulted in a huge immigration of Catholic workers and the town and its population steadily increased with housing for over 200 people built between 1881 and 1891. The land was badly drained and liable to subside so that much of the housing was of poor quality. The majority of the people of Tilbury lived in poverty. Immediately it was decided that a school should be built to educate the children living here. It was then standard practice to build a school first so that through education, the heart of the parish would be formed. A site nearly two acres in size had been purchased.

Canon Keens was supported by a benefactress, a wealthy Australian convert named Ada Mary Auguste Stephenson, and a school for over two hundred children was built, dedicated to 'Our Lady Star of the Sea'. The school building consisted of five classrooms, and it was opened by

Cardinal Manning, the Archbishop of Westminster on 8th September 1887. This date marked the beginning of the new parish. A section of one of the classrooms was screened off for use as a chapel. The building work cost £1,300. The parish itself consisted of a few streets with small houses and a school.

The school chapel continued to be served from Grays and the first priest-in-charge of the Tilbury Parish was Rev. Joseph Upton, who had resigned as Rector of Grays in order to become the first resident priest in Tilbury in July 1901. He had no presbytery and his home was the school. Approval for the building of a new presbytery, at a cost not to exceed £750, was given by the Westminster Diocesan Council for Temporal Administration on 5th February 1902, although some records show that the presbytery was built in 1901.

Sisters from the La Sainte Union Convent in Grays taught in the school, but by early 1902 a very serious conflict had occurred between the Superior of the Sisters and the Parish Priest. In a letter dated 15th January 1902, Fr. Upton begins

> Since the Sisters have been here the state of the Mission has completely changed for the better. The reports of H.M. Inspector have steadily improved. The attendance of the children has also steadily improved. We have not a single Catholic child attending any school but our own. The attendance at Holy Mass and the reception of the Sacraments has increased 300%. The Sisters have now the esteem and respect of every class in the docks.

However, he then suggests that because of the current conflict the work of the Sisters in both Grays and Tilbury should be separated. This eventually took place in 1905.

In October 1904 the Rev. Jules Van Meenan, born in Belgium but now a priest of the Diocese of Westminster, was appointed. Fr. Van Meenan, a very young priest at the time, also celebrated Mass at Corringham and Vange, visiting his extensive 'Mission' by bicycle. A new appointment to the Tilbury Mission was made in July 1905 - an assistant priest, Father Joseph Lynch, a newly ordained priest from Oscott, appointed to Tilbury from 1st September 1905. *(Westminster Diocesan Council Minutes July 1905).*

In October 1905 Fr. Van Meenan stated that he would like to relinquish Corringham which he felt could be served from elsewhere. On 19th March 1906, he stated that he could not continue to serve Corringham for a monthly Mass as there were just 50 Catholics living there. However, a certain Mr. Curtis paid the interest on the parish debt on condition that Mass was celebrated there monthly. The Bishop replied that there could be no change before Easter and that Father Van Meenan should get a supply priest to say Mass in Tilbury when he celebrated Mass in Corringham, so that Tilbury was not deprived of its late Mass. This suggests that Father Lynch did not actually arrive in Tilbury.

On 7th May 1906, the Diocese agreed to give 10 shillings per week towards the saying of Mass at Corringham for a period of three months. In August, a suggestion was made that perhaps the Franciscan Conventuals might wish to enter the diocese and take on Corringham. Finally the Corringham saga ended just over a year later when on 15th November 1906 it was stated that Corringham would be served from Grays. *(Westminster Diocesan Council Minutes)*

It was during Canon Van Meenan's residency that, in 1905, the Sisters of Mercy came to the parish, primarily to teach in the school, replacing the Sisters from Grays. They also agreed to pay the parish £50 per annum on a one year agreement. Fifteen baptisms took place in 1907 and one person over fourteen and sixteen people under fourteen joined the Church. There were no weddings in the parish as Tilbury was not registered for weddings, and these still had to take place in Grays. Canon Van Meenan remained in Tilbury until April 1907. The Westminster Diocesan Council Minutes of 25th July 1907 noted the appointment of a Father Herlihy to Tilbury.

On 29th January 1906 the Tilbury Mission received a grant of £20 from the Williams Fund and less than a month later, on 19th February, plans for a new church in Tilbury were examined. Father Van Meenan was responsible for the building of the church, the foundation stone of which was laid on 21st June 1906. The church was built in the Early English style, in yellow brick with red dressings. The roof was constructed out of timber trusses and the windows had a timber frame with leaded lights. The interior included a balcony. The church had a solid wood block floor. Again this project was largely funded by Ada Stephenson, but before the church construction could take place forty ferro-concrete piles were driven sixty feet down through the marsh and joined together to form a raft strong enough to hold the new church building.

High in the gable end of the church, overlooking the docks, was placed a statue of Our Lady, a copy of the statue of Notre Dame de la Guarde near Marseilles, so that she could 'watch over all those who go down to the sea in ships'. The church was opened on Ascension Day, 9th May 1907. Inside the church are memorial tablets to Canon Keens, founder of the Tilbury Mission and to Ada Stephenson, the church's benefactress. A donation towards the cost of furnishings also came from Canon Keens' legacy where the balance of £358-1-9d was to be used to pay for a site at Rainham and the remainder to go to furnish the church at Tilbury. *(Westminster Diocesan Council Minutes 15th November 1906)*

In 1908, when Rev. J. Mulcahy was in residence, there were two Masses on Sunday at 8 a.m. and 10-30 a.m. and a boys' choir, comprising boys from the school who were taught by the Sisters to sing in church. There was a weekday Mass at 8 a.m. Catechetical instruction took place at 3 p.m. on Sundays and was attended each week by about seventy children. The average congregation in May 1908 included fifty four men, fifty eight women and one hundred and eighty children. There were one hundred and sixty five children at the parish school and the Sisters achieved an 'excellent' grade in every area of the religious examination that year. During the first week of Lent, a Franciscan preached a Mission in the church. *(Second Triennial Visitation Returns 1908)*

On 21st May 1909 Father Mulcahy asked for financial assistance for Tilbury. He stated that he had had £100 from various sources but did not receive any support from the convent. On 23rd July 1909 the Reverend Mother was asked what the convent could do for the 'Mission' and she replied that the Sisters of Mercy would 'offer £26 per annum for a weekly Mass and honorarium to confessor.' *(Westminster Diocesan Council Minutes 23rd July 1907)*

Around September 1911, an Irish regiment arrived in the area, remaining for three years. The soldiers requested a Sunday Mass and Father Deady asked permission to reduce the Masses at Tilbury by one. The Westminster Diocesan Council rejected this proposal and stated that some other arrangement would have to be found. The minutes of 4th November 1911 stated that the War Office should be asked to place a commissioned chaplain at Tilbury pro tem.

A form completed by the 'Rector', Rev. Jeremiah Deady on 9th March 1912 showed that the Parish Bazaar in 1911 had raised £259-15-3d and Sunday Concerts a further £1-10-1d. Repairs on the presbytery, in an attempt to keep the rain out, had cost over five pounds. A visitation was made to the parish by Bishop Butt in December. The total population was about 6000 and of these the Catholic population was estimated at

520, of whom 108 men, 116 women and 199 children came to Mass. At the end of 1913, the Sisters of Mercy increased Father Deady's salary to £36 per annum. In 1914, the parish had a debt of £1,220, with interest payable at 3&1/8th%.

At this time the school was in a bad state of repair – it was desperately in need of being painted on the outside and the roof and drains needed attention. There was also a clubroom made of timber, which was decaying. *(Fourth Triennial Visitation Returns 1914)* In February of 1914 the question of the parish boundaries was raised but no definite decision made concerning the northern boundary. The River Thames formed the southern boundary, East Tilbury the eastern extent and Grays the western boundary.

In 1917 the Diocese of Brentwood had been formed and so the parish was no longer under the jurisdiction of the Archdiocese of Westminster. The Visitation Return to the new diocese for 1917/18 shows that the Catholic population included 330 adults, of whom about 100 attended Mass, and 170 children, of whom 90 attended Mass. About 20 adults and 40 children received Holy Communion. Confirmation took place on 7th December 1917. The church itself was open daily from the 8 a.m. Mass to nightfall. The parish first became a 'parish' on 2nd August 1918 and Father Hannan, the first Parish Priest, later wrote

> Due to the slackness of dock labour, consequent on the war, and the absence of these Catholic Sailors, who in pre-war days were a great source of income, the Mission is at present suffering a very considerable financial loss. *(Visitation return to Diocese of Brentwood 1917/18)*

Following the resignation of Father Michael Hannon from his post in Tilbury due to ill health – he subsequently lived for some time at the Orsett Union Workhouse – Father Patrick O'Donnell was asked to report for weekend duty. He remained there for the next thirty-one years, having been appointed as Parish Priest on 10th January 1922.

In the following year *(24th May 1923)* Father O'Donnell wrote to the Bishop to suggest changes to the northern parish boundary. The current boundary, although straight and well defined, ran straight through what was to become the heart of the village which now was officially known as 'Tilbury North Ward', a change from Chadwell, being the predominant residential area at the time of the building of the docks. If the boundary remained the same, then the 'Tilbury North Ward' would be in the Grays or Stanford-le-Hope Parish. Fr. O'Donnell wanted Chadwell St. Mary to remain in his parish. The parish debt stood at £900 in 1924.

By 1925 the Visitation Returns state the Civil & Ecclesiastical names of the parish as Chadwell St. Mary, Tilbury. The population of the area was now 10,000 and the Catholic population included 326 adults, of whom 200 attended Mass, and 286 children, of whom 90 attended Mass. At this time about 45 adults and 40 children received Holy Communion. It was also stated that the ships in the docks were visited every Saturday and Tilbury Hospital visited occasionally. *(Visitation return to Diocese of Brentwood 1925)* Father O'Donnell frequently visited the homes of his parishioners.

Guilds which met in the parish in 1926 included the Children of the Angels, the Children of Mary, the Apostleship of Prayer and the St. Vincent de Paul Society. The debt on the parish was now down to £750. *(Visitation Return 1926)*

There were quite a number of letters between Father O'Donnell and the Diocese. One dated 19th October 1927 stated that the Bishop would be coming to the parish on 4th December 1927 and that the Mass would include a special sermon on the life of St. Francis Xavier. This would suggest that the Goanese Seamen were already featuring largely in the life of the parish (see three paragraphs below). Father O'Donnell said that the church had recently been internally redecorated by the parishioners and electric light installed. He added

> Our beautiful altar has been cleaned and renovated and four statues have been renewed. The chess board design in paint has been removed from the sanctuary floor thus revealing a fine wooden block floor. The total cost will be about £300 and though we started with only a few pounds about 2/3 is already paid from ordinary income – less £20 contributed by the Children of Mary.

He also implies in this letter that there was criticism about this work in some quarters as the school was very much in need, and concerns had been raised about spending scarce resources on the church. Father O'Donnell explained that

> the money contributed week after week would hardly have been given for the school extension as it has largely come from McAlpine workers and from seamen'. *(Letter from Fr. O'Donnell to Diocese 19th October 1927)*

The reorganisation of St. Mary's School was also predominantly due to the efforts of Father O'Donnell. The present junior school was built in 1929, and his continued interest and work in this sphere resulted in St. Mary's becoming the first Catholic voluntary secondary school in Essex. Although predominantly a poor area, the parish continued to grow. This was partly due to the generosity of the Goanese seamen, many of whom felt the parish was their parish too, contributing both pastorally and financially to its development.

Father O'Donnell had a special care for seafarers and their families and was instrumental in establishing the work of the Apostleship of the Sea in the Diocese of Brentwood. He did much to secure the provision of Mass aboard liners and other ships berthed at the docks and, via an arrangement with the shipping companies, ships were supplied with altar requisites. He spent many Saturday afternoons in the docks talking with the seafarers, and amongst the Goanese seamen he became quite a legend. An older story relates that, in earlier days, Canon Van Meenan when told that the Goanese seamen would like a statue of St. Francis Xavier said he would get them one. When the Goanese saw the statue they said, 'That's not St. Francis!' and on their return they brought with them a statue of St. Francis - in black.

A report made on 10th February 1930 stated that £16-16-0d had been spent the previous year on a bus to bring parishioners from Chadwell to Mass in Tilbury.

Despite his initial thoughts that he did not want a curate, Father O'Donnell was very pleased when, in 1932, Rev. Francis Brennan, from the Diocese of Kilmore, Ireland, became the first assistant priest to arrive and help with the work in the parish. Our Parish Priest hoped that Father Brennan would put new life into the parish. 20,000 people lived here in 1933 with a Catholic population of about 1,400. The population had more than doubled but the parish income had hardly increased. Father O'Donnell wrote

> The newcomers are of the very poor, with a few outstanding exceptions, and of necessity they are more of a burden than a help.

A letter from Fr. O'Donnell in March 1933 recorded that the collections averaged £3-9-8d but expenses were greater than income. In 1933, the Sunday Mass attendance was approximately 600 - 700 people each week and by 1935 Mass was celebrated at 8 a.m. and 10-30 a.m. in Tilbury with additional Masses at Chadwell at 8-30 a.m., and at East Tilbury at

9-45 a.m. There was also a weekly class for children who attended non-Catholic schools. The debt on the church stood at £750 and on the school at £2,800.

Every three years the exterior woodwork and iron work of the church was repainted. In 1934 much of the paint for the work was donated to the parish and the actual painting was carried out, in their spare time, by 'certain men and boys of the parish'.

The Golden Jubilee celebration for the parish was held on Monday, 18th October 1937. Prior to the celebration, Father O'Donnell had asked the P & O Company if he could hire a ship for the reception after the Mass. The office staff laughed at this request but, because the P & O Company greatly appreciated the efforts made by Father O'Donnell for the welfare of the Goanese seamen, they were delighted to entertain the Bishop and other guests to luncheon on the SS Strathard, served by the Goanese. This lunch followed the Golden Jubilee Mass, which was celebrated by Bishop Doubleday with the singing led by the schoolchildren and a priests' choir. In the evening a social was held in the junior school for 'parents and old folk' with the young people acting as hosts. Two days later the young people had their own celebration holding a dance and on the following Saturday the children 'had a treat'. The next evening the celebrations came to an end with an outdoor torchlight procession. Part of the purpose of the celebration was to reduce the debt on the parish which originated as a loan of £2,600. At a parish meeting held the previous year, it was agreed that every adult should try to contribute £1 over the next twenty months. By the time of the Golden Jubilee the debt was down to only £400.

Another Tilbury story related by the Bishop during the Golden Jubilee celebrations tells that many years ago an elderly lady arrived at the port a day early and went to the priest to ask where she could spend the night. She was so disgusted by the poverty of the priest's quarters that she said, 'I will give £1,000 to build a presbytery'.

The parishioners suffered a great deal during the Second World War and many of the children from the parish were evacuated to safer areas. A transit camp was also established in Tilbury and there were many Polish and Canadian soldiers passing through. During war time bombing, the church suffered only superficial damage. However, in September or October 1940 Fr. O'Donnell wrote that the church was now practically isolated from the people by a ring of 'time bombs'. He added that most of the parishioners would have to take a very roundabout route and was wondering what would happen the following Sunday. On 2nd November 1940 there was just one Mass at 8 a.m., followed by Confessions and then Mass at 9 a.m. at Chadwell. Father O'Donnell also noted that all the Goanese seamen had left for the duration of the war.

Another connection between Tilbury and Stanford came to the fore around 1948 but was not settled until early 1950. The parish boundary was once again causing concern, but this time it was the East Tilbury boundary. Here, the Bata Shoe Company was extending its housing and the present parish boundary ran straight through the estate. The factory was in Tilbury Parish and the new residential area predominantly in Stanford Parish, where Father O'Donnell celebrated Mass in the Bata Estate Hotel each Sunday. Both he and Fr. Snell, Stanford's Parish Priest, felt that the whole of East Tilbury should be in one parish and as Father Snell could not provide a Mass there it was agreed that East Tilbury should be entirely in the parish of Our Lady Star of the Sea, Tilbury. This was agreed by the Bishop.

Also in 1950 approval was given for an early morning Mass to be celebrated at Tilbury Hospital on one weekday each week. Father O'Donnell informed the Bishop on 23rd April 1952 that the Council had promised an acre of land in Chadwell for the building of a church but that they had not yet fixed the price or the exact location. He was also seeking land in East Tilbury, but here, the Bata Shoe Company would not sell any land and he was seeking a site on the perimeter of their estate.

On 13th July 1952 the Bishop briefly visited the parish on his return from a Seafarers' Meeting and unveiled a memorial statue of the Sacred Heart in the church grounds.

Tilbury suffered once again with the disastrous flooding on Sunday, 1st February 1953 but there was no damage to the church, school, convent or presbytery. However, over 7000 people were evacuated from their homes and 2500 out of a total of 2,750 homes were flooded. A £200 donation was given by the Holy Father via his Apostolic Delegate for flood relief to help both Catholic and Non-Catholic victims of the flood. A month later a £500 donation was received from the Canadian Hierarchy and the Bishop of Luxemburg.

The Consecration of the church of Our Lady Star of the Sea took place on 8th June 1954, by Right Rev. George Andrew Beck, Bishop of Brentwood. By this time the care of the parish had passed to the hands of Father John Byrne and a special booklet was produced for this momentous event. Although the Consecration took place in June, the Consecration Feast Day was to be celebrated annually on 14th May.

At the beginning of 1957 Father Byrne asked the Bishop for permission to celebrate an evening Mass every Sunday, because many of the men in the parish were unable to attend Mass on Sunday as they had to report for work in the docks in the morning. He also added that this too would benefit the Goanese seamen as many of them also had to work on Sunday mornings. At the time of writing the letter there were three P & O ships in the port, with a total of 500 Goanese on board. Permission was given by the Bishop on 11th January 1957, and on 3rd February 156 people attended the evening Mass, with 25 receiving Holy Communion. These were mainly dock workers, seamen, nurses and people from Chadwell, of whom about 40% formerly attended morning Mass.

The Brentwood Visitation Form dated 29th June 1958 states that every family in Tilbury was visited each month and families in Chadwell and East Tilbury visited every four months by the two priests. The Sisters taught in the schools, cleaned the sanctuary weekly and prepared the altar for Mass. Two confraternities existed in the parish, those of the Blessed Sacrament and Christian Doctrine. The Form relates that 'When the boys leave school they join the Squires. There is a youth club for 11+ boys. ... To encourage conversion the laity are encouraged to bring Non-Catholics for instructions'. The church was open from 6-45 a.m. to 9 p.m. Nor was the parish in debt; in fact there was a credit of £1,327-1-7d.

In 1961, it was reported that 350 families were visited each month and there were now lots of new families moving to Chadwell. The Sisters were noted as visiting the sick when asked to do so. Confraternities were now the Pages and Knights of the Blessed Sacrament, looked after by the Sisters. After leaving school both boys and girls were asked to join the Young Christian Workers.

Three years later there were still many new families moving to Chadwell and 58 children from there travelled by coach to St. Mary's School. The Catholic children from East Tilbury travelled to St. Joseph's, Stanford. Two youngsters from the parish were mentioned as interested in becoming priests. A Mission was held in the parish in May 1966.

By 1968 the Sisters' role in the parish now included instructing converts and visiting the sick at home and in hospital. The church hall in

Chadwell had opened in March 1968 and Mass was now celebrated there and occasionally on a weekday in Tilbury Hospital.

A Mission was given in the parish by the Redemptorist Fathers between 21st September and 5th October 1969.

In 1971 the parish had a debt of £4,247-13-10d on St. Joseph's Church Hall, Chadwell St. Mary. By 1973 a Parish Council existed and a youth club which met once each week.

The parish boundaries were once again altered in 1975 when the parish of St. Joseph, Chadwell St. Mary was formally created. East Tilbury was then finally transferred to the parish of Our Lady and St. Joseph, Stanford-le-Hope and Tilbury no longer had a need for an assistant priest. In 1983 these boundaries were once again redrawn when St. Joseph's Chadwell ceased to be a parish in its own right.

Having had just two Parish Priests in sixty two years, things changed with the death of Canon Byrne in 1983. He was replaced for the next two years by Father Donal Donegan, but ill health meant that he was replaced in 1985 by Father John Duckett. Father John was instrumental in the reordering of the church but there was a great deal of opposition from many members of the community who wanted the style of the sanctuary to remain the same. The Second Vatican Council closed in 1965, but the church still had a temporary altar placed in front of the old ornate plaster altarpiece.

Father Duckett was replaced by Father Bob Hamill who completed the reordering of the church. Father Bob also encouraged and supported social events in the parish and established a social committee that did a great deal, especially for the sick and housebound. Their weekly Lenten lunches, the monthly lunches for the Senior Citizens Club and the regular outings to Aylesford and beyond were looked forward to by many of the older members of the parish.

As time passed, the church once again needed redecoration and in 1990 the church was reordered and the new altar was consecrated by Bishop Thomas McMahon on 7th September 1990.

Father Bob Hamill was replaced by Father Paul Bhanji in 1994 and in the following year he was replaced by Father David Clemens. Five priests had now served the parish in just twelve years and when Father David left in 2000 the parish would be served by four more Parish Priests in the coming ten years – Father Peter Connor, Father James McShane, Father John Meehan and now Father Paul Dynan.

On Mothers' Day, 18th March 2007, a beautiful framed icon of Our Lady Star of the Sea, which had been embroidered by Gwen Perkins, was unveiled.

B. The priests who have served the Parish of Tilbury

Archdiocese of Westminster:

1901 -1904	Rev. Joseph Upton
1904-1907	Rev. Jules Van Meenan
1907-1911	Rev. John Mulcahy
1911-1917	Rev. Jerome Deady

Diocese of Brentwood:

1917	Rev. Jerome Deady
1917-1921	Rev. Michael Hannan (1st Parish Priest 1918)
1921-1952	Rev. Patrick O'Donnell
1952-1982	Rev. John Byrne
1983-1985	Rev. Donal Donegan
1985-1987	Rev. John Duckett
1987-1994	Rev. Robert Hamill
1994-1995	Rev. Paul Bhanji
1995-2000	Rev. David Clemens
2000-2004	Rev. Peter Connor
2004-2009	Rev. James McShane
2009-2010	Rev. John Meehan
2010- present	Rev. Paul Dynan

Assistant Priests:

1932-1937	Rev. Francis Brennan (Kilmore)
1937-1940	Rev. Hugh McGrail (Kilmore)
1944-1950	Rev. Denis Petry
1950	Rev. Kevin Vincent Connolly (Armagh)
1950-1951	Rev. Martin Kirvan (Killaloe)
1951-1953	Rev. Philip Finnegan S.S.C.
1953-1954	Rev. William Caffrey (Melbourne)
1954-1957	Rev. William Luby
1957	Rev. John Ryder (Derry)
1957-1961	Rev. Christopher Nigel Collingwood
1961-1962	Rev. Gordon Godfrey
1962-1969	Rev. Donald Mills

1969-1970	Rev. Gerard Butcher
1970-1972	Rev. Joseph Tuohey S.D.S. (Incardinated 1971)
1972-1973	Rev. Albert Fitzgerald

Chadwell St. Mary:

1975-1983	Rev. Donald Mills

C. St. Mary's Primary School and St. Mary's Secondary Modern School, Tilbury

The first Catholic school in Tilbury, which was opened on 17th October 1887, began as an 'all-age' school with just sixteen pupils. Poverty was a major problem from the start. On opening day the school equipment consisted of four dozen slates, one box of pencils, six dozen exercise books, three and a half dozen copy books, three and a half dozen Longmans new readers, a box of chalk, a gross of holders and a box of nibs. There was one teacher, the Headmistress Miss Nora Sullivan, who was a member of the Congregation of La Sainte Union des Sacres Couers de Jesu et Marie (a French Order from Douai) who was based in Grays. She would walk to the school each day. The sixteen children, all taught by her, were 'classified' on the first day as follows - three standard V, two Standard111, four Standard 1 and seven Infants. Part of the school was used as a chapel.

By 1888, forty-eight children attended the school. The School log book indicates the sad story of the school conditions and poverty of the area. On 16th January 1888, Father Doyle visited and heard the children of Standard 1 read – he found them very backward! On 16th March 1888, Standard 111 were examined in Arithmetic – one child failed and the rest had three or four sums right. On 23rd March 1888 the Board Officer (a man to be feared!) visited the school for the first time. The attendance that day was low 'on account of the dirty state of the roads owing to the bad weather'. By July, many of the children were absent because they had gone 'pea-picking' but there were sixty children on the roll at this time.

In May 1889, nearly one hundred children were 'at school', officially on the registers, but many were often absent. Absences were caused by illnesses such as 'the blight', Typhoid Fever, Scarlet Fever and Diphtheria, pea picking or hop picking depending on whether it was July or September, poor weather conditions and the sheer poverty of the people resulting in a lack of shoes and clothing.

In August 1889, cement paths were laid down in the playground 'to prevent the children getting wet feet'. In January 1890, the School Attendance Officer said that he could not compel parents to send their children to school on account of the mud – there were no roads or footpaths built across the marshes. On 1st May 1891 the School log book records – 'The first drawing lesson given today'. However, a far more notable event took place in September of that year as parents no longer had to pay to send their children to the Catholic school. It was now free and there were three members on the teaching staff.

As time passed conditions in the town did not appear to improve. A note on the state of the school buildings on 28th September 1893 included the comment , 'the playgrounds and offices are defiled by cattle' and on 4th June 1894, 'twenty nine windows found broken this morning in the school'. In September 1894 four children were admitted to Standard 1 - the big school - not knowing their letters and an extract from H.M. Inspectors' Report of 12th June 1895, a time of payment by results for teachers, stated

> Nor are the children so zealous in their work as they should be and hence the full Grant under Art. 101(b) of the Code has been barely earned.

In April 1896 the school was closed for a month because of Scarlet Fever in the district. All however was not gloom. On 10th July 1894 a half holiday was given on account of the visit of the Duke of York to Grays and another holiday on 15th January 1896 on account of a treat in the parish.

The first major change to the school came in 1897 when, after an examination on 12th April, the Infant Class was changed into an Infant Department, which was placed under the charge of Miss Margaret Sullivan. The Infant Department consisted of two rooms on the south side of the building. Tilbury continued to expand so much that by June 1898 the Managers were told that the accommodation was insufficient for the average attendance. The school's official name was now Tilbury Dock Road R.C. School.

The population in the area was always fluctuating and children came and went. Times were hard, work often difficult to find and many families needed much help. After a tea party on 11th January 1901, a New Year's gift was given to each child 'consisting mainly of clothing'. There were now 183 children on roll. In March 1901 the school was visited by Cardinal Vaughan.

On 1st October 1903, in accordance with the new Act of Parliament, the school was reorganised by the County Council. There were now 260 pupils on roll with the Infants school providing accommodation for seventy seven-children. The remainder of the school was known as the Thurrock Tilbury RC (Mixed School).

In 1905 Canon Van Meenan, the Parish Priest, became Manager of the schools and on 9th January 1905, at his request the Sisters of Mercy took charge of the schools, replacing La Sainte Union Nuns from Grays. Miss Bridget O'Connor was the new Headmistress. In August 1905 there were 285 children on roll and on 24th August the children had their photographs taken 'amid some excitement'. There was then a staff of eight. On 9th May 1907 the school ceased to be used as a chapel as the new church had been opened. It was a holiday for the children.

In the coming years many people left Tilbury as they were unable to find work. In 1908 it was recorded that the 'poverty of the children is so great that many have to remain away while their mothers are out working'.

By 1911, there were 150 Catholic and 85 non-Catholic children on the school roll. 90% of the children attended Mass and 60% Catechism Classes. *(4th Triennial Visitation Report 1914)*

The outbreak of war in 1914 had little immediate effect on the school. However, Diphtheria and Whooping Cough did. In 1915 there was a new influx of children and a new teacher from Belgium, possibly escaping from the effects of the First World War. In July 1915 there was a Zeppelin raid and subsequent raids caused the children to be sent home. The school was closed for a variety of reasons, due to a lack of coal to keep the fire burning, for the children to see a pantomime and because of an epidemic of influenza.

Tilbury grew rapidly between 1919 and 1924 and the number of children grew too, with the accommodation problem becoming acute. In 1922 there were 61 Catholic boys, 55 Catholic girls and 44 Catholic infants attending the schools. 30 boys, 33 girls and 37 non-Catholic children also attended. *(1925 Visitation return to Diocese of Brentwood)*

In 1926 Sister Aloysius Leonard became the Junior Head Teacher and every child left the school able to read and write. Sister Aloysius also taught the girls needlework, knitting and craftwork. Concerts were put on for parents and the Sisters took an interest in the home life of the pupils. By 1927 there were 320 children on roll, and the shortage of accommodation was acute. This was eased in 1927 when a temporary wooden building was placed at the disposal of the Managers of the school by the McAlpine Company, who had originally provided the building for the use of their workers enlarging the Docks. Before this, the Infant Department had accommodation for only 62 children but there were 120 on roll!

Father O'Donnell, the then Parish Priest, wanted to build a new Junior school and despite the financial implications, building of the new school began. In December 1928 the school was closed for two days as the school rooms were being prepared for a bazaar, the proceeds of which were to be used to pay off part of the debt on the new school. This was opened on the Feast of Our Lady of Lourdes, 1929, when 141 children were transferred from the old Infant school. The official opening took place on 19th March 1929. Lord Eustace Percy, President of the Board of Education, officiated and the Bishop of Brentwood was also present. There were four classrooms in the junior school. Sister Borgia Colahan became Headmistress of the Senior school and Sister Angela Colahan was appointed as the Infant Head Teacher.

Tilbury remained a very poor area but despite this the number of children in the school continued to increase. However, on one day in November 1929 only 96 out of 187 were present – there was an outbreak of Diphtheria in the area. In January 1930 the Dock Police began to provide about 30 of the poorer children with hot milk. In 1931 the Dock Police provided some of the children with boots and in 1932 a Relief Committee was formed to try and relieve some of this poverty. Free school meals were provided for up to 60 children. According to the school's log book, 'the teachers wait on the children and the caretaker assisted by the senior children, has kindly undertaken to do the washing up'.

Between 1929 and 1934 most of the £383-1-8d spent on repairs to the school was on playground surfacing and fencing. Men from the parish volunteered to carry out the work, saving about £150.

By May 1932 there were nearly 200 children on roll between the ages of eight and fourteen. There were four classes and a four year age range in most, with plans for 100 extra places approved by the L.E.A. Father O'Donnell asked the Diocese for permission to borrow about £1,000 and stated that the old McAlpine Hut had been removed so that the new building could be built there.

Notable events for the children during the thirties included a tree planting ceremony, when six children from the top class planted a tree each; a netball court being marked out for the first time; the football team winning the local Cup Final match; a visit to Grays Regal Cinema to see the film 'Twenty Five Years a King' and a visit to the Docks to see the destroyers, 'The Crusader' and 'The Cygnet' and the Submarines, L21 and L53.

The result of a medical examination in 1935 was that the doctor

> expressed appreciation of the general cleanliness and good manners of the children but found many of them were under nourished and quite a large number ill clad and ill shod.

In September 1936, the Infants school was known as Tilbury R.C. Infants School and from February 1937 the Junior school was known as The Thurrock, Tilbury R.C. (Mixed) School. On 18th October 1937, the staff and children of both schools took part in the celebration of the Golden Jubilee of the parish and schools. The title 'St. Mary's R.C. Primary School' was conferred on the school to mark the occasion.

The imminent outbreak of war in the summer of 1939 caused drastic changes to the normal school routine. In July, registration forms for an evacuation scheme were distributed and on 2nd September 1939 the Sisters and many of the children were evacuated to Holt in Norfolk. Much later, one of the evacuees, twelve year old Kathleen Hurdle, recalled

> To us it was a great adventure. My brother and I were being evacuated. Each of us carrying a brown paper parcel, tied up with string, containing a change of clothing, we were taken to school at 9 a.m. There we boarded a coach which took us to Tilbury Riverside. Here we were shepherded along a gangway and found ourselves, to our delight, on a boat – a paddle steamer – which took us to Yarmouth. We were then taken to a school where we had to sleep on sacks filled with straw. We had a great time having pillow fights with them! The next day, Sunday, war was declared and that night the sirens sounded. On Monday morning we re-boarded coaches and travelled to a small village called Holt. We were taken to another school where all the local people were assembled. Here, we were 'sorted out' and allocated to the villagers in ones and twos. I was separated from my brother.

St. Mary's School was closed on 4th September 1939, due to the danger of possible air raid. In October, the teachers who had returned from Holt began instruction in the parish church for those children who had not been evacuated and who wished to attend for one and a half hours, three times a week. In December, correspondence classes commenced for the older children and tutorial classes, for children under seven, were opened in private houses.

In January 1940, some of the Sisters returned to Tilbury and on 4th March the school re-opened, operating on a half time shift system for all children over seven. On 3rd June the children in Holt were transferred to Leek, Staffordshire and on 18th June forty three children left for Wiltshire, accompanied by Father O'Donnell, Sister Francis Boyden, Sister Margaret Mary Kelly and Miss Knott. On 20th June the school re-opened again with only five children present. In the course of the day teachers visited the children's homes to ask parents to send the children still in Tilbury to school but found many of them in the pea fields – life was going on as normal! On 1st July the school re-opened for full time instruction.

As time passed some children began to return to their own families and in 1941 there were seventy children on roll. From 5th January 1942 the two schools resumed their normal independent existence. The school staff began fire watching duties two nights each week and on Saturdays and Sundays. On 1st September 1942 Sister Bernadette Roche became Headmistress. Throughout the rest of the war there were many bombing raids on Tilbury and a great part of the town was badly damaged. Fortunately, the school itself suffered little damage. The number on roll increased back to 250, with two extra classrooms once again needed.

Not long after the end of the war a new chapter in the life of the school in Tilbury began. A Secondary Modern school, St. Mary's, was opened on 9th September 1947, with a roll of 168. The children came from the Catholic primary schools in Tilbury, Stanford and Grays. There was a staff of five, the Headmaster and four assistants. The school itself included the old school building, together with three prefabricated huts, the H.O.R.S.A. huts. In these huts were a Woodwork room, a General Science room, a Domestic Science room and two classrooms.

As from 21st January 1949, St. Mary's Primary School was granted Aided Status. In 1952 there were over 200 pupils on roll and it was hoped that a new school would be built in Chadwell St. Mary but the economic conditions of the time put an end to that idea. The school had to be closed yet again in February 1953, this time for a very different reason. The River Thames had breached its banks and there was extensive flooding. This led to a visit to Tilbury by Her Majesty the Queen on 13th February. She passed by the school and everyone was outside waiting to see her.

In a report made in 1954 the state of the schools was described as fairly good but the offices and the children's toilets were said to be in a rather poor condition.

As from 1st January 1957, the official name of the school became 'Tilbury, St. Mary's R.C. Primary'. By 1961, the primary school which had been built in 1929 consisted of four classrooms and one extra class taught in a nearby Council school - Lansdowne. There were 190 children on roll. The secondary modern school consisted of ten classrooms with 280 children on roll. More space was desperately needed and the first phase of the school extension was begun in April 1963. The hall and a new classroom, Junior Four, were completed first but by now there were 231 children on roll. In June 1966 a second classroom, which later became the nursery, was ready to use.

By now, the secondary school was giving great cause for concern. The actual classrooms as well as toilets were reported to be in a very poor condition. It was expected that the boys would eventually transfer to a school that had closed earlier, Ockendon Courts in Aveley, and that the girls would go to Grays Convent School.

In the early 1970s secondary education in Thurrock was reorganised and St. Mary's Secondary Modern School closed in July 1971. The children from there transferred to either Grays Convent School, run by the Sisters of La Sainte Union who had taught at St. Mary's at the turn of the twentieth century, or to St. Cedd's Secondary School in South Ockendon.

The primary school continued to flourish and on 3rd May 1973 the demolition of the old school began making way for a new Infant extension that opened the following year. 1974 also saw the end of another era when Sister Bernadette retired as Head Teacher. She was replaced by Sister Agnes Williams. In September 1975, the school kitchen and new offices were opened. In March 1979, a Parents' Association was formed and in the same month thieves stole lead from the roof of the Infant school, the kitchen and the hall – an on-going problem to this day!

Sister Agnes remained in post until 1981, when Sister Patricia Staunton took over the leadership of the school. During her headship, on 3rd September 1985, the Nursery school was opened. There was provision for 20 children each morning and 20 children each afternoon. In October 1986 a decision was made to form a Parent Teacher Association and at the end of October 1986 an extensive programme of improvement commenced in the Junior school. The asbestos ceilings were removed and replaced by suspended ceilings. The hall and classrooms were re-wired and everywhere redecorated. In the following year, on 13th October 1987, the Centenary Mass for both the school and church was celebrated by Bishop Thomas McMahon.

In 1993 Sister Patricia retired from the school and this brought to an end the daily role of the Sisters of Mercy in the life of St. Mary's, which had spanned over ninety years. Mrs. Anne Ennefer became the first lay Head Teacher in January 1994, and ten years later Mr. Jonathan Shields took over this role.

D The Sisters of Mercy

The Congregation of the Sisters of Mercy was founded in Dublin in 1831 by Catherine McAuley. They had a special mission to help women and children and it was through their work in education that they came to Tilbury.

At the turn of the twentieth century, the Parish Priest, Canon Van Meenan, wanted the help of a resident Community of Religious Sisters who would teach in the school and undertake the visitation of the Catholic families in the area. He arranged with the Superior of the Sisters of Mercy in Macklin Street (now known as Tavistock Square), London to send some Sisters to open a new convent in Tilbury. On 8th January 1905 three Sisters, Teresa O'Connor, Camillus Ryan and Ethelburga Dwyer moved to a house in Dock Road, Tilbury, now named Trevor Villas, They started work teaching the very next day, with Sister Teresa O'Connor appointed Headmistress. Later on, the adjoining house was also acquired and, in 1909, the present convent in Malta Road was built. There were now seven Sisters in the Community, but sadly one young Sister, Sister Clare Joseph Phelan, had died in 1908.

The Tilbury Community continued to flourish as a 'branch house' dependent on the 'mother house' in London. However, once the Diocese of Brentwood was formed in 1917, the Sisters in Tilbury were unsure which Bishop held authority over their convent. It was finally agreed that the convent in Tilbury would become an Independent House as from 8th January 1923. Sister Aloysius Leonard was the Superior and seven other Sisters formed the Community. All the Sisters were teaching in the school and they continued to carry out pastoral work. Tilbury remained a very poor area and there was much need across the parish. Sometimes the Sisters would visit families carrying bread and other foods hidden in the large sleeves of their habit! As well as teaching and visiting families in need, the Sisters always supported the annual Parish Bazaar. Altogether fourteen Sisters joined the Sisters of Mercy through entering the Order in Tilbury.

At the outbreak of war in 1939 the Sisters were evacuated with the schoolchildren to Holt in Norfolk, and the Convent of Mercy had to be closed for a few months. However, in 1940, some of the Sisters returned to re-open part of the school for those children who still remained in Tilbury. Later that year a second evacuation took place, and Sisters Frances Boyden and Margaret Mary Kelly accompanied the children to Wiltshire. Throughout the war the convent suffered little more damage than cracked walls and ceilings.

The seeds of a new role in the life of the Sisters of Mercy based in Tilbury were sown in May 1952, when Bishop Andrew Beck visited the Sisters to ask if they would consider opening a branch house in Thorpe Bay. This happened in July 1952 when 34 Burges Road, Thorpe Bay was opened with Sister Therese Connolly appointed as the first Superior. A year later, in May 1953, the house next door was bought. It became a rest home and a house for holidays for both Sisters and other ladies. In October 1953, Sister Angela Colahan suffered a stroke and she subsequently retired in March 1955 and went to live in Thorpe Bay. The branch house eventually closed in December 1963.

In 1954, there were plans for a second branch convent to be opened at Chadwell St. Mary to serve the needs of the church and parish which was to develop there when the Council's new housing estate was built, but this never came to fruition.

On 7th April 1958 a statue of Our Lady and the Divine Child was erected over the front door of the convent.

In the early 1960s a reorganisation of the Sisters of Mercy was being considered and in June 1961 the Sisters found themselves being urged by the Bishop of Brentwood to join the Westminster Amalgamation, which they did in November 1961. It didn't appear to be a popular move amongst the Sisters in Tilbury and some Sisters asked to be moved elsewhere, with changes for the Sisters continuing throughout the decade. In 1965 the Bishop of Brentwood suggested that Tilbury become a branch house again, but this time as a branch house of Wanstead. Soon after this happened, on 9th February 1966, some Sisters were sent from Wanstead to join the small Community in Tilbury.

The next change for the Sisters came in May 1969, when the Federation of the Sisters of Mercy was formed, with the Sisters in Tilbury joining this Federation. Then, from 1973, there was the recognition that it might be good if the Sisters of Mercy across the country joined together. This finally happened in April 1983, when many Communities, including those in Tilbury, voted to become part of the Institute of Our Lady of Mercy.

Many changes in personnel began to occur as Sisters moved across the country. Sister Carmel, who had taught at St. Mary's School for many years and established a much needed Youth Club in the parish, moved to South Yorkshire and Sister Agnes, the former Head Teacher of St. Mary's, went to Frinton. Sister Emmanuel headed for King's Lynn, Sister Annunciata to Charlton and Sister Patricia, on her retirement as Head Teacher, went to Wanstead. Over time, in their places came Sisters Dominic Gollogley, Imelda Keena, Anne Waugh, Mary Keogh, Concepta Guidera, Rita Lynch, Teresa Croston, Stanislaus Culligan, Veronica Walker, Paula Cleary, Christine Mather and Deborah Stokes.

With the closure of the Convent of Mercy in Stanford-le-Hope in 2005, Sister Monica Cremin moved to Tilbury, although she continues to work in the parish of Our Lady and St. Joseph, Stanford-le-Hope, yet another connection between the two parishes. The Sisters no longer teach in the school, although they continue to work there in a voluntary capacity. They continue to visit parishioners in their own homes, in hospital or in sheltered accommodation, work with refugees and seamen and support the parish in any way they can.

In the early 21st century a new role began with the development in Tilbury of the Mercy Associates, a group of lay parishioners, sensitive to the charism of the Sisters of Mercy, who now support their work across the parish. At the time of writing, 2012, they are led by Sister Teresa Croston.

The work of the Sisters of Mercy in the parish of Our Lady Star of the Sea continues as does the legacy of all they have done for the people of Tilbury.

Acknowledgement to:
Sister Barbara Jeffery, Mercy Institute Archivist, for her writing in the Centenary Booklet – 100 Years in Tilbury.
Bishop Andrew Beck, Rev. John Byrne, Rev. Jules Van Meenan and Sister Bernadette Roche for their writings in the Souvenir Book of the Consecration of the Church of Our Lady Star of the Sea, Tilbury.

E The Parish of St. Joseph, Chadwell St. Mary

The history of the Catholic Church in Chadwell dates back nearly 900 years, but the existence of a Catholic parish in its own right has a much shorter time span.

The needs of the people of Chadwell St. Mary were first mentioned in 1923, when Father O'Donnell suggested changes to Tilbury Parish's northern boundary. He wrote

> Chadwell is the most important place in this neighbourhood and is rapidly growing, as a sort of residential district.

He stated that there were fifty houses there already and rafts had been laid for 200 more. He went on to write, 'A year ago there were no Catholics there. Today there are at least twenty'. His final comments in this letter were

> Everything points to the fact that Chadwell St. Mary will need development from the Catholic point of view in the not-distant future but if the three parishes of Grays, Tilbury and Stanford-le-Hope meet right in the heart of it, there is a chance that it will become a sort of no-man's land and be neglected. *(Letter to the Bishop dated 24th May 1923)*

Later in 1932 Father O'Donnell wrote that his foremost problem is 'what to do with Chadwell St. Mary' where there were about seventy Catholics. About thirty of these attended the early Mass in Tilbury travelling by private motor coach, and a few others walked or cycled to the later Mass. He went on to write that he

> would like to bring back the Mass to Chadwell, which was the centre of the faith in the old days, for all this area.

He debated whether a room could be hired in a club or the local Council school. He added

> The provision of a building of our own or even the buying of a plot of land is out of the question with the school burden so heavy upon us. *(Letter to Diocese dated 12th October 1932)*

Mass was offered in Chadwell for the first time since the Reformation in January 1933, under the papal sign of the Cross Keys. The licensee of that public house offered the Catholics of the area the use of his hall, which was soon filled to overflowing. Chadwell St. Mary thus became a Mass centre served from Tilbury, from 1933 to 1975. As over seventy people attended Mass at the Cross Keys, it was necessary to move to a larger hall, the Working Men's Club across the road, where the rent charged was ten shillings per week. This remained the Mass centre in Chadwell for many years.

In the early 1950s the Sisters of Mercy considered opening a convent here, a branch house from Tilbury, but this never materialized. In 1952, Thurrock Urban District Council promised an acre of land for use as a church site but they did not locate the exact site. At the end of 1953, the Chadwell Hall Building Fund had begun, and by 1965 £4,000 had been donated.

By the 1960s, with the building of three large Council estates and a private estate, Chadwell had a nine hundred strong Catholic community and Father John Byrne decided that the people of Chadwell should have a Mass centre of their own. At this time, a Ladies Guild was started under the leadership of Annie Hill and meetings were held weekly in members' homes. One of the chief objectives of the Guild was to raise money for the building of a church hall as well as giving an opportunity for new parishioners moving to the area to get to know one another. The Ladies Guild used the hall at the Working Men's Club for jumble sales and dances in order to raise funds.

As the membership of this Guild increased, the members began to meet in the new village hall in Waterson Road and Christmas Bazaars as well as jumble sales were then held there. Canon Byrne attended the meetings regularly and supported the Guild in every way. Tote tickets were also sold to raise more money for the building fund.

Eventually, Thurrock Council set aside a one acre site in Defoe Parade for the building of a Catholic church, hall and presbytery. Only the church hall ever came to fruition, a cedar wood building on a concrete base, built between 1967 and 1968. The hall was designed by Henry Bingham Towner, from Uckfield Sussex and the contractor, who was later to become a parishioner, was Michael J. Greenan. The hall cost £21,000 to build and could seat 250 people. As money was in limited supply, another parishioner, Arthur Matthews, made a wooden altar for the hall. The Lady Chapel to the left of the stage, which later became the Blessed Sacrament Chapel, had a small altar, a gift from the Sisters of Mercy.

The church hall was officially opened on 17th March 1968, with a Mass celebrated at 10.00 a.m. on the thirty inch high stage. Initially Mass was celebrated here twice on Sundays, at 10.00 a.m. and 4-30 p.m. and also on Tuesday evenings at 7-30 p.m. The hall was now used by the Ladies Guild for their meetings, for Bingo on Sunday nights (beginning on 6th October 1968) and for social events, including a dance held on 27th September 1968 which raised £173-3-0d for the Building Fund. Des Pearson was the chief organiser of this event, with the Ladies Guild providing the refreshments and Father Pat Heekin, the Port Chaplain, supplying the bar. On 2nd October there was a Beetle Drive which raised £4-13-0d and on Wednesday, 30th October a Halloween Social. For many years there was also an annual pilgrimage to Aylesford, organised by Winefride Pollard, to celebrate the Feast of the Forty Martyrs of England and Wales.

On 18th March 1975, Father Donald Mills became the first and only Parish Priest of St. Joseph's, Chadwell St. Mary. A series of parish boundaries was redrawn at this time and the Woodside estate in Grays, together with Orsett and Bulphan, became part of the new parish. As well as daily Mass at St. Joseph's, Mass was now also celebrated at Orsett Hospital. It wasn't long before a Youth Club was opened.

A notable date in the parish history was Sunday, 3rd June 1979, when the Annual Civic Service was held in the church hall at 11-30 a.m. A parishioner, Patrick Bolger, had been installed as Mayor and his Chaplain was Rev. Donald Mills.

Father Mills remained in post until the parish was once again incorporated into its mother parish, that of Our Lady Star of the Sea Tilbury, in 1983. At the same time, the Woodside estate reverted back to St. Thomas's Parish, Grays.

In 1982, St. Mary's Youth Club, under the leadership of Sister Carmel McEnerny, began to meet at St. Joseph's and they continued to meet there for the next twenty years. For most of this time it was organised by Pauline Lacey and Mary Pollard, with numerous other helpers. Although Chadwell was no longer a parish in its own right, the hall continued to be used for Mass each Sunday and for a Saturday morning Mass. It was also the centre of many of the parish's social events, with jumble sales, beetle drives, dances and quiz nights regular features, and later the weekly meetings of the Senior Citizens' Club and the annual bazaar. The hall also hosted many private functions. The hall had a superbly well equipped kitchen and this was used extensively by the Care Committee to provide monthly lunches for the Senior Citizens' Group as well as weekly Lenten Lunches. The Chief Cooks, Diane Connolly and Pauline Lacey, ably assisted by a small band of faithful and hard working colleagues, also organised outings to Aylesford, London and elsewhere, an annual Mass for the Sick, followed by lunch, and wonderful Christmas Lunches for the elderly and housebound.

In 1993, on 17th March, the Silver Jubilee of the opening of the church hall, a joint social was held with the parishioners of St. Michael's, East Ham and on 28th March a Silver Jubilee Mass was concelebrated by Bishop Thomas McMahon.

For the next seventeen years, Sunday Mass was celebrated at the church hall. Sadly for the people of Chadwell, the last Mass was celebrated at St. Joseph's at 9.00 a.m. on Sunday, 29th September 2010, and since then the hall has remained empty.

In the course of the research that was conducted to write this commemorative book, one idea kept appearing. It was stated by so many different people, and contained in so many written records and letters. People had recognised that our parish of Stanford-le-Hope is special. Yet what makes it so special? It is true that we have a pleasant church in Our Lady and St. Joseph's. We have a well organised and successful school. We are surrounded by some lovely countryside. We are close to the sea. We even have quite good transport links. Yet many parishes might make similar claims. No, the special quality is the people, the parishioners, who have created such warmth in their friendly and kind relationships with each other. I do not understand how this has come about, but I do know how fortunate we all are that this is so.

This chapter has been created to give some of our parishioners the chance to say a few words of their own. Some of the pieces are taken from letters and jottings from over eighty years ago. Others were recorded in conversations during the last couple of years. Now at last we hear directly from some of the members of our own, very special parish.

An Old Pupil Remembers (Molly)

When the Sisters came to Stanford-le-Hope, they were warmly welcomed by the Catholic people. They had little money and limited accommodation in a semi-detached house. On Saturdays, some Sisters went by train to the village of Vange to instruct the young children who were not in Catholic schools. When Father Snell got a car, he took them on this Visitation, and in 1945, when Father Snell was ill, this old pupil, Molly, drove the Sisters. The Sisters took food to the very poor in outlying villages when the priest went there to hear Confessions.

Sister M. Benignus was sent from the Convent of Mercy, Commercial Road, to teach Seniors in the "Upper Room", (which was a room built over the Sacristy, and used as a temporary private senior school).

Sister M. Bernadette, Head Teacher, was highly regarded by children and parents. If children misbehaved, she had only to look displeased, and they felt abashed; discipline was very firm but kindly and when the school day was ended, and the teaching Sisters returned to the convent, it was very rarely, and only for a serious reason, that they were disturbed by parishioners calling at the door.

At first, when the Sisters went on Visitation, mud was flung at them by non-Catholic boys, and stones were thrown at the convent door, but the Sisters soon earned the respect of the people of Stanford-le-Hope.

(Molly was the church organist at Our Lady and St. Joseph's from 1930 onwards.)

Terry Duggan : Pupil of St. Joseph's 1936 to 1940

I started at St. Joseph's with my elder brother, Keith, in 1936, when my family moved from Cardiff to Fobbing. My younger brother, Philip, started school a year later.

There was no bus service from Fobbing, nor school buses in those days, so we walked to Corringham, where we could catch a bus to Stanford-le-Hope. We moved to Corringham later, which made travelling easier. When Keith moved on to the senior school, I was responsible for getting myself and my younger brother to school and back. I can recall that on one occasion, on coming home from school, I left my brother at the bus stop. There was great panic when I realised this, until the conductor stopped the bus, and I was able to run back and grab him using a few choice words about younger brothers.

The teaching staff consisted of Sister Bernadette, Head Mistress, who taught the older children, Sister Joseph (Juniors) and Sister Columba (Infants). Our schoolboy assessment of the staff might be described as: Sister Bernadette – formidable but fair, Sister Joseph – strict disciplinarian (watch your step), and Sister Columba – try it on (you might get away with it). The most severe form of punishment would be to report to the Head, for slaps on the arm; the number and intensity depending on the gravity of the misdemeanour. "Roll up your sleeve" was almost akin to the judge donning the black cap.

Sister Bernadette had a somewhat automatic response of "I doubt it", when some excuses for certain actions were given. I didn't know what this meant in my younger days, until I finally asked my parents.

I would hasten to add that, in adulthood, one got to know and recognise the Sisters for the dedicated and loving nuns they were, and one thinks of them with nothing but affection and gratitude.

Externally, the buildings were virtually as they are now, with the two original classrooms, separated by a partition, and the addition of a hall in the late 1930s. (*Note: This was written before the school was relocated to the other side of Scratton Road.*) My brother Keith, who entered the senior school in 1936, recalls that his classroom was in what is now the boiler room, indicating that the hall was not built in 1936, but my memories always include the hall.

Sister Columba's classroom was that nearest Scratton Road, the other was Sister Joseph's. The corridor was lined with pictures of sailing ships, which I never tired of looking at. The cloakrooms were at each end of the corridor. Two classrooms were furnished with small tables in regimented rows, with the girls occupying one half and the boys the other. In the hall there were 'proper desks' with ink wells! Ink wells were collected and distributed as required. The Head's desk was on a raised dais. Blackboards were on easels, not wall-mounted, and were assembled and dismantled as required.

There was a very strong emphasis, of course, on Religious Instruction (especially the catechism) and prayers. The bell for the Angelus was rung, until the outbreak of war, when bell-ringing was not allowed. Church bells were to be reserved for sounding the warning of the German invasion, if it occurred. Our instruction in the 3 Rs followed the normal course. P.T. was taught and rounders were played, but there was no instruction in football or cricket for boys. Examination in the catechism seemed to be a traumatic event for both staff and pupils. It was carried out, I believe, by Canon Cameron, whose reputation for a stern and exacting examiner preceded him. For weeks before his visit we were taught how to respond if he asked a question, and threatened with dire consequences if we deviated or, dare I say, failed to answer. I think the visit always seemed to be an anti-climax, and no excommunications or charges of heresy took place.

In our final year we took the Scholarship Exam, the 11+, in order to try to gain entry to a grammar school. If successful, your education continued to the age of 16, with the aim of passing the School Certificate, or Matriculation Examination. Failure of the Scholarship meant attending a local Council secondary school to the age of 14 years (school leaving age) with a more restricted syllabus.

One of the highlights of our primary school education was First Communion. As well as the excitement of this spiritual event in our lives, I think a high proportion of anticipation was generated by the thought of breakfast in the school after Mass. I think that a boiled egg featured largely in the menu served by the Sisters. Fasting, then, of course was from midnight, so I believe we received our First Communion at the 8.30 Mass.

Random memories

- Collections in class for Missions and "Black Babies". Ha'pennies and pennies (old money) were standard donations.
- Father Snell visiting the class.
- Serving Mass and Benediction and being given sixpences by Father Hopkins – a fortune!
- May procession at Tilbury with a brass band leading the hymns.

This concludes some of my boyhood memories of a period in the development of St. Joseph's School, and enables me to express my thanks for the foundations I received in both my religious and general education. The school has developed and modernised over the years to reach the high standard and well-earned reputation it holds to-day. I think that the Sisters of Mercy must be very proud of their contribution to Catholic education in the parish, and equally the parish can only be extremely grateful to them for their major contribution for so many years.

Recollections of Sister M. Aquinas (in lighter vein) 1935, 1936, and 1937

Stanford-le-Hope in the late thirties was the only holiday resort of the Wanstead Novices; the Novice Mistress, of course, accompanying us. As there was no chapel in the original semi-detached house, we used the 'Front' room as Oratory, when we were not "praying to the trees" as some of the locals supposed, for we spent most of our time out-of-doors. To get fresh air must have been the object of our holiday, as well as looking after the house while the three resident Sisters were on a real holiday by the sea. My first 'holiday' I can vividly recall, because as we were leaving Wanstead (with most of our belongings up our big sleeves), the Reverend Mother, M. Xavier R.I.P., bade us farewell and announced that I was to be the cook! I had never even lit a gas cooker, let alone cook on one. That needn't have worried me, because very little cooking was done, except for Sunday, when the 'leg of lamb', cooked then, did us for the rest of the week. There was plenty of lettuce and spinach in the garden, so we had fresh vegetables. As it was August, the local plums were cheap, and they, plus windfalls were the only desserts I can recall.

One Summer we did have a cook, but fared no better, as we had to spend so much time out-of-doors, and the cook was only allowed back half an hour earlier than we were to get the meal ready. This occasioned the famous question : Novice Mistress to Sister Cook, "How long does it take to stew plums?" to which Sister Cook innocently replied "Until they are done". Previously Sister M. Dominic and I had searched the village for the best bargain in plums, as we were told by the Cook "keep the change", knowing that it was unlikely that there would be any. However, we did manage to have one penny change, and again 'did the shops' for something cheap for a penny. Yes, we bought a Milky Way.

The sea, or rather the Thames Estuary, was about a mile away, along an unmade track, and behind the sea wall. We set out each morning for 'our day by the sea' (!) and had our lessons and spiritual lecture as we sat on the slopes of the grassy bank. If the tide was in the grey muddy waters were relieved by the sight of the ships, tugs, coastguard vessels and dredgers, but when the tide was out, there were miles of black mud, where gulls and waders foraged.

One warm afternoon, Sister M. Dominic and I thought we'd get away for a while from the 'hedge school', by suggesting that we would walk out on the now hard mud. There were no other volunteers for the excursion, so the two of us took off our shoes and stockings, and walked across the caked and cracked morass. Here and there were pools of soft mud, which gave way and we sank, but were able to regain our footing fairly easily. Not realising the danger, we intended to go out to meet the incoming tide, so as to wash off the stinking mud before we could face back our jeering companions. We soon discovered the imminent peril of being sucked down into a muddy grave, when the first wave washed over the hitherto solid mud.

By the providence of God, the tide was coming in at right angles to our retreat route, and not straight towards us, so we were just able to pull each other to firmer mud after each swish of water which overtook us. We had no free hand to tuck in our voluminous skirts, as we needed both hands to help each other out of the black holes. We were out of earshot of our companions, and even they didn't realise our danger or look for help for us. After strenuous effort, and many fervent ejaculations (as we thought our last hour had come), we beat the tide and regained the firmer mud. We dragged ourselves to the bank, away from our companions, and made for home to have ourselves washed and disinfected before their return. Our Novice Mistress must have felt that we had endured enough punishment, as I don't remember any 'after effects'. We knew that nothing short of a miracle had saved us from a horrible death.

Another highlight of our holiday was the opportunity to see one of the Anglican Brothers of Divine Compassion, who had a monastery in the parish. These were the days before Ecumenism, and I regret to say that the brothers were much more inclined to be friendly than we were. We couldn't but return their salute when we met – "accidentally on purpose" – on the road. I am glad to say that a few years later two of us got an invitation to be shown over the monastery, and were given all the garden flowers we could carry. My early interest in these Anglican Monks has developed into an ongoing friendship with various Anglican men and women all over the country.

No recollection of the early days at Stanford-le-Hope would be complete without some reference to Father C. Snell. After much prayer and negotiations he succeeded in getting three Sisters to form the nucleus of the school, and he continued to support the Sisters in every possible way. He took a special interest in "new faces", and often joined us at recreation in the evening, which we enjoyed in the garden in those summer holiday times. One Sunday evening, his presence wasn't as welcome as usual, but he wasn't to blame for that. It was a Sister's Feast Day, and we had begged the Novice Mistress all the week to buy a quarter pound Cadbury Fruit and Nut Bar, for the occasion. To, needless to say, our intense delight, the 'blue' bar (costing eight pence) was produced when we were all seated outside the door and the Hail Mary duly said. Our Novice Mistress carefully divided the Bar, and we all had just received our square when Father and another visiting 'supply' Belgian priest appeared round the corner of the kitchen. As we weren't supposed to eat in public, we hastily put the chocolate behind our backs, and welcomed our visitors. Only one daring Novice popped hers into her mouth while pretending to move her chair. As it was a very hot evening, I could feel mine melting through my fingers, but I carefully guarded the piece of nut till the visitors left.

Ten years later, when I came back as a teacher to the now-flourishing school, Father Snell was both distressed and amused to hear my tale. His gentleness and generosity endeared him to everyone who came to know him in those days.

Recollections of Sister Barbara Jeffery

After spending two years in the Joint Novitiate in Harewood Avenue, London, part of which time was spent in community experience in Croydon, I made my First Profession on 14th July, 1984. A few weeks after that, I moved to Stanford-le-Hope, to become a 4th Year Junior teacher, replacing Sister Philippa.

To say I was apprehensive was putting it mildly, as I had never taught 4th Year Juniors before. But nevertheless I muddled through my first year without too many mishaps. I was very fortunate in having a well-behaved 4th Year class. The highlight of the year was taking them on an educational week-long visit to north Essex, and they had opportunities to visit a windmill, a cave, a stately home and the historic city of Cambridge and its university.

I had '4th Years' the next year too, but felt a little less confident in handling them. So by the end of that second year I decided that I needed a change in age group, and I asked Sister Monica Cremin, who was Head then, if I could move down a year or so. This decision actually coincided with the decision of Sister Helen Furness to go on Mission to Kenya, and so I found myself taking over 1st Year Juniors, much to my surprise. It also happened to be the First Communion Class, and so meant a great deal of organisation. I followed the format left by Sister Helen for the first year, but now having just completed a second year in this year group, I have made the programme much more my own, adapting the Christiane Brusselmann's programme, "We Celebrate the Eucharist", as well as "We Celebrate Reconciliation".

Apart from school work, I have worked for a couple of years as the church Sacristan, and helped to get the church ready for the big feasts of Christmas and Easter.

A recent development after a Mission in the parish in March, 1987, was my involvement in the 16 - 18 year old group in the parish. We now meet weekly on a Monday evening from 8.00 to 9.30 p.m. approximately, and there is a steady turnout of about 10, which is quite a success rate in this day and age. We follow a number of activities : discussions, using material from the Young Christian Workers' movement, fund raising activities, social outings, videos, social and justice issues plus a weekend away at Walsingham House occasionally. We hope also to use the House of Prayer near Brentwood for an evening of prayer at some stage, and we keep very close links with Margaret Magennis, The Deanery Youth Leader.

So life is very full and busy for me, and the time has certainly flown since I made my First Profession in 1984.

Reminiscences of Sister M. Stanislaus Culligan

On January 31st, 1987, the A1 road led to an A1 Community at Stanford-le-Hope, on my arrival as new Superior. For some weeks before, telephone wires were buzzing with surmises, conjectures and finally certainties. The heavy January snow in Essex that winter prevented the usual pre-view visit. Travelling south that day, the damp biting cold came as a surprise after the more temperate Yorkshire climate.

On arrival I received a very warm welcome from the Sisters, and I can honestly say that I felt at home right from the start. The convent is small but very comfortable: no wasted space or "hidey holes". The chapel which has been built on more recently to the existing building, is both peaceful and prayerful.

The parishioners were most welcoming, but it took some time before we really got to know them. Sister Carmela, from a Sheffield Community, also arrived in Stanford that same day, so we were 'dubbed' the two new Sisters. On the first Monday, with the aid of a local map, we located roads and avenues. We must have looked like two surveyors mapping out new territory.

As a Eucharist Minister I am able to take Holy Communion to the elderly and house-bound. I was very impressed by one dear old lady, who has now gone to her reward, for she had her church collection of £4 ready on the mantelpiece at each visit.

We were surprised by the extent of the parish, which has four Mass centres, but only one priest, so there is a great need for Sisters and, Thank God, their presence is much appreciated.

Sister M. Dolores : The Case of the Missing Turkey

Having been at Stanford-le-Hope since July 1987, and having got to know the Community, I was looking forward to sharing my first Christmas with them. However it was more entertaining than I could have foreseen.

Preparations were in full swing a couple of days before Christmas, and we expected our local-reared turkey to be delivered from Mickey Dunne's farm on 23rd of December. Several phone calls were made to ensure its delivery, but 23rd came and went and 24th came and almost went, before our turkey could be tracked down. In answer to our urgent enquiries, we were told that the turkey had been delivered, together with four dozen eggs, and that Mickey was frantically searching for a lost farm dog and for a lost pet duck, and had no time to search for a lost turkey. But as a goodwill seasonal gesture, Mickey said that he would deliver a 12 lb. capon, and four more dozen eggs. He was completely mystified as to the whereabouts of the turkey, and he promised to contact the lady who had delivered it.

In the meantime Sister Philippa and I decided to investigate, by holding a torchlight procession round the garden to see if the turkey had been left in some unusual place. On our rounds we decided to enquire at the presbytery just in case Father Gostling had accepted our turkey as an unexpected gift, not realising our plight. We received a firm denial from the P.P. but he offered to look round the exterior of his premises, in case the bird had strayed.

To our delighted amusement and relief Father Gostling found the elusive bird buried in a manhole – disused – under a cover, and accompanied by four dozen eggs. Father did not bat an eyelid, or seem to find the episode at all unusual, which attitude only served to add to our amusement.

Making our triumphal return, with the bird held aloft, not forgetting the eggs, we arrived back at the convent to find that the capon and the eggs had already been delivered, and Mickey had gone, still in search of his dog and duck. Our hilarity increased as we now realised what a good Christmas we were going to have. When we telephoned Mickey Dunne, he told us to keep the capon and the eggs, and to enjoy them, for he was worn out by the whole proceedings. We just had enough time to stuff the turkey and put it in the oven, before going to Midnight Mass.

P.S. We learnt later that the duck had probably provided a good Christmas dinner for a lucky fox, and the dog had run away from the house – probably, too, the sight of so many turkeys had driven him to seek solitude.
P.P.S. We kept the capon in the deep freeze until Easter, and it was a great relief to know that we did not have to search for it.

Mrs. Lilian Webb remembers the chapel at Horndon on the Hill

There was a small chapel in Horndon before the Sacred Heart Chapel was built. It was constructed mainly of wood and asbestos, as were the homes of the families brought by Miss Green to live in what was known as The Priory, as she wished to form a small Catholic settlement. The little chapel was very plain, some wooden seats, rough uneven stone floor, and the only lights were oil lamps.

For me, at least, it had a wonderful atmosphere, especially at the Christmas Midnight Mass: easy to imagine the Stable at Bethlehem in such a place. A harmonium was played by Mr. Banks, a non-Catholic music teacher. He was also present at a Club, run by a lady-companion of Miss Green, for young members of the Community. I looked forward to that entertainment on Saturday evenings even though I was only a week-end visitor.

I must add here that my future husband's family had removed from London to live at Horndon – hence my being there at week-ends and holidays.

A very narrow winding path led into The Priory from Oxford Road, and at a bend in the path was a large Crucifix, almost life-size. When I arrived in the dark of a winter's evening – there were no lights – I was always startled to come upon it suddenly. There was also a Grotto, with a statue of Our Lady of Lourdes, and the Angelus bell was rung twice daily. The present Sacred Heart Chapel was built before my family finally came to live in Horndon, then I was happy to take a turn at cleaning, and at arranging the flowers. For a short time during the war, we had Mass only on alternate Sundays.

The chapel was not licensed for marriages, but our Banns were called on the three weeks before our Great Day. As we were a small Community, we all knew each other, so there was much interest and many good wishes. It is sad to think that after so many years, there will no longer be a Catholic chapel in Horndon. Circumstances have brought about what the German Airforce failed to do, for one night, after the 'All Clear' sounded we went to bed thankful that there had been no damage. Luckier than we realised! Next morning on our way to Mass, we were stopped from getting to the chapel, for a land-mine had been dropped during the raid, but it caught in the branches of a tree close to the chapel, and so had failed to explode : a miracle it seemed to us.

(Note : Mrs. Lilian Webb is a sister of Dave Arnold, who spent so much of his life devotedly looking after the chapel. Such was his involvement, he became affectionately known as the Bishop of Horndon.)

Letters from Kenya

Some of our Sisters of Mercy have responded to the call to work in the African Missions, principally in Kenya. In a 1972 edition of the *Parish Quarterly*, we were able to learn of the work of Sister Monica, who was based at the Mission field of Koru.

"Sister Monica seems to be enjoying the adventurous life in the tropics, making light of the hazards of her unusual way of life. Teaching there has its problems, but it is never dull. Sister reports that when school re-opened after the Christmas holidays the grass had grown up through the classroom floors! No, not parquet or tiled floors, but well-beaten clay ones, or at least that is what they should have been. Yes, the remedy is obvious (to us): wait for the children to trample it down. Those of you who have tried to cultivate lawns and rear young footballers know how quickly one can overcome the other. This remedy could not be applied in Koru, Kenya, as it was not the grass, but the hidden population of "creepy crawlies" that was the difficulty, and I suspect a greater threat to teachers than to children. One Sister has already experienced the inconvenience of "Jiggers" as they call the leeches that take up residence under the toe-nails. So the floors had to be mown and the surface restored to its original well-baked appearance, before the new entrants arrived.

And surprise, surprise! Each pupil advanced carrying his own seat – a large flat stone. Another unusual feature of school-life there is the age of people who come to school in their thirst for education, or at least for the advantages which it will bring. One class of "Upper Juniors" had an age range from 10 to 30 years. The "mature" juniors are no trouble as they are so anxious to learn – the quicker they acquire knowledge the sooner they quit.

During the holidays the Sisters visited the Big Game Reserve, and they were full of admiration of the animals, birds and scenery which defy description. They also visited other convents and Mission schools to exchange ideas and discuss ways of becoming more efficient Missionaries."

In April 1985, there was a special appeal from Father Miskella who ran the Barkorwa Mission in Kenya. He asked for Sisters who could give a few years of their time to help the Mission. One of our Sisters of Mercy, Sister Helen, showed an interest in this venture and was given permission to withdraw from her teaching post to prepare to play a part in the Pioneer Project in Secondary Education at Barkorwa. The following extracts are from letters that Sister Helen sent back to the parish in the years that followed. They give an indication of the range of challenges that the Sisters of Mercy readily undertake as part of their vow of service.

October 1986
The time is going very quickly and we are kept busy. We're getting used to the heat, but we stay in the house when we can, it's cooler. We're getting used also to the few deprivations, so we'll soon be part of it all. Our visit to school was very fruitful, especially Koru, where we spent four days. We even got a chance to teach there.

We're going to the Kerry Mercies next week for two weeks. They started from nothing like we are doing, so it will be interesting to see how they do it. We have to write detailed schemes of work, and detailed lesson notes, so we are going to be kept busy. We've been into Kisumu a few times. There is a nice hotel there with a swimming pool and a shower – what luxury!

The convent is not ready yet, so we're still in Father Miskella's house. He is so good to us and really appreciates our being there. We went shopping for curtain material and sheets yesterday, so we've made a start. We should move in by mid-November. We haven't even unpacked our big cases yet.

We visited the Training College this morning. We've been invited back at the weekend to a display of Visual Aids for teaching. That should be useful. The schools I've seen are totally lacking in V.A. material. The primary schools haven't even got benches. The children sit on stones and write on their knees.

March 1990
The Blessing and official opening of St. Barnabas Girls Secondary School, Barkorwa, Kenya. Headmistress : Sister Helen

Our opening day went very well. The Bishop was in top form, and promised 10,000 shillings – but unless he has changed drastically, a promise it will remain. He was dressed like the Infant of Prague statue we use to have years ago. I don't know how he could bear all those robes in the heat. The new Minister for Foreign Affairs also came. We were delighted and he spoke to the parents and girls. The Bishop blessed every corner of the school, with me walking beside him.

And everyone got fed – it was like the feeding of the 5,000. People had donated gifts of food: chickens, goats, sheep, lots of maize, vegetables and fruits. We bought a bull, so everyone had plenty. It was a beautiful day and every place looked lovely

July/August 1991
The most significant event that took place this term – and indeed since the opening of the school – was the visit of His Excellency, President Daniel Moy. On 30th July we were informed by the Education Office that the President would visit our school on Thursday, 1st August. For nearly two days the school was a hive of activity – washing, digging, planting, painting etc. Even the workmen left the building to help in the preparation.

On the morning of the 1st we put up banners, flags and bunting, and made paths of white stones. The place sparkled – fit for a King! By 12 noon the girls were all lined up on both sides of the road, but the President didn't arrive until 4.30 p.m. We forgot the heat and frustration as cries were raised in welcome.

I received His Excellency at the gate and introduced my Staff. I then walked with him to the office, surrounded by tight security. I got close to the President at one stage and I was pulled away by his personal bodyguard. At the office I posed for a picture while the President signed the Visitors' Book. He then sat outside while he was entertained by the girls with singing and dancing.

I made a speech of welcome, after which the Minister for Foreign Affairs and M.P. for Kisumu spoke and invited the President to speak. He showed his pleasure at what he saw by praising Irish Missionaries, and knew they were good workers, even if they were hot-tempered! He then burst into song, "It's a long way to Tipperary", to loud applause. He finally made us a gift of two hundred thousand shillings (approx. £4,000). Then the President added a further twenty thousand shillings (approx. £400) for food for the girls – they went wild!

I then walked the President around the school and he was very impressed, especially with our labs and practical rooms. The Permanent Secretary was overheard saying: "These people are serious". The visit was supposed to last 15 minutes, but he stayed one hour. As he was leaving he thanked us again and said he would return next year!

Sister Corona : Eulalia

But of all the stories that came back to us from the African missions, none made more of an impression than Mother Corona's account of an experience in Zambia. Sister Corona is, of course, well known in our parish, as is her family. The account became the feature article in our *Parish Quarterly* in March 1971. Despite its length, I make no apology for including it in its entirety. Those who have not heard this story before will see why.

"Thank God we are finished on time tonight" I said to Sister M. Leo, as we locked the Labour ward door of our small hospital in Kasaba, Zambia and prepared to go over to the convent for supper – but we never got that supper, we got triplets instead.

This story goes back to a hot January evening four years ago. During the previous few weeks we had had a span of difficult maternity cases, desperately sick babies and endless hours of work day and night and to put it quite bluntly we were dead tired.

On this particular January evening as we walked off down the covered way, with our thoughts on an early supper and early bed, we saw some men coming in through the main door carrying an improvised stretcher. It was already dark so I shone the flashlight onto the stretcher and saw a young woman there. I asked the men what was the matter, silently bidding goodbye to my supper and bed. "One baby out, one baby in" was the matter of fact reply. I unlocked the Labour Ward door once again and they took her inside. After a preliminary examination I knew the second baby would not be too long getting himself born, so I wrapped the first baby up warmly and put him into the little cot in the corner and then concentrated on delivering the second one.

She, for it turned out to be a girl, came without any difficulty and was soon placed beside her brother. I then turned back to the Mother and immediately knew that things were not yet finished. I did a quick examination and found another baby waiting to get out. I broke the news to the mother and the grannie heard me and ran from the room to tell all her friends outside that triplets were being born in the labour ward. The excitement was tremendous but I was a little apprehensive because as I listened in to the unborn baby's heartbeat I could detect that he was not doing so well, he was suffering from the delay. I wished that the people would not rejoice until I had the baby safely out, but there was no stopping them, so I turned my full attention to delivering the Mother of this last baby.

It all took some time, there were some attendant difficulties, but eventually a limp little parcel lay in my hands, heart only just about beating, slowly and faintly, no other signs of life at all, no breathing, no movements. It was a case of White Asphyxia, a dreaded neo-natal condition. It was now 7 p.m., and as Sister was seeing to the Mother and the other two little ones, I concentrated on number three.

I did everything in the book and many things not in <u>any</u> book, but nothing helped. One whole hour passed and I myself was almost exhausted from the mouth to mouth resuscitation I had been keeping up. At this time we had no oxygen supply in the hospital. This mouth to mouth breathing for babies has to be so controlled in order not to damage the tiny lungs that the resuscitator becomes more and more deoxygenated as a result! But with this baby it was the only thing that brought a flicker of strength into the thin wavering slow heartbeat. As soon as I paused for a few moments to regain my own breath the tiny heart would slow and grow faint again.

I continued until one hour had passed and still there was not the slightest indication of any effort on the part of the baby to take over his own breathing. I checked his record card again to see if there was anything else I could possibly give. There was nothing. He had received everything. I returned to the mouth-to-mouth breathing. The next time I checked the clock I realised I had been at it for 190 minutes. Was there any point in going on? He had not made a single effort of his own, not one gasp, not one flicker, not one anything.

The initial excitement of the relatives had long since given way to anxiety and they all sat round the walls, quietly watching me.

Weariness has its own peculiar force and because I was weary, very much so, I began to think things that are not normal to my mentality. I sat down on the low stool and just stared at this baby. The Mother after all had four other healthy growing youngsters, as well as the other two new borns. She was a simple village woman who would surely find it quite enough to bring up these <u>two</u> tiny tots, when after all she had only been expecting one! They could well do without this last one. In any case, all such considerations aside, I had done everything I could possible do, there was nothing else I could think of and, what was more, even if I could think up something else that might bring life into this lifeless little body, would it ever be a real baby, a real child, a real human being. After all this time it must surely be suffering from cerebral anoxia (lack of oxygen to the brain), there must surely be irreversible brain damage by this time, so what was I trying to keep alive, a baby or a vegetable? I had seen babies that had been revived after much shorter times of anoxia and their brains had never recovered.

"Mother?" a voice broke in on my thoughts. "Would you not like to go over and have some supper, you have done everything possible, there is nothing more to do is there?" I looked at the baby again. Sister was voicing my own thoughts. "I'll try a little longer" I replied. His small heart was so brave, it was trying against desperate odds not to give in. It was fluttering faintly yet appealingly like the wing of a dying bird. He did not want to die, this little fellow, he was craving to live and I knew I had to go on helping him. For one more hour I went on with the mouth-to-mouth resuscitation, and by this time I was seeing stars I was so giddy, and just then as I paused to regain my breath, he gasped!

It was now 11 p.m., four whole hours since he was born, and this was his first effort, but it was an effort! The whole atmosphere in the room was charged with hope. Grannie and her companions sat up, alert, intent. From that moment I knew in my heart against all my better medical judgement and knowledge that we were going to win. Gradually the gasps became more frequent and then gradually they gave place to real breathing, slow and laboured to be sure, but real breathing nevertheless. The yellowy/white skin began to change to a purply/blue and then slowly to a dark pink and eventually to a lighter pink. His tissues had become oxygenated and he was breathing regularly and strongly without any help from me. His heartbeat was quick and firm. It was now 11.45 p.m., four hours forty-five minutes from the time of his birth, and he had only just established his own breathing.

This little Bush baby whose passing would have been mourned for only a short time would have gone back into the earth from which he came, nameless and unknown. Limbs fashioned for action would never have been used and the Labour Ward record book would have carried a simple statement, "All efforts at resuscitation failed, still-born" and that would have been that. But it did not go that way, that tiny heart had refused to stop beating, refused to accept the death sentence, the little body was determined to live as anything conceived of a woman has a right to do (a fact forgotten these days is some of our so-called developed countries). Throughout the night he continued to breathe, although his first cry was not heard until a full twenty four hours after birth.

However, I was still worried, brain damage would not necessarily show for some time. I still wondered if I had saved a baby who was capable of a full human existence with his little brothers and sisters or a child who would never function normally. But as the weeks went into months all my worries subsided. He had a lustier yell than the other two when he was hungry which was always! He had a temper no other baby could match (could it have been my breath in him that did that?), he gained weight, slept and smiled just as the books say a baby should behave. The father of the babies kept insisting it was a miracle, and no amount of talk would convince him otherwise. It was a miracle and that was that! He had heard from Grannie all that had taken place and he knew a miracle when he met one whatever I tried to tell him!

These babies were by name Peter, the eldest, Ephrasia (shortened to Efa) the little girl, and Eulalio the little vegetable. They all stayed in the hospital for two years with their Mother and we saw them grow into fine healthy children. During this time the father, to whom we had since given work in the hospital grounds, had with the help of the Brother on the Mission fixed up one of the small mission houses ready for his family, and then came the day for the departure ceremony! Off they went, discharged from the hospital, the three of them in little red and white suits we had made for them. They turned and waved at every half step even though their new home was only 500 yards away and as we walked back into the hospital it seemed like a tomb. That was over two years ago.

Just a few days ago, I heard a lot of noise outside the office window where I was working. Stepping carefully over Nshele – another little long term baby we have who was methodically emptying my waste paper basket onto the floor, I looked out of the window and I saw Eulalio, my little "brain damaged" baby streaking up the path with a tiny box in his hand that he had obviously just snatched from his brother, who was in hot pursuit. The last view I had of them before they rounded the corner was of the soles of their feet as they sped along kicking up a powerful exhaust of dust and shouting anathemas at each other! Aged four if you please! "Vegetable" I said to myself half under my breath, as I turned away from the window. "Pardon Mother?" came a voice. Sister had walked into the office. "Did you say something about vegetables?" "Not in the plural, Sister" I replied. "Just one rather special vegetable." "Eulalio?" said Sister. "Eulalio" I replied.

Sister M Joseph R.I.P. (Article in the *Parish Quarterly*, March 1972)

It has been said that life is like a ship passing through the waves. The ship leaves a trail in its wake – a trail that quickly vanishes and leaves no evidence of the ship's passage.

Sister M. Joseph has just died at the age of 69. When a Sister dies, the Community rejoices and prays. We rejoice that another person has gone to God. Once we used to wear white festive cloaks, but these have been discarded by modern trends. We pray that she may enjoy the vision of God.

Sister M. Joseph was the first new recruit or postulate of the Wanstead Community when it became independent with the establishment of the Brentwood Diocese. She came from County Limerick, Ireland, and was one of a family of seven. She was educated in a boarding school run by the Sisters of Mercy at Ennis and graduated at 19. She decided to become a Sister of Mercy and entered Wanstead Convent in 1920, being later joined by her sister who is still a member of the Community.

It is well known that Sister spent most of her active life in Stanford-le-Hope and was one of the founder members of the convent here in 1930. She taught children of various ages until her retirement in 1968.

Many will remember Sister M. Joseph – as we remember our first teachers – because of a cryptic remark, a reprimand or a word of praise. I remember Sister M. Joseph as a teacher, as a person and as a religious.

As a teacher she had excellent discipline and one was always sure that children got a thorough grounding in the basic subjects in her class. Trained in Selly Park in 1928, she saw methods changing radically in her years of service. She kept abreast of the times, though not prone to jump on every band wagon, and was not a little perturbed when the "New Maths" began to reach Stanford-le-Hope. With the assurance of experience she sagely remarked "We will come back to the four rules one day!" She was sympathetic and industrious and had a deep understanding of children. A boy once told his mother that Sister said he need not wash before going to church on Sundays. He interpreted this in his own way.

As a person, people have found her approachable and kind. If it were possible for her to help someone in need, she did so at once, never leaving a request on the long finger. She was a gifted needlewoman, and made several altar cloths, vestments and other sacristy requisites through the years. Each year she made a considerable contribution to the Parish Bazaar.

As a religious – and this she regarded as her foremost calling in life – she was certainly dedicated, and an example in her appreciation of Holy Mass, fidelity to prayer and religious customs. Yet she accepted change with an open mind and had a great loyalty to the Order.

Sister M. Joseph got ill on St. Stephen's day and was anointed by Father Collins. She was sent to Orsett Hospital, where she was given every possible treatment and care. She recovered sufficiently to be allowed home but she deteriorated rapidly. As we became aware that she was incurable, we had a Mass said for a happy death for her. That is just what she had. For the last fortnight the Community at Wanstead took care of her and she received Holy Communion frequently. On Sunday 26th March, just as the Sisters surrounding her had said the prayers for the dying, she went to God. Our prayers are all the help we can give and that is all Sister Joseph would wish for from us. May she rest in peace.

(Written by a Member of the Community)

Reminiscences of Sister Monica Cremin

In 1954 I transferred from Canvey Island, where I had spent four busy years in the newly opened convent primary school. The Housing Authority in London's East End decided to rehouse a number of its young families to Stanford-le-Hope and consequently there was a sudden influx of primary school children. I was sent – not asked or consulted – (unheard of terms in those days) to join the Community of seven Sisters. My first assignment was a mixed class of lively seven year olds. It was well into the Autumn term before I met all my pupils as some were away with their parents in the Hop Fields of Kent. When I called the names of the missing pupils I would be hailed with a chorus of "gone 'opping, Sister". I spent thirteen happy years at St. Joseph's before answering the call to teach at St. Bedes, Chadwell Heath, and then to the Mission Field of Koru in Kenya, East Africa.

After an absence of eight years I returned to Stanford-le-Hope and it was during this time, with the help of a very dedicated Staff and a supportive Parish Priest, Father John Taylor, backed up by an experienced Board of Governors and an enthusiastic, imaginative Parents Association, that changes were able to take place. Permission was finally given to transfer the entire school on to the Scratton Road site.

In 1985 a major operation was a contributing factor in a decision to resign my post as Head Teacher of St. Joseph's. A beautiful Mass, celebrated in the open air in the school grounds and attended by a large congregation, marked my departure from a beloved school.

During the Autumn of 1986 I was privileged to attend a Spiritual Renewal Course at Hawkeston Hall, near Shrewsbury. This was a most enriching, enjoyable experience and I met Sisters, priests and Brothers from many parts of the world. A visitor to the Centre while I was there was "Dana" – a former winner of the Eurovision Song Contest. As she was educated by the Sisters of Mercy she was happy to be photographed with the Mercy Sisters who were on the course.

Nearing the end of that happy, carefree term at Hawkestone Hall, our Provincial, Sister M. Rita Lynch telephoned, asking me to meet her at a nearby convent and the result of that consultation – cajoling, requesting – was that on 2nd February '87 I would go to St. Joseph's at Horsforth, approx. five miles from Leeds. St. Joseph's is a convalescent home, and the Matron was Sister Carmel Farrell, who is now one of my very valued colleagues. (I'm jumping ahead.) I quickly settled down and I was helped, guided and made to feel at home in a situation which I had hitherto never experienced.

Seven years passed very quickly and once again the call came from Sister Rita to pack my bags and move nineteen miles further south to Wath on Dearne, close to Rotherham. My assignment there was to do parish work in Herringthorpe in the Rotherham area. This necessitated supplying me with a little Renault 5 car for my use. One of my companions was Sister M. Aidan O'Neill, my former Head Teacher at St. Joseph's and whom I succeeded when she was Missioned to Kenya.

At the end of two years I was invited to return to my beloved Stanford-le-Hope and without hesitation I said "Yes". I feel as if I have come home. I received a very warm welcome from Sister M. Bernadette Roche, whom I had lived with during my previous sojourn and who was a "tower of strength" and support. Sister Josephine Ryan also gave me a great welcome and it was good to find that Sister Carmel has settled in her new home in the South.

Serious Fire damage to St. Joseph's Church

On the afternoon of Saturday, 28th October, 1989, about 5.30, two teenage boys reported to the Sisters that black smoke was pouring out of one of the windows of the Parish Church. The fire brigade was called, and two Sisters went round to the church to investigate. The Parish Priest, Father Gostling, who was due to celebrate Mass at the chapel at Horndon, asked them to give any possible assistance to the Fire Officers.

In a few minutes two Fire Brigade Crews arrived and, using breathing apparatus and hoses, they managed to put out the fire, which appeared to have started in or near the Confessional.

The woodwork, including the sacristy doors, in that area is badly burnt, and the beautifully carved statue of St. Joseph is destroyed. Plaster work and flooring are badly damaged, the Altar, furnishings and fittings are blackened to such an extent that it could take months before the church can be used again.

The Sisters and parishioners gathered round to prepare the Parish Hall for Sunday Mass next morning, at which the congregation appeared to be distressed and shocked by the tragedy. To add to the gloom, it was the last weekend that Father Gostling was to officiate as Parish Priest here, as he had been appointed to Chadwell Heath Parish. He expressed his thanks for the many messages of supportive sympathy from local churches and Denominations. He had the sad task of breaking the news to the incoming Parish Priest, Rev. D. Ashton, who was expected to arrive on the evening of 2nd November.

It was announced that Masses on the Feasts of All Saints & All Souls would be celebrated in the School and Parish Halls. On Friday evening, parishioners who arrived for the evening Mass found that the Parish Hall was occupied by the Youth Club, so the Knights of St. Columba, plus the usual Friday evening congregation, arrived unexpectedly at the convent chapel, which was speedily prepared. Everyone was provided with a seat, and all ended happily. Weekday Masses were either celebrated in the convent chapel or in the School Hall.

Father Gerald Gostling

My next appointment after St. Joseph's was to St. Bede's in Chadwell Heath, where I was Parish Priest for eight years, and then my move after that was to Most Holy Redeemer, Harold Hill. I thank God that I have been happy in and retain great affection for all the parishes I have served as a priest.

I volunteered in 2003 to come to our Twinned Diocese of Dundee in South Africa.

(The twinning of Brentwood with Dundee was forged around 1985 when Michael Rowland became Bishop of the newly formed diocese of Dundee. Bishop Michael was born and brought up in Grays, Essex. He became a Franciscan priest and has spent much of his working life in South Africa.

He came to visit Bishop Thomas when he was newly ordained a Bishop and they forged the twinning at that time. The twinning was originally envisaged to be one of spiritual support and friendship but over the years it has taken on different forms, including the twinning of parishes and schools.

The Holy Father has appointed Father Graham Rose to succeed Bishop Michael Rowland as the new Bishop of Dundee. He is a South African, born in Evander, which is in the diocese of Dundee, and he was ordained a priest for his diocese of Johannesburg, where he was involved in setting up the Catholic University. His Episcopal Ordination took place on 30th August 2008 in Newcastle, within the diocese of Dundee.

Priests and Deacons have been exchanged for a time. Our parish enjoys regular contact with a Polish priest, Father Tomasz Wargacki, who is in charge of Breyten and Wesselton Parishes.)

One of the reasons I volunteered was because I firmly believe in this special bond between the two dioceses, and at the time when they were asking for another Brentwood priest there were no other takers…so I put my hand up ! I came here in 2004, initially for two to three years. It is now over seven !! Here in South Africa I was appointed to the area of Evander and Secunda, but in January 2012 I am due to move to Newcastle. It's a little too near the 'engine room' as the Bishop lives in Newcastle and the Offices are there. Actually it will be great. This is part of many necessary moves in the diocese. We have only five incardinated priests, and only three locally ordained priests working in this Diocese of Dundee at the moment. But wonderful things are happening, even if it is a struggle at times.

I have shared about life and Mission here in many letters and articles. But briefly my work has been parish work, and then very soon I had responsibilities for Home Based Care which has started and thrived in this area (Township based) since I have been here. Fr. Giorgio Masa and I worked very closely together, and I really thank God for this. He was my neighbour and taught me a huge amount, but now he is back in Italy.

Life is extremes, from well-to-do people, to the very depths of poverty in parts of the Township – orphans, HIV/AIDS, poor services (water, sewerage, electricity etc.). The needs at times can be quite overwhelming! I have come to love the people in the Townships, including the smells, the noise, the dusty roads, the suffering, the great faith, and big smiles that get us through the struggles. What Zulu I have is Township language, but I manage. I and our communities have been supported by the prayers and love of SO many people in parishes where I have served. I think it is true that I have asked for nothing, but when we've needed practical help somehow it has just come along. Fund raising is certainly not one of my gifts!

Whoever is reading this please pray for us and our Dundee Diocese. Graces will flow all round. One day, if God wills, I would like to spend a time in the Brentwood Diocese sharing about the work here in this diocese – and St. Joseph's would be on top of the list !! God bless and love you all – and be a good 'missionary' just where you are at any moment.

Margaret Kennedy

I married in 1956 and moved to East Tilbury, which came under Tilbury Parish at that time. We had Father Byrne, who was then made a Canon.

Before I was married I lived at Horndon on the Hill. We had our own chapel down at the Priory until it was sold and is now a private house, along with St. Augustine's at Corringham Town Centre.

I used to go to Mass at East Tilbury when our two girls were young, then my husband would cycle from East Tilbury to Horndon on the Hill; he loved that chapel.

Thomas Bata was Managing Director of Bata Shoe Factory. He said that Sunday Mass would always be available. It was in the Managers' Dining Room, then the Ballroom in the Hotel.

When the Hotel was made into flats and shops we used the Social Centre (which used to be a Cinema). That was too costly. We then had Mass at Linford in the Methodist church, until recently.

Also Sean Parsons lived in East Tilbury. He went to St. Joseph's School, Stanford-le-Hope, and was ordained at Our Lady and St. Joseph's, but was sent to Leeds.

My late husband Tom Kennedy would take Marie and Eileen to Our Lady and St. Joseph's on Good Fridays for a procession around Stanford then I would go to 3 p.m. Mass.

Ann Grant

I started the St. Joseph's playschool around 1975. At the time, my two children, Marie and Ian, both attended the parish's primary school. Starting the school a few years beforehand had been quite a traumatic event for them as they did not know any other children attending, and it was this observation I took influence from when starting the playschool.

If the children due to start the infant school in the coming years had already met and made friends with fellow future pupils at a playschool of some sort, transcending over to the primary school would not be so daunting a task. I asked fellow parish member, Mary Hall, if she would like to help me with the project and she quite thankfully agreed.

Before we could get under way, Mary and I had to go through several official checks. The parish community also proved vital in these early days, and thanks to their generous donations we were able to acquire toys and other starting equipment.

Alongside making friends, our aim was to give the playschool children a taste of the 'big school' which they were due to attend in the near future. We initially began in the Parish Room, although the playschool eventually moved over into the infant school's classrooms. This way, the children were introduced to a school environment, complete with toilets, basins, coat hooks, pigeon holes etc.

At the end of term, teachers of St. Joseph's Primary School would invite the playschool pupils over for 'story time'. This gave the children the chance to meet their future teacher. We also made use of the infant school's playground area, to introduce the children to the rather daunting experience of playtime!

As the playschool increased in popularity and numbers increased, in 1976 Margaret Spoors and Pat Pennycook joined us for what would be the next 8-10 years.

I am told that the playschool still runs today under the local government. This is, of course, a very rewarding fact. Many of the children I once looked after are parents themselves now, sending their own children to the playschool. I really do hope their children continue to reap the benefits I aimed to provide them with all those years ago.

A Priest's Story

A few years ago, the Diocese created a booklet entitled *A Priest's Story*. Diocesan priests were asked to give their reflections on what was important to them in their life as a priest. Some of our priests responded. Here is what each wrote.

Father Bartholomew Lynch

I had already started my working career when the nagging began. I kept thinking about the priesthood. No matter what I did the idea would not go away. In desperation I went to a priest who said "Stick with your job, Bart, and the nagging will go away!"

At the time I was attending Judo classes at a Catholic club. There I met another priest who, being a keen photographer, asked me if he could take a snap of one of my judo sessions. I found him much easier to talk to about the repetitive calls the Lord seemed to be making, and with his encouragement I eventually entered the seminary.

One Saturday evening in Holy Week, some years later, I was preparing for the 11.00 p.m. Vigil Mass. It was about 9 o'clock in the evening when the doorbell rang! Outside stood an old man, scruffy and unkempt. To all appearances he was just another beggar, knocking on the presbytery door. I invited him in, and had to exert all the patience I could muster as he told me his tale of woe and the huge problems he had with drink. He was desperate, depressed and lonely.

I offered him sandwiches and cups of tea which he gladly accepted. Eventually I told him I needed to go and say the Vigil Mass for which, by this time, I hadn't been able to prepare at all.

Two years later, the old man returned. He reminded me who he was and revealed that he in fact was a priest. He continued: "I was on my last legs that night, but your kindness and hospitality meant so much, that I have been able to sort out my drinking problem and carry on my priestly ministry."

What better way could I have prepared for that Vigil Mass, I thought!

God grant me the serenity to accept the things I cannot change, the courage to change the things I can and the wisdom to distinguish the one from the other. ***Reinhold Lebuhr***

<u>Father Gerald Gostling</u>

In my ordination card in 1969 I quoted Our Lord from St. John's Gospel: "TRUST IN ME". Then I had cards printed for my 25th anniversary on which I had the original words and added "I DID TRUST, AND IT WORKS!"

Trust in God is the foundation of my life, and as a priest I trust that He is the one who has called me to this particular ministry. Obviously we have worked together and I have willingly and as best as I can responded to the 'Call'.

What happens within that 'Call' is a big act of trust and faith.

The first thanks I give to God is for bringing me into being and letting me be me – this is my first act of gratitude to God every day. I then thank him for what he has called me to do with this one unique precious life, and that this new day will see me faithful, discerning and happy.

I firmly believe that a good priest is one that is first very human and therefore it has been crucial for me, often weaving in and out of authority, to keep myself up-to-date and enthusiastic just as a human person!

I thank God that he has helped me to be clear that my priesthood is identified with His will and not a conformity to the organization or structure of the 'Parish' or 'Diocese' or any other kind of organization.

Of course we all need some kind of structure (and nothing will ever be perfect!!) but I try and allow God to work freely in me in whatever way he wishes. Celebrating Mass with the Community gives me the meaning of who and what God is, the meaning of the whole of creation, and what I and all these other people are doing here on this earth, spinning in the vast Universe. I and my priesthood are part of this massive and wonder-filled mystery.

Father Paul Dynan (written as a Seminarian at Allen Hall, Chelsea)

As a student for the priesthood, my view of priestly life is governed, not only by previous parish life and experience, but also by a life of prayer, study, and formation in the seminary.

I have to ask, where do I come from, and what is it that I bring with me? Where am I now, and where, and in what ways, will God's call lead me in the future? What is it that the Church is asking of me and what evidence is there that God has revealed Himself in my life? A life that I willingly yield to His service. The gift of self, in order to be of service to others.

Service has been integral to my life story. A full and busy career in the Health Service and the years of being father to my children since the loss of their mother when they were relatively young. These, and other examples of working for the community, mean that I am well acquainted with the concept of serving others.

My current ministry, however, is mainly one of study, but I look forward to that day, once ordained, that I may more fully serve God's people. To be an instrument in the lives of others, to assist them in turn, to reap the fruit of their own vocations and to minister in Word and in Sacrament in order that Christ is manifest in their lives, and those to whom they in turn will evangelise the Good News.

Heavenly Father, we pray that by your Grace, we may come to fully understand the mission that you have bestowed on each one of us, through the life, death and resurrection of your Son, our Lord Jesus Christ. By the gift of the Holy Spirit, may we obtain the zeal and tenacity to act upon, and remain in your service, that we, and all whom we serve, may come to dwell with you forever in your heavenly kingdom.

An Interview with Father Dick Ashton
(On the Occasion of the Thirtieth Anniversary of his Ordination to the Priesthood, printed in the *Parish Magazine*, Autumn 1996)

Father Ashton was born in May 1931, in Ilford, Essex. He was the eldest of two boys born to Alfred and Joyce Ashton. He was baptised – Richard James – in the Church of England, Barking Abbey by a lady Deaconess and was brought up in Ardleigh Green, Hornchurch (near the present Campion School).

Richard attended Wanstead High School from 1942 to 1949.

Three weeks after leaving school, he was in the British Army, the Royal Inniskilling Fusiliers. During this time he served in Jamaica, Cyprus, Egypt and Northern Ireland, leaving the forces in May 1953. This was followed by a further spell of part-time service in the Parachute Regiment (Territorial Army) 1955 – 1960.

On leaving the Army in 1953, Richard Ashton joined the staff in the General Office of Briggs Motor Bodies, Dagenham and stayed until 1956 when he entered Newland Park Teacher Training College, Bucks., for a two year course.

1957, to use Father's own words, marked a watershed, as he became a Catholic while in the College, the date of his reception being 15th October 1957. Asked what led up to him becoming a Catholic, Father says "I became more and more interested in the Catholic Church; I discovered that whatever its faults, in it resides all truth".

1958 – 1960 found Richard Ashton teaching in St. Mary's Catholic School, Hornchurch.

In 1960, he resigned from everything to study for the priesthood. Asked what led to this decision, his reply was one given by many men wishing to become priests. It was simply "to be nearer to God, the centre".

As for his parents' reaction, his mother was thoughtful but said nothing, and his father after a few moments' thought, said "Well I suppose it could have been worse, he might have considered being a burglar". Father Ashton adds "As an East-Ender, Dad was not joking …"

And so in 1960 Richard Ashton left this country once again, but this time bound for the Venerable English College, Rome, to study for the priesthood. Studies were in the Gregorian University, in Latin. He recalls "It was tremendous to be in Rome while the 2nd Vatican Council was on. The whole Church began to blossom anew". These studies continued for the next seven years and then on the Feast of Christ the King, 30th October 1966, Richard James Ashton was ordained priest, with both of his parents being present.

For the next two years Father Dick, as he prefers to be called, was Parish Priest at Barkingside, and from 1969 until 1972 he was Parish Priest at Westcliff-on-Sea. 1972 – 1973 found him at the Corpus Christi (RE) College after which he was assistant priest at Gidea Park for a year and then went on to East Ham Parish 1974-1976.

For the next thirteen years Father Dick was at Holy Trinity, Basildon, where he was responsible, along with the parishioners, for planning and building the church.

In 1989 he arrived here at Stanford-le-Hope and was responsible, along with the parishioners, for planning and building a new church. (*This is not a typing error*.)

Our Parish Priest is also Chaplain to the Old Comrades Association of the Royal Inniskilling Fusiliers, London Branch, and conducts their Service of Remembrance at the Cenotaph each year. (He looks quite distinguished, standing in Whitehall, robed in his alb and stole, next to the Cenotaph.)

Looking back over the last thirty years, there have been many changes in the Church. Father Dick recalls that in the year he was ordained the Liturgy was in process of changing from Latin to the vernacular. He continued: "Great hope was in the air. The Catholic Church was opening up to the world. Not all the hopes have been fulfilled but we still live in the love of God and our neighbour. We are still in the service of all, we hope".

In 1991 on the Silver Jubilee of his priesthood, Father Dick, thinking of the future, said "I think I can plod on a bit farther – watch this spot in 2016 – with the help of God and our brother and sister parishioners".

Another quote at that time, from Bishop McMahon at the end of a Mass to celebrate the occasion: "A man of great understanding who accepts people for what they are".

From us to you, Father Richard James Ashton, on this your Thirtieth Anniversary to the priesthood, we wish you well and ask that God may bless you and guide you in your pastoral duties and grant you happiness and satisfaction in the work that you are doing for Him (and us).

After his work at Stanford-le-Hope, Father Ashton moved in 1998 to Canvey Island as Parish Priest, retiring in 2000. He died in November 2011, and his Requiem Mass was held at St. Basil the Great, Basildon on November 29th. In the Order of Service for that Mass there is a brief outline of his life which I include here, especially for the many people in our parish who knew and loved this fine man.

Fr. Dick Ashton, RIP

Fr. Dick was a devoted Parish Priest, who will be sadly missed. His great loves were Rome, the Royal Inniskilling Fusiliers, the Parachute Regiment, the Venerable English College, and Education, notably church and military history. He was a fierce champion of Justice and Peace issues, praying and working for peace in the conflict between Israel and Palestine. In his priesthood, he had a particular devotion to Our Lady, and he was also the builder of two churches: Holy Trinity, Basildon and Our Lady and St. Joseph's, Stanford-le-Hope. The former was a new church, the latter to replace a church that had been destroyed by fire.

Fr. Dick's parents, Joyce and Jimmy, met on the boat from Australia to London; his grandparents had emigrated to Australia and history repeated itself as his only surviving brother, David, now lives in Australia.

Fr. Dick was a life member of the Essex Recusant Society, and an avid member of the Catholic Record Society. In the diocese, he served as part of BRES (Brentwood Religious Education Service), and ran encounter groups for young adults that were some of the beginnings of the Brentwood Catholic Youth Service.

Fr. Dick formed close links with a number of religious communities: the Brentwood Ursuline Sisters, the Missionary Sisters of Our Lady of Africa, the Sisters of Sion, and the Benedictines of Quarr Abbey, where he would spend his annual retreat.

Military links remained important to him, and he was chaplain to the Royal Inniskilling Fusiliers Regimental Association and the Combined Irish Regiments Association until his death.

Key dates in Fr. Dick's life were:

Born 10th May, 1931, in Ilford
Baptised (in his words) "by a Deaconess at Barking Abbey" C of E, 1931
Childhood in Ardleigh Green, Gidea Park

1942 – 1949	Wanstead High School
1949 – 1953	British Army – Royal Inniskilling Fusiliers
1955 – 1960	Parachute Regiment (Territorial Army)
1956 – 1958	Teacher Training
15th October 1957	Received into the Catholic Church
1958 – 1960	Teacher, St. Mary's School, Hornchurch
1960 – 1967	Seminarian, Deacon and Priest, Venerable English College Rome
30th October 1966	Ordained Priest in Rome by Cardinal Heard
1967 – 2011	Ministry in Brentwood Diocese, including time as an Assistant Priest at Barkingside, Westcliff, Gidea Park and East Ham, and as Parish Priest at Holy Trinity, Basildon, Our Lady and St. Joseph, Stanford-le-Hope, and Our Lady of Canvey and the English Martyrs, Canvey Island. He also spent time at Corpus Christi College and Elm Park, and served as Chaplain to Anchor House. It is very clear that Fr. Dick was held in great affection by parishioners.

At the Vigil Mass at St. Basil the Great on November 28th 2011, Father Andrew Hurley delivered the eulogy on his friend and colleague.

Father Dick and I were good friends. We both studied for the priesthood in Rome. Dick was at the Venerable English College; I wasn't. Quite unexpectedly and almost unnecessarily, probably because we were both studying for the Brentwood Diocese, he turned up at my college just to visit me. From that moment we became firm friends. From that moment there began a long, strong and warm friendship. I always had a great respect and affection for him.

On several occasions I went to the Holy Land with him. He was the organisational brains behind the escapade. He used to say, in his own inimitable way, "If you haven't found Jesus here at home you won't find him in the Holy Land". I have a recollection of starting out early in the morning about 6 o'clock and walking up to Jerusalem. It was very hot even at that hour and must have been the Sabbath. Singing or chanting was coming from the open windowed synagogue which we passed. In the distance was a hill and the sun already up. I said to Dick "What's that?", as though making a casual comment about the weather. He said, "Mount Zion". My reaction was "Wow". But that's where the eternal banquet is going to be at the end of time. The banquet open to all peoples, not restricted to a few. Everyone is invited. The kingdom is for all. That would have appealed to Dick who was a people person. He loved people.

When we arrived at the top of the hill in old Jerusalem I was tired, hot, hungry and thirsty and wondered why on earth I had come. I don't think it affected Dick in the same way what with his army training in the Inniskilling Fusiliers. Once in the old city I saw a plaque on the wall which said "If anyone wishes to be a follower of mine, let him deny himself, take up his cross every day and follow me". I seemed to take on a new lease of life at that moment.

On one occasion when we returned to England we received news at the airport that Dick's mother had died. I was glad that I was just able to be with him at that moment.

If there were only one person to testify how dedicated and pastoral Dick was, that would be enough. There would probably be many other examples that we don't know about. A lady who lived in East Ham when Dick was there said that for the last few years of her father's life Dick visited him and brought him much peace and comfort. His visits created a strong bond between them and eventually her father returned to the faith. Dick was also instrumental in bringing the same lady to the Church. I think Dick's faith was what the Italians call "una fede vissuta"– a faith lived out in practice in his daily life.

A friend, Edna D'Lima, said that young and old alike owe a lot to his kindness, understanding and his great ability to listen to everyone. He was non-judgemental and never had a bad word to say about anyone.

A debt of special thanks is owed to Isobel Parks who befriended and cared for Dick in the latter years of his life when he was failing and suffering considerably. Father Bob Hamil was also a faithful friend. I think mention should be made, too, of two friends from his Rome days who kept in touch over the years, Tim Firth and Clyde Johnson.

I am sure that Dick now knows that, in the light of eternity, not one single second of his suffering was in vain. It was united, especially in the Mass, to the redemptive Suffering, Death and Resurrection of Christ.

I often think that our life is like a tapestry and most of the time we are conscious of the reverse side, chaotic with no beauty, the untidy criss crossing of threads, the dark side reflecting the negative things of our life, the suffering. But one day, at the end of our lives, the front of the tapestry will be revealed to us. So beautiful. Up to now seen only by God, who all the time has been at work weaving that tapestry and creating a masterpiece. So it will now be for Dick.

Jesus said "If anyone loves me, the Father and I will come to him and make our home with him". How often, especially in Mass and Holy Communion, had Jesus and the Father made their home in the life of Father Dick. Now it is different. Jesus has come to take Dick home to be with the Father for ever. What joy now fills his heart.

We pray now in this Mass that Dick will experience that peace, that perfect peace, which is beyond our understanding, of being with God and the saints and his mother and father for ever and ever.

Joseph Foroma : Parishioner : January 2012

In August 2006 I went on a holiday visit back to Zimbabwe, my birthplace. On my return here with many emotional memories, I approached Fr. Martin Nott, the Parish Priest, and made a request.

A local Catholic Community in one of the impoverished regions of Zimbabwe, Chivhu rural area, met monthly for Mass under a tropical tree. Many of the faithful travelled long distances, some up to 20 miles, to the congregating point where Mass was celebrated by Franciscan priests from the nearest Mission. The congregation, numbering 200 or 300 Catholics each time, would spend the day together participating in Guild activities, Choir practice, Confessions etc., and eventually the Holy Mass. In any event, they would have to spend enough time before the long trek back home. Those who could manage it would bring some food so the Community would share after Mass.

My request to the Parish Priest was if it would be possible to arrange a retiring collection at some point to assist this Community in their efforts to build a church at the place where they met each month. Very understandingly, Fr. Martin listened to my story. He responded by saying that he would try his best, as God's Church was a universal Church. He explained, however, that there were already many financial demands on the Community at Stanford-le-Hope and Linford. The earliest slot for a retiring collection would not be for a couple of months.

Franciscan priests, Father Thomas Makamure and Father Walter Sean, at the new church site in Zimbabwe

Before this could happen, however, Fr. Martin was transferred to another parish. The new Parish Priest, Fr. David Clemens, was briefed about this in the handover on his arrival. On the appointed Sunday, I was offered an opportunity to briefly explain the essence of the retiring collection to the Congregation at all Masses. For some time, to help our parishioners understand the context, I had displayed photos at the back of the church of the Zimbabwean Community worshipping under a tree in the hot, tropical sun.

The response of the parishioners was truly phenomenal. On Sunday, 28th January 2007, an amazing £972 was raised from the retiring collections at all Masses. Father David said that he would round up this tremendous response to £1,000.

The money was transferred by Father David to the Worldwide Head of the Franciscan Missions in Dublin, Republic of Ireland, to ensure a safe and transparent transmission to the beneficiaries. The Franciscan Headquarters in turn transferred this gift over to the Head of the Franciscan Missions in Zimbabwe.

A worthy story of the tremendous generosity and selflessness of the Stanford-le-Hope parishioners that deserves to be recorded. God Bless.

Music in the Parish : Peter Preston and Gareth Outen : Parishioners

In the parish, we have been fortunate to have had our liturgy enhanced with much music and singing. An example of this was the ceremonial opening of the Sacred Heart Chapel in Horndon on the Hill in 1938.

In the old church in Stanford-le-Hope, the choir and organ were finally situated in the gallery to the rear of the church. Early photographs show the original site of the organ on the left of the altar. In the time of Father Carless the church organ at Our Lady and St. Joseph's was played by Mrs. Fitzmaurice, who retired in 1930 after many years of loyal service. Her place was taken by Miss Margaret McDade, known to her many friends as Molly. Many are the services that have benefited from her enthusiastic playing. Mr. Hagger was the choirmaster in those early days and under his able leadership the choir reached a very high standard and quality. He continued till well after the Second World War. For a year or so during the War, the choir was reinforced by German and Ukrainian prisoners of war, who in due course nearly all returned to their own homelands. Mr. Hagger later retired and went to live in London.

With Molly still playing the organ, Mr. Dennis Treston, the son of two of the original parishioners, took over the choir. Later, Terry Duggan was asked (or as he termed it "manouvered") to take up the reins of the choir. When Molly McDade retired, she moved to the south coast of England.

The make-up of the choir, like many others of its kind, has fluctuated over the years with members moving on, sometimes to the ultimate House of God, but it has remained very active with a standard of music and singing of a high quality in what might be called the 'more traditional' style.

The 11.00 a.m. Mass in the church of Our Lady and St. Joseph was often referred to as the "Parish Mass" and was usually a High Mass. This form of the Mass was used for Sunday and special occasions, and always had music and singing to embellish the liturgy. High Mass, for those who may have forgotten, had incense, acolytes and of course the music and singing, whereas Low Mass was a shorter, all-spoken Mass.

Some of the Sisters of Mercy were accomplished musicians. Sister M. Gertrude Horrigan, who taught at St. Joseph's School from the mid 1950s to the later 1960s, was a brilliant pianist and an organist. A great friend of the church organist Molly McDade, she often helped out at church services, especially when the schoolchildren were involved. In the nineteen seventies and eighties, Sister Philippa Kohlbecker, class teacher and then Head Teacher, promoted music in the school. It was her class of children who composed a song which won a county-wide competition and was frequently played on Essex Radio. Many will remember Sister Carmel McEnery who used to teach the violin, both at St. Joseph's School and at Hassenbrook Music School on Saturday mornings.

With the building of St. Augustine's in Corringham, a separate choir began. From the small beginning of one guitar played by Mike Coy, a small group of musicians was formed in 1977. This consisted of two guitars, Mike Coy and David Farrell, and a bass, played by Peter Preston. The singing part of this choir was made up in the main of the players' wives or partners. This new group expanded with the encouragement of some of the schoolchildren to join in, first on recorders but later violins and flutes. The music was in the modern idiom often referred to as Folk Mass, a bit of a misnomer as it was just a music group.

When Mr. and Mrs. Coy left the parish, Peter Preston took over the running of this choir, taking a lead role in parish music that was to extend through to the Autumn of 2011. Like its counterpart at Our Lady and St. Joseph's, the membership fluctuated over the years. There were invitations to the music group to play at the 175th anniversary of the local Methodist church, an event organised by Father Glynn, and to perform at the Fellowship of Churches' festivals. The group also played at the Aylesford Youth Day celebrations. After the closure of St. Augustine's the group then provided music for one of the weekend Masses in Stanford-le-Hope. Mr. Preston also provided accompaniment for the Masses offered in the Methodist Chapel Mass centre in Linford until it closed as a Mass centre in 2010. The group continued to serve in the new church in Stanford-le-Hope until the Autumn of 2011.

In the Sacred Heart Chapel at Horndon on the Hill, the Mass was often accompanied by the small organ there. At the Saturday evening vigil Mass, it was played by Jane Wheatley. When this Mass was transferred to St. Augustine's after the chapel was sold, Jane continued to play at the Mass.

Small music groups have been formed from time to time in East Tilbury, but a permanent choir did not emerge. Sister Barbara from the convent played her guitar at many of the Masses here, often accompanied by children on recorders. When Sister Barbara left the parish, the St. Augustine's music group visited the East Tilbury Mass centre quite often, to provide their own accompaniment to the Mass.

The organ that we hear in Our Lady and St. Joseph's, a Norwich "Sprowston", was badly damaged by smoke during the fire in the old church. After careful restoration by Norwich Organs, Norfolk, the organ was resited to the left of the altar in the new church, near to the choir seats.

Other church organists included Robert Sanders, who assisted Molly McDade and Mr. Mauro Shehan. The current organist and choirmaster is Mr. Gareth Outen.

Gemma Norris : Parishioner : Mother of Marc, Victoria and Annabelle : Memories of the Parent Teacher Association

I look back with great affection to the time of my involvement with the school, some thirty years ago, when my children were young.

In 1984 the P.T.A. organised the first mini marathon, which was held on a Sunday in March. The route started off at the Stanford-le-Hope recreation ground and then went all around the seawall and back via Manor Way and Billet Lane. It was an open event, which besides lots of people of parish and church attracted a great number of local and not so local people. In total, 289 took part and all of them finished the course, either running, jogging or walking. Sister Monica recalls walking the course together with Sister Helen Campion, but a few hundred yards from the finish Sister Helen got into a competitive mood and put on an impressive sprint to the finish. Everyone's time was recorded by head marshal Chris Meads and his team. Back at the church hall, a small team of volunteers made up certificates for everyone with their recorded time. The *Thurrock Gazette* published an article of the event with a photo!

Marathon Runners Raise £500

STANFORD-LE-HOPE'S first mini-marathon was a runaway success. The event attracted nearly 300 runners and raised about £500 for the town's St. Joseph's Church.

A total of 289 competitors set off from Stanford-le-Hope recreation ground on Sunday on the 4.8 miles road and cross-country course.

The first man to finish, Paul Emery, arrived back at the recreation ground after 27.3 minutes. He received a £10 cash prize from head marshal Chris Meads.

The Parent-Teacher Association of St. Joseph's School, in Scratton Road, Stanford-le-Hope, organised the race to raise money for a new public address system for the neighbouring church.

Mrs. Gemma Norris, the association treasurer, said the event raised £325 in entry fees alone, and the final total would be about £500.

She continued: "All the 289 that started finished the course. Between first and second it was very close. It was quite a keen contest."

Thurrock Gazette : Friday March 16th, 1984

At the time I was involved with the P.T.A., another Dutch family joined St. Joseph's by the name of Hendrikx. We were often asked about the Dutch traditions around St. Nicholas and before Christmas one year we prepared a little play for the children, called *St. Nicholas Meets Father Christmas.* Peter Hendrikx (the dad) was in the role of St. Nicholas and I can't remember who took the role of Father Christmas. St. Nicholas's helpers have to be very acrobatic and very colourfully dressed, so the pupils who were in the gym club played these parts. They somersaulted and did cartwheels all the way through the hall to the stage. Quite spectacular. Little Jordy Hendrikx, who was not in school yet, but allowed to come with his mother, was most impressed and never recognised his dad. Jordy Hendrikx is no longer little, the family moved to New Zealand, and Jordy is now a professor of geology at one of the universities in America.

There was a time that pantomimes were organised and played by members of the P.T.A. It was such good fun. One pantomime in particular springs to mind, when the pantomime imitated a Punch and Judy show. Instead of the puppets, we used the heads of the P.T.A. who pretended to be puppets. Lots of one-liners, I can't remember them, but one did include something about a flying nun!

Jan Goona (nee Spoors) : Parishioner

I was born into this parish in 1966 and have lived in Stanford-le-Hope all my life, attending St. Joseph's School and celebrating all my Catholic passages in our church. I made my First Communion in 1974 when Father Bart Lynch was curate and he officiated at my group's First Communion Mass. I recall he said it was the first of many things he could assist us with in our Church lives and said he would "marry" us in later years. He was a great communicator with us as children, seeming young for a priest!!

When I got married in September 1992, Father Bart was Parish Priest at Holy Trinity, Basildon. It was during this time that the new church in Stanford was being constructed, so my husband Paul and I were married at Our Lady Star of the Sea, Tilbury, and Father Bart did indeed, at my request, marry me!! It was so important to me that I had a link to my parish when I married as "my church" was unavailable to me, and Father Bart provided that link. A great man, sadly missed. RIP Father Bart.

Maureen Foulkes : Parishioner : February 2012

I suppose my first impression of Stanford-le-Hope was before I even moved here. It was when I was at school at Grays Convent. There were girls who came from Stanford-le-Hope on the train. The name Stanford-le-Hope seemed very exotic, it sounded like a romantic, medieval name. The girls from Stanford-le-Hope were very nice and very kind.

Before I came to live in the parish, I met Fr. Bart Lynch, who was the chaplain at Orsett hospital. During my first pregnancy, I was in hospital for a long time and he was a regular visitor. Everybody at the hospital loved him. He seemed to know all the nurses by name. Everybody used to spruce themselves up when they knew he was coming. One very down-to-earth lady from Tilbury Parish stated: "I don't know why you're all bothering. He isn't allowed to get married".

I had a difficult pregnancy and had gathered enough of little snippets of information from medical staff to make me very concerned. Father Lynch knew this. On the morning I was to be induced, I was very frightened. Father Lynch came in at half past six in the morning, and sat with me, holding my hand, until nine o'clock when the nurses came in to take me off to be induced. I never forgot his kindness. You could say that he revived my faith.

We had lived in London in the first few years of our marriage. In the parish there, nobody spoke to us. We went to several socials and nobody spoke to us there either. In fact the only contact we had with the parish was the week before we were leaving, when someone called round to try to sign us up to the tax covenant scheme. Although our next parish at Chadwell St. Mary was more welcoming, the sense of warmth when we moved to St. Joseph's was a wonderful surprise. I remember the first Mass we attended at St. Joseph's. We were welcomed at the door by George McNamara, who smiled at us and nodded. The second week he spoke to us. The third week it was as if he had known us all our lives. It was such a change for us.

The Parish Priest was Father John Taylor. He always had time for you. He had this gift of concentration which made you feel that he had absolutely nothing else to do in the day but listen to what you had to say. He was an excellent listener.

When Father Gostling arrived, there was some concern about his ascetic appearance. We need not have worried. At one of his first Masses at St. Joseph's, one of the very little children called out "We know that Father Gostling drinks Ribena". The delighted smile that slowly grew across the face of our new Parish Priest reassured us all. And this was the priest who was seen to genuflect in a London theatre as he left the main aisle to find his seat. As he afterwards explained "It was the red colour of the furnishings that reminded me so much of St. Joseph's".

I was pleased when the parish pilgrimages to Aylesford were organised. I now had two young children, and new friends in the parish would help me with my sons when we went to Aylesford. Anne Groody, Mary Stockwell, Peggy Sharp and others became friends and we shared the looking after of our children in a kind of kibbutz system. I remember how everyone rallied round when my father died and arranged the food for the reception, making quiches, sandwiches and cakes, and even organising the cutlery.

When my husband left and I was to bring up our three children on my own, the parishioners, and particularly the Sisters, were wonderful. For a while I told nobody of my plight; I was simply too embarrassed. It got to the point where I had no food to give my children. I remember walking along King Street one night, wondering how to feed the children, when I met Mary, a friend and fellow parishioner, coming out of the butchers. For the first time, the story came out. Mary was carrying a pound of mince, which she put into my hand with the words "There's the dinner for tonight". Mary went straight off to the convent, and by the time that I had walked home Sister Philippa was waiting for me with a box of groceries. The Sisters must have raided their own cupboards. They were so kind to us and the new Parish Priest, Father Dick Ashton, was just as kind, always willing to listen to me. He was such an intelligent man, so interesting, with such a fund of stories.

My friends organised that the children could be looked after on a Wednesday evening so that I could attend CDOT, the opera group in Grays.

As a member of the P.T.A., I recall the pantomimes we did for the children at St. Joseph's School. The children seemed to enjoy the sight of their parents making idiots of themselves. We did a spoof of the Muppet Show, and there was a version of Jack and the Beanstalk. At one of the Christmas plays, Cinderella, my son David played a Chancellor. There was a running joke that everyone pushed him over, until his younger brother, Colin stood on his chair in the audience and shouted "Don't you hit my brother!" It brought the house down. And then there were all those summer fetes. We always used to say that Sister Monica had a direct line to the "Clerk of the Weather" as I can hardly remember a rainy day when we were all out in the open air.

In 1999 we all went, as usual, to the Forty Martyrs celebration at Aylesford. There had been a craft fair earlier at Aylesford for us to look around. During the Mass, the Stanford parishioners were sitting on the first two benches in front of the High Altar. The Bishop was giving the homily, and as he said the words "As the bells ring out for the millennium" there was the sound of bells. We were all a bit disconcerted about where the sound was coming from. Then we saw Hazel Earl frantically trying to stuff her gloves and her scarf and her woolly hat into her handbag. We realised that the noise of bells was coming from her handbag. And nothing would stop this wretched noise. Hazel was fiddling with something, apparently trying to turn it off. The Bishop was watching and everybody turned to look at her. Doug Iles nearly fell off his bench with laughter. Hazel Earl was a lady of immense dignity, so she picked the bag up, turned, genuflected to the altar and went off down the aisle in front of the amazed glances of everybody there. This klaxon was banging away like a fire alarm. We could hear it gradually disappear into the distance. It was an alarm clock that Hazel had bought at the craft fair.

I remember Father David Clemens. He had a very dry sense of humour, he was so funny. When people turned up at the presbytery, they could be met with the words "Oh no, not you again!" He was great fun and so interesting to listen to. I gather he was quite a gourmet cook. They used to have deanery meetings, and the local clergy were always keen to come to St. Joseph's! When I was very ill in Basildon hospital, Father David visited to give me the Last Rites. Father Paul also came to see me, and he remembered my name when he came to our parish many years later.

I recall a Mass on a Holy Day of Obligation, when all the schoolchildren were present in the old church The church was full and we were almost at the back, on the right, near to an enormous statue of the Sacred Heart. My son David, who was then a toddler, got bored and moved into the aisle. His eye level was at the base of the statue, so he leant back to look up. "Oh, it's you, Jesus" came the little voice. "You've no shoes on, Jesus". Then we all heard "This little piggy went to market …" Sister Monica was sitting in the pew just in front of us, and we saw her shoulders shaking as she tried not to laugh out loud.

Among the many school trips when parents were asked to help, I particularly remember those where the children wore costumes, whether Tudor (Kentwell Hall at Long Melford, Suffolk) or Victorian (Colne Valley). In some places they were not allowed to bring a packed lunch in a plastic bag or box, or carry a canned drink, as these were not available in those times. The children were intrigued about paper wrappings for their lunch but were not so keen on the curled up sandwiches which were the result. One of the actors at Kentwell Hall, dressed as an Elizabethan gardener, stole a kiss from a teacher. She slapped his face and called him a "saucy knave". The children were open-mouthed. We all had a few children to look after, and I taught my little group to bow and curtsey. When they did this to the 'Lord of the Manor' he responded with the words "Thou hast well schooled children, Dame. Dost thou whip them oft?"

One year, the Advent wreath caught fire at the Vigil Mass. The first Advent candle had burned all the way to the bottom, and the flames began to consume the leaves. One of the parishioners noticed and hissed to my son, Richard, who was an altar server. His attempts to put out the fire with the sleeves of his cassock were less than successful, and the flames were eventually quenched with Holy Water.

Apart from all the fun and laughter over the years, my main impression of our parish is its wonderful sense of family. There is so much genuine warmth here. There is an atmosphere of being part of a small village. The parish has also given me so many good and true friends. I feel I would do anything for them, just as they have supported me with such kindness.

Matthew and Pat McDonald : Parishioners : February 2012

We were married at our Lady and St. Joseph's during the War, on 13th June 1943. Father Snell married us. We got married on Whit Sunday afternoon, which I don't think was really allowed. There was only Pat's family there as none of my family could come over from Belfast.

In the early fifties, we used to go around the parish doing house collections for parish funds. I think it was on a Sunday. We had notebooks with the names of the people and the amount of their weekly donation. It was usually just a few pennies from each family. I remember that another helper was Angela Byrne, who must have been very young at that time. We would take the money back to Father Watson at the presbytery. We often just left it on the table there because Father Watson would be outside doing his gardening.

Many years later, when our son got married, Father Hibbert mentioned that we had been married during wartime, when services were rather plain, and asked if we would like a proper Nuptial Mass. Pat asked the Parish Priest if she could wear white and was told she could wear white with a purple sash. After the Mass, Father Hibbert asked us to pop into the presbytery. Pat said "Oh no, not more jobs" because we sometimes helped him. But when we went inside, there was a nice wedding breakfast laid out for us. A lovely Irish wedding breakfast. He was a lovely man, very down-to-earth. You could speak straight to him and he would speak straight back to you.

Before St. Teresa's Mass centre was opened, we used to walk from Corringham over to St. Joseph's for Mass, and our children walked with us. We would even do this for Midnight Mass at Christmas. It was no hardship as we had the kids with us and we might call in at a few houses on the way home, and arrive back at two in the morning, when the children would open their Christmas presents and then fall into bed.

We had a Youth Club down at St. Teresa's, which was open to all young people from the area, whether Catholic or not. There were about seventy young people who attended regularly. I bought a couple of small billiard tables, we had an old gramophone, and there were quite a few games, including quoits and darts. Pat ran a canteen which was just at the door where the youngsters came in. I remember we put up a notice that said PARK YOUR WEAPONS HERE, so it gives you some idea of a few of our regulars. There were some knives, the occasional bicycle chain and even a ring with a spike. This was at the time at the end of the nineteen fifties when there were gangs of youths coming into the area just to start trouble. But I have to say we never had any bother at all. An assistant priest, Father O'Brien, used to call in each Wednesday night and talk to the young people, and when he wasn't there they would ask for him.

You have to say that St. Teresa's Hall was a really rough building. It was concrete, and there was always a lot of dust, no matter how many times it was swept. On wet days, this soon turned into mud. We started a building fund committee down at St. Teresa's, to build a proper church on the site. We raised funds by running a Tote, selling tickets as far away as Fords in Dagenham. I remember Pat well into her pregnancy, perched on the back of a friend's scooter as they went round collecting the Tote tickets. There was Bingo on the Saturday night, when St. Teresa's was packed to the door. Tom Stocks used to call the numbers. (*Tom was also the treasurer of the Building Fund Committee, and it was his job to ensure that all the money raised was safely deposited in a special bank account.)* After each Bingo session, we had to clean the hall and get it ready for Sunday Mass, putting away the tables, organising the chairs and kneelers (concrete floors) and arranging fresh flowers.

There was a wonderful big wooden Altar, solid mahogany, which I think came from the East End. We got a boy to sell the local weekly paper for a penny at the door, and raised money to buy yards and yards of material from Pitsea Market which we made into an Altar Cloth and curtains. It was all green and white. We scrubbed up all the stage until it came up white. There was a big fire in the middle, but we never lit it. The people kept the hall warm just by being there. There were a few leaks through the corrugated iron roof but we managed to patch them up. There was a big congregation every Sunday, including a lot of Catholics from Fobbing.

The St. Teresa's Building Fund Committee members were really keen on what they were trying to achieve, and there were a few non-Catholics there as well. There were plans drawn up for the new church, with a model and everything. It looked lovely. They were going to put in a centre for midwives and a clinic to serve the community. These were real plans, not pie in the sky, but it all came to nothing when the old Mass centre was sold on to a house building company.

We went to St. John's for a few times, when the Vicar offered his church to be used for a weekly Catholic Mass, but we soon got back into the habit of going back to our Lady and St. Joseph's. It was a lovely church for us, we liked it. After all, it was where we were married.

Of course a lot of the little chapels and Mass centres in the parish were closed down over the years. Apart from St. Teresa's and then St. Augustine's in Corringham, there was East Tilbury, Horndon, Orsett Camp and Orsett Hospital, Vange and Linford. It looks more like one of those business plans than anything else, having one big church in the middle and nothing else. Just like what they are doing in the National Health Service.

When it came up to our Diamond Wedding Anniversary, Father Martin Nott asked us if we would like a full Nuptial Mass. He organised a special service just for us, and led the clapping when we walked out at the end of the Mass. We shall never forget that kindness. Gareth Outen organised the music. It was beautiful. Five years later we had another Mass to celebrate our sixty-fifth anniversary. Father David Clemens was the Parish Priest then. When I went up to the altar with my husband, Father looked at me very carefully, then asked "Are you sure you weren't a child bride?

<u>Doug Iles : Parishioner : February 2012</u>

We lived in St. George's Avenue, Grays, in the parish of St. Thomas, where our oldest children started school. When our seventh child, Christopher was born, there were too many of us to live in this three bedroomed house and so we moved to Southend Road, Stanford-le-Hope in 1971. Our younger children started their education at St. Joseph's, when the Sisters were a real presence in the school. Now that the Sisters have left the school, we do miss them terribly.

We were just over the road from the old church; in fact we were so close that we could see the Sanctuary light burning from our front lounge window. We could almost have gone to Mass in our pyjamas. My mother lived with us in a granny flat, and she would walk out into the traffic on the way to Mass, holding up a commanding hand to stop the cars.

The first thing we noticed when we moved to our Lady and St. Joseph's was the lovely, family atmosphere. It was so family orientated. I had visited the church to go to Mass before we moved into the parish, and it seemed so intimate and family centred, not at all like the feeling of some bigger churches or the impersonal coldness of a cathedral.

I remember the old gas heaters that hummed away in the background, trying to keep the church warm. As we lived so close to the church, my wife Monica and I soon got involved in the maintenance of the old building and the repairs that were always needed. Often these were quite minor things like changing light bulbs or putting up the odd shelf, but there were also things to do at the presbytery. I remember that Father Martin was not very good at DIY and was really grateful for some help. John Flitcroft and I went down to see him at Dunmow after he left our parish. He was so delighted to see us. Thinking about it now, I always got on well with all of the Parish Priests since my own arrival in the parish.

When we first moved into our Stanford home, I bought a square scaffolding platform that could rise to sixteen feet. It was used to decorate and repair our own house, but then it was quite easy to move it over to the church. Every two to three years, we had to paint the interior of the church from head to toe, after first cleaning off all the mould. Because the walls were solid concrete, mould grew very readily. We had to use green scourers and hot water to remove the mould before the painting could begin. It was a bit like painting the Forth Bridge. We had hardly finished one repainting before we had to gather another team of volunteers and start all over again. It was a real struggle to keep that church clean.

On one occasion, I made a bit of a mistake with some electrical cable that fed into a fan heater. When Father Bart Lynch went to switch off the fan heater, there was a great tongue of flame. I don't think he ever touched that switch again. Whilst we're on the subject, I should tell you that I was the one to install the electrics for the heater in the Confessional which later caused the church to catch fire! People were supposed to switch the heater off at the wall, but some chose to switch off on the heater itself, leaving the flex live. When the flex frayed, the fire began. (*To be fair to Doug Iles, our old church never did actually burn down. When experts were called in to assess the extent of the smoke damage, they discovered something much more serious. The concrete shell of the church was suffering from concrete cancer, rendering the building unsafe. Left untreated, it could have caused sections of the walls and roof to fall away and even collapse. Who can say what trouble was averted by this early diagnosis. With the benefit of hindsight, we may now see the enforced demolition of the church as a blessing in disguise.*)

I remember during one school holiday when I was doing some repair work in the church, high up on an aluminium ladder. My ladder bent over and then broke, and I was thrown back onto the Altar, where I cut my head open. Fortunately, my next door neighbour was a doctor and he stitched up my head, doing quite a good repair job himself. The funny thing is, I didn't like to tell anybody about it at the time. I mentioned it only many years later, because I didn't want anyone to get upset about what had happened.

On one occasion, I took Father Bart and one of my sons sailing in my little Mirror Dinghy. We sailed from Mucking Creek Wharf down to Southend and back. Father loved it. Our only problem was the lack of toilet facilities in the Dinghy, so we had to improvise!

I still get bulletins from Father Gerald Gostling in South Africa. That's a really tough job. There are terrible conditions out there. He writes about female children who are not valued and who sometimes simply 'disappear'. And of course AIDS is rife. Fortunately, he is still in good health, much like our own Bishop Thomas and there are no signs of Father Gerald retiring.

John Flitcroft and I used to go to our Essex Austin 7 Club meetings in Chelmsford, and our route would take us past the Bishop's house in Stock. "Hello Bish!" we would call out from the car window as we drove by or "Goodnight Bish!" as we returned. When John became too ill to drive his own Austin Seven, I bought it from him. He wanted a friend to look after it.

Over the years I was a member of the Parish Council and the Premises Committee and a School Governor, although I am not a meetings person. I tend to fret at meetings, and sometimes I just want to get on and do things rather than spend too much time talking about them. They did serve the function of bringing us up to date with what the current problems were, although we didn't often solve them.

I recall the chaos after the old church caught fire and we had to make interim arrangements for parish Masses. We used St. Joseph's Hall and Corringham, whilst the new church was being built. Fortunately for the parish, Hazel Earl's bequest in 2011 reduced the mortgage debt substantially. (*Note: The remaining debt of £22,000 was almost completely paid off in the twenty months to June 2012.*)

There was quite a lot of maintenance of buildings and grounds needed in the parish, and I think that that is why Monica and I each received the Benemerenti medal in 2001 for thirty years service to the church. We used to joke it was for thirty years of undiscovered mistakes. I think that the biggest contribution we made was when Monica took over the instruction for First Communions after the Sisters left the school.

We finally decided to move up to March in Cambridgeshire to be near our narrowboat, saving us a hundred miles round trip each time we used it. It was now moored outside our front door on the River Nene. Later on, when Monica became more ill, I realised that we had to go back to Stanford, to be near our friends and family.

In the old days there were quite a few parish Socials, probably about once a month. I remember Peter and June Preston helping to organise many of them. There don't seem to be quite so many Socials these days. All we old stagers are running out of energy. Perhaps it's time for the youngsters to take over.

We are so lucky to have Father Paul, and it's lovely to meet his children and grandchildren too. It's obvious he adores them. That little one dressed up as a donkey in the Nativity Mass! His experience helps to make him such a lovely priest. He really understands life.

Kevin Greenan : Parishioner : February 2012

My father owned a company called Greenan Contractors, and he built the first St. Augustine's Hall, roughly where the supermarket is now. It was round about that time that he died. Greenans seem to have had a longstanding contract to build many of the churches in Thurrock, mainly because he didn't charge enough! One of my brothers said that if we were atheists we would have made a lot more money.

I was born in County Monaghan in Ireland. We all had to come to England for a series of operations for my sister, who was partially blinded when building lime got into her eye. We lived in a little terraced house in bombed out Woolwich. Coming from the Irish countryside and seeing all the bomb sites, I just thought that this was what England looked like. I knew I didn't like the place, so when I was five and a half I ran away from home to get back to Ireland on my own. I knew I had arrived by boat, so I got onto a boat down the river. It turned out it was the Woolwich ferry. The police found me wandering the streets and took me home. My mother, always very respectful towards the law, thanked the young policeman for returning her lost son. As soon as the door closed, I got a hiding down the hall for the shame of having the police on the doorstep.

There were seven children then, and three more children were born in England. We moved out to Belhus Park. Although the family split up a little when the children grew up, the whole family lives in Esssex, apart from me here in London and my son who owns the flat above me.

My wife and I eventually bought a house on the Homesteads in Fourth Avenue and later had a house built in Central Avenue. That was about the time that my involvement in parish life really began. It would have been the early seventies. I remember Father Collings and Father Taylor and, of course, Father Bart Lynch. A fine priest, the finest priest I met in my whole life. He had a natural Irish warmth He didn't have any airs and graces. He exuded kindness and he never saw bad in anybody. He wasn't a holy man in a pompous, pious way and he had a great sense of humour. If the homily wasn't up to much I would say to him as I left the church "There's another sermon you can bury". And he would reply "Thanks for the encouragement, Kevin." Father John Taylor, there was another brilliant priest.

My one, overriding memory of Stanford-le-Hope, Corringham, Horndon and East Tilbury was that it was a community parish You don't see that very often. It really pulled together and the attendances at Masses as well showed that. One of the advantages of the parish that it would be easy to overlook was having the convent there. The Sisters were so brilliant. I remember when they decided to send Sister Mary Aidan to Africa I nearly went up to the Mother Superior's house to ask her what on earth she was doing. Of course, in time Sister Aidan grew to love Africa and her work there. And then there is Sister Monica. I don't know anyone who doesn't love her. Running through all of these people there is a fund of humour.

I remember when Father John Taylor first arrived in the parish. There was a rat problem in the presbytery. One morning he walked into the kitchen to be met not by a priest or a housekeeper but a huge, fat rat that was in no hurry to leave the kitchen. It had obviously been there longer than he had. When Father Taylor went into the church, he stated "Either the rats go or the priest goes". My dad came out on an emergency call. The floorboards were undermined by all the rat runs, and a new concrete floor had to be laid. My dad was convinced that there were also rats in the garden shed, and went in there with his two Jack Russells to root them out. As a joke, his mate locked the door on him. The Jack Russells scented rats and set up a racket and my father was cursing in the dark. Fathers Taylor and Lynch came out to see what all the fuss was about, but when they realised it was just Mick Greenan locked in the shed with the rats, they went back into the presbytery and left them to it.

There was often a Parish New Year's Dance down at the Bata Hotel in East Tilbury. One year, when Father Lynch came back from Ireland, he asked everybody what the dance was like. Everyone told him what they thought he wanted to hear. The music was wonderful, terrific, lovely. In fact the band was so good that the drummer kept his sandwiches and a beer on top of one of his drums. I told him that the band was rubbish. Since he heard from a hundred people that the band was good and only one person said it was bad, he booked them again for around Easter time. He couldn't sell any tickets at all.

In the seventies and eighties there was a surge in the Catholic Church which also affected our parish. Following Vatican Two, there was a renewed interest in Human Rights. We parishioners came out of our shells, but in a positive way. I formed a few Human Rights groups and found the parishioners in Stanford so receptive. If you asked for help, you got help. One example is that at that time there was a terrible persecution of Soviet Jews. There was one case of two married professors who lost their jobs and were relocated to the edge of Siberia with their young children, where they barely survived. We organised a campaign for people to write to them. They had to be postcards, so that the letters did not need to be opened by the authorities, and there could be no hint of criticism of the regime, just words of encouragement, prayer, kindness. This was a London wide campaign and there were many postcards, but particularly from one place: Stanford-le-Hope. People had such open hearts. There was so much mail that eventually the entire family was kicked out of Russia and they went to live in West Germany. On another occasion, I organised a parish coach into London to a demonstration where the women from Northern Ireland were talking about the Troubles there. We had complete backing from our priests for such things. There was an atmosphere of complete trust.

One of the nuisances of the old Parish Church in Stanford was that after the Masses you just couldn't get out. There were so many people at the only exit, meeting and greeting each other. It's not really a criticism but something of a wonder. The parish was a community. I loved that old church and was heartbroken when I heard the news of the damage to it. I admit that it could be cold inside, but it did look something when you came along Southend Road and saw the building with the crucifix in front of it. When there were processions, hundreds of parishioners turned out.

When I started a parish magazine, I chose the name *Link*, because I wanted to link together the people from Stanford, Corringham, East Tilbury and Horndon. The close links within the parish made it easy for all people to speak to each other, including the Parish Priest. One disadvantage of having Westminster Cathedral as my local church is the sheer size of the team who serve it. There isn't that ease of access that I remember in Stanford-le-Hope. Now you effectively have to organise an appointment to talk with someone.

When my son Mark started at St. Joseph's School he had a great time at the school. He loved it. He couldn't wait to get out of the door to go to school. He became an actor in adult life, but he was an actor from the age of four or five. In the School Nativity Play he was given the role of the Innkeeper. They soon realised that they had given the longer line parts to the wrong people, because within a day Mark knew all the lines of the play perfectly. In the rehearsals, he acted as an unofficial prompt, quietly supplying lines when others forgot them. The play was going to be presented in the big hall at Hassenbrook School. The night before, I heard him crying in his bedroom. My wife and I talked to him. "What's wrong?" we asked. "It's the school play." "Don't you want to do it? Have you forgotten the lines?" "No." "What's wrong then? What are your lines?" "There's no room in the Inn." "Well, what's wrong with that?" "But Daddy, I wish there was." I told the Sisters at the school. The next night in Hassenbrook Hall, Joseph goes up to the Inn to knock at the door and one of the Sisters reaches over and grabs my hand and whispers "For God's sake, don't let them in!" I remember how he would look up and beam at me in Mass when the priest announced that the reading was from the Gospel of St. Mark.

We had great Christmas Bazaars in those days. They were big social events as well as raising a lot of money. One year there was a problem. The queue to see Father Christmas snaked all the way through the school, and the queue wasn't moving at all. There were hundreds of kids trying to see Santa. Sister Mary Aidan went down to Santa's grotto to see what was happening. Santa had an Irish accent and was saying to one child, "And dear Baby Jesus …." He was telling every child individually the full story of Christ's nativity. Of course, he couldn't see the queue. Sister Mary Aidan pulled back the curtain and said "Skip the story, give them the gift and get on with it!"

We used to organise a St. Patrick's Day Dance every year in St. Joseph's Hall. We never hired a band, just playing records and having a good time. One year, the windows were wide open as there was no air conditioning, and the music floated outside. The petrol station next door was owned by an eccentric lady who had a pet duck that followed her around. She went to the *Thurrock Gazette* complaining that we had played IRA music at the St. Patrick's Night Dance. It was headlined in the next edition of the paper, as this was the beginning of the Troubles in Northern Ireland. I seem to remember the headline "Catholic Church Plays IRA Music". We had no warning that this was to be published. I called the *Gazette* and they came over to St. Joseph's. I showed them the albums I'd played. We went through them all. The only album that could possibly have been interpreted in this way, and it was a long way from what had been alleged in the paper, was a record of old Irish Ballads, the sort of record that used to be on sale at petrol stations. And yes, I had bought the record from the shop in this lady's petrol station! The next week, the *Thurrock Gazette* published that story. For the next few weeks parishioners stopped calling into the petrol station to fill up their cars after Mass. They had their own ad hoc boycott.

They were great days, and the community spirit was just as strong when someone suffered loss. I recall a lovely young couple from Northern Ireland who moved into Corringham. They hadn't been in the parish long when they lost their little boy in a tragic accident at home. They hardly knew anybody, but when the little white coffin came into St. Joseph's Church there wasn't even standing room, as the church was packed to the door. The entire parish attended the Requiem Mass. There was just total love and it was hard for everybody. I spoke to an old member of the family who came over from Northern Ireland, expecting to be the only people at the service. The family was so grateful for the support.

These days, I don't get to visit Stanford-le-Hope very often, but if I do meet up with a parishioner we often spend time reminiscing about the parish. It really is such a special place.

George and Maura McNamara : Parishioners : February 2012

We first met in England at the Thomas McCurtain Hurling and Football Club Dance in a Parish Hall in Dagenham. We were from neighbouring districts in Ireland, and so we did know each other beforehand. We were married in Ireland in 1956 and moved into the parish in 1957. I remember that there were fourteen nuns in the convent then. We were in the parish forty nine years before we moved over here to Chelmsford. Maura was a nurse in the National Health Service for forty years and I worked for the Ford Motor Company.

We bought a house in Abbots Hall Chase. It was all fields in those days, there was no Abbots Hall Estate then. Of course, later came the big developments of the East Ham and West Ham housing estates, which were built very quickly. I remember the Londoners moving in and asking me where were all the red buses. Some of them couldn't believe it and went back to London after just a few days.

Maura was a midwife on the district for a while and she cycled around from Fobbing to East Tilbury to help the families. When she went out at night she would ask her patient to leave a light on in the front part of the house so she would know which house to go to.

Father Hibbert was our first Parish Priest in Stanford. He was a lovely priest and he had a great sense of humour. His mother was his housekeeper at the presbytery. He used to go on holiday to Ireland quite a lot. We would ask him where he was going and he would say "Canvey Island to Liverpool" because he travelled with a fellow priest from Canvey.

One of the things I liked to do was to meet and greet people when they came into the church. I used to look out for any new faces and make sure they were made welcome. One young couple, Will and Mary Dollard, came out from Dagenham to live in our parish. They were dreading it as they didn't know anyone in the area. They told their local councillor, Councillor O'Dwyer, that they were moving to Stanford and he told them "George Mcnamara is there, you'll know him when you get there. He'll be at the back of the church organising something." When I greeted them they said "You must be George McNamara."

When the saying of Mass in English was introduced, the nuns would sit together in the church to make their responses, and they had their own ideas about the speed of those responses. Some people in the congregation thought that they were "dragging it out", but the nuns were keen to show how it should be done and there was no way to make fourteen nuns speed it up a bit.

During those early years, a lot of Irish people came over to live and work in England. With them came quite a number of priests from Killaloe, who worked in the Diocese of Brentwood. Some of them stayed in the diocese, whilst others returned to Ireland as Parish Priests or as teachers. Quite a few of these priests, being young men, were keen to play a game of Irish Football at the Club we had set up in Dagenham, if only to get on the pitch for a few minutes. We would say to one of the players "Pretend that you're injured and we'll let Father X on for a bit of a game."

We remember Father Bart Lynch when he was like a youngster, shaped like a beanpole. He had lots of sisters, seven or eight, and they were all very slim too. Father Bart married all four of our children. The Parish Priest then was Father Taylor. They made a brilliant team. Father Taylor was a lovely man. I remember that we bought him a new Ford car so that he could drive around the parish, but then the Bishop moved him to another parish. We kept in touch with him after he left. Father Taylor was a man of the people, very down-to-earth. Of all the time we spent in the parish, that was the best time. Father Taylor and Father Lynch were such a driving force in the parish.

Our four children all went to St. Joseph's School. In those days it was run by Sister Aidan. She was very strict but the school was good. Our children must have had a good grounding there because they all went on to university later. We remember the School Sports Days and the Christmas plays. One year, in the mid seventies, I recall the children went out into the street in Stanford to perform their Nativity play. The Christmas Bazaar was another big event for the parish, and sometimes we would raise two thousand pounds, which was a lot of money in those days. Everyone would muster in. Maura used to make cakes and raffle them, and it was possible to make as much as a hundred pounds on a cake.

When Father Ashton first arrived in the parish, we went down on the Friday evening for Mass, but there was no church there because of the fire. I knew Father Ashton from his work at the hospital in Basildon and he said "Where can I say Mass?" I said to him "Father Gostling has made some arrangements at the presbytery. I think he said he built an Altar there." Father Ashton replied "Well if he did he took it with him!" We rushed over to the convent and arranged with the Sisters for Mass to be said at the convent chapel that evening.

For a while we had Mass said in St. Joseph's Hall, with the big room on the other side of the corridor as an overspill when the hall became too crowded. We made what use we could of St. Augustine's in Corringham.

When the new church was built, they left the grounds in a terrible state. There was rubbish everywhere, and the presbytery garden didn't look good. I didn't like the idea of the neighbours looking at all the mess. I got onto the Probation Service to see if they could help. A supervisor came out to take a look and he said "I can give you ten men, one day a week, for as long as it takes to clean this all up." It worked really well.

Three Parish Stalwarts : John Flitcroft, Geoff Helm and George McNamara

One of the workers saw that we were hiring skips to take away the rubbish, and he arranged to do this with his van. He couldn't read or write, but I had an agreement written out and his friends read it to him.

When it was all cleared, I decided to have a lawn laid to make the presbytery garden look better. The Knights of St. Columba helped me to lay this lawn whilst Father Dick Ashton was away on holiday. A couple of days after his return, a friend of Father Dick called round at the presbytery and saw the lawn. "Doesn't the lawn look lovely!" he said to the priest. "Where?" asked Father Dick. He hadn't even noticed.

At the time of their Golden Wedding Anniversary, George and Maura were presented with the Benemerenti medal for service to the parish. Father John Taylor, Maura Mcnamara, Father Bart Lynch, Father Martin Nott, George McNamara

About 1965 I had a chat with Father Hibbert about starting a tax covenant scheme for our weekly church collections. I think they call it Gift Aid now. After a while, he said to me "If you want to start up a scheme, do it". So I did. I ran the scheme for twenty-eight years. In those days we didn't have computers, so there were all bits of paper to be signed. Our daughters used to call in at houses after school to get the necessary papers signed. Now my daughter runs a Gift Aid scheme here in Springfield Parish.

I used to go down to the church early on Sunday morning with a set of keys to open up the church. Sometimes it would be raining and there might be a couple of people with mobility needs, and I didn't like the idea of them getting wet as they waited for the church to open.

When the old church had to be pulled down, there was the question of what to do with the various items of religious furniture in the building. It was decided to store them away safely until the new church could accommodate them. Amongst these items was a life sized statue of Our Lady. It was kept in a garage on the church site for a few years. When it got to the time to place it in the new church, it was discovered that someone had given it a new coat of paint. Unfortunately, they had chosen whitewash. As you can imagine, it looked quite a sight. George and I took it over to our house, where we stored it indoors until the whitewash had quite dried out. Then it was washed down and the repainting began. When the white, blue and purple colours had been applied, we noticed that the thumb on the statue of the infant Jesus was missing. Using my cake decoration skills, I built up the thumb, using sugar paste. After the painting was completed, you would never have been able to tell.

When we began to look for a home here in Chelmsford, George wouldn't even look at a house as he loved Stanford so much. I had to do that with my son-in-law, because George didn't want to move. We were both very sorry to leave the parish after so many years.

George and Bridget Sanders : February 2012

I (Bridget) was born into the Sharp family in Forest Gate and baptised at St. Anthony's. There were eleven children in our family, and I was number five. My grandparents found a house for us in Stanford and we left London at the beginning of the War. That house has now been in the family for over seventy years.

I started going to St. Joseph's School during the War. I made my First Holy Communion there in 1944. I've still got the Prayer Book I was given by my parents for my First Holy Communion. For our First Communion breakfast, we were taken into the school by the nuns and we had boiled eggs and bread and butter. At that time, fresh eggs were hard to come by, so it was a real treat. There were only three nuns in the school at that time. There was Sister Bernadette, who was the Head Teacher. Sister Columba had the Infants. Sister Joseph had Standard 1 and Standard 2 (Juniors) and Sister Bernadette, besides being the Head, also taught Standards 3 and 4. At that time there were less than 100 children in the school. Stanford was still only a village in those days. Mother Vincent also lived at the convent. She would sometimes look after the children at playtime. She was a real dear, and we all loved her.

To begin with, I was taken to school by older brothers and sisters, and later on it was my turn to take younger brothers and sisters. With so many children in the family we all helped out. By the age of eight I would think nothing of feeding the baby and changing its nappy, and helping with shopping and cooking. We all had more common sense in those days.

At school, discipline was quite strict. You couldn't talk during lesson time, even to the person sitting next to you in the double desk, although we did whisper now and again. I remember later on in the senior school I said "Ta" to a child who had lent me a piece of blotting paper, and I was told off for that. The double hall opposite to St. Joseph's Hall had a partition drawn right across to make two classrooms. One classroom was the Infants and the other was Standard 1 and 2. Standard 3 and 4 were in St. Joseph's Hall, where we have the coffee mornings now. When I was in Standard 3, Sister Aquinas joined the teaching staff. She was introduced to us by Sister Bernadette.

When we were naughty, each of the nuns had her own way of punishing us. One used to poke you with her finger. Another had very long fingers and when she slapped your arm her hand went the whole length of your arm. One Sister would knock you from side to side, by hitting you on one shoulder and then the other. People would not do that nowadays but then we thought it was quite normal.

We had school dinners, but they weren't cooked at the school. The meals were brought in a van. There was no choice in the food we were given and we were made to eat it, whether we wanted to or not. But then again, during wartime everyone was glad to have a meal. You ate what you could get in those days. They didn't make you eat the skin of a jacket potato, so we would turn the skin upside down and hide things like onions underneath.

During the War we used to see the German prisoners who came to Mass on Sundays. There were thirty or forty and they pretty well filled one side of the church. The Germans were on the left hand side and the rest of us were on the right hand side. Older members of my family remember the German soldiers smiling at us and they remember them singing 'Silent Night' in German at Christmas. They thought it sounded really beautiful. At the Sunday Mass, a German officer would read the gospel in German after our priest had read it in English. As far as having the Germans there, I think we just took it in our stride.

I remember an Air Raid when we were at school. The shelter was out in the playground, near to the wall next to the old convent. Some of the children were taken into the cloakrooms. Our teacher had been teaching us 'Hail Holy Queen' and she was so nervous that when we got into the shelter she couldn't remember the next line of the prayer. She must have been traumatised, worrying about getting the children safely across the playground to the shelter. My sister Margaret, R.I.P., was the only one of the whole lot of us who could remember the next line.

When we were eleven we left St. Joseph's and went to the senior school. There was no money for transport to the Catholic school in Tilbury so I went to the Council school for two and a half years. Then the Council provided money for transport and I was able to go to St. Mary's at Tilbury for the last year and a half. We all left school at fifteen then.

When Father Hibbert came to the parish, we all started up the Youth Club, the Guild of Angels, the Children of Mary, and the Legion of Mary. Years later, we used to run coffee mornings about once a month in the Parish Room, where the garage and sheds are now.

George and I met on a blind date. Our sisters worked together, and one wanted to get rid of a brother while the other wanted to be rid of a sister, in the nicest possible way of course. Little did they know that their teenage pranks would lead to so many years of happiness. I went along on the date as a bit of a giggle. We were married in about eight months, quite a whirlwind romance. We spent the first year of our married life down in Westcliff, which was the only place we could afford to get a flat. After that year we moved into the parish and we have been here ever since, over forty six years.

George : In 1968, I joined the Knights of St. Columba. My father in law took me. I didn't know what they were. He said "Come on, you're coming with me." He took me up the road to enrol and I've been with them ever since. I was Treasurer for about fourteen years, Grand Knight more than once and Chancellor. A few years ago there were fewer and fewer members, but there was still the same amount of work to do, and it got to be too much for the ones who were left. In 2006, they closed the Council here in Stanford, but I didn't want to lose my service, so I transferred my membership to Basildon. I'm not able to go to any Knights meetings these days, but I'm still a member. I still do some work for the parish, by ordering the Christmas and Easter posters. We even organise their distribution to other local churches. The Knights used to do a lot of charitable work and helped to organise processions in the parish. We would help out at the Parish Bazaars. I remember particularly all the older members of the Council, especially those who were members when I joined. They and their wives worked very hard, a lot of it behind the scenes.

A Quiz Night organised by the Knights of St. Columba, and yes, the Ladies won! Congratulations to Mary Stockwell, Maureen Foulkes, Shelagh Orritt and Peggy Sharp

Bridget : Sister Monica taught my two youngest sisters at the old school. Our oldest son and daughter started school in the same old building. I think it was just the Infants left there by then. In the old school you couldn't see out of the windows, and it was very cold. If you sat near a radiator, you were really lucky. When I was a child, the Parish Bazaars were organised to raise funds for a new school building.

The new school was much more modern, much better. Another change was that there were now lay teachers in the school.

As each new priest arrives in the parish, everyone expects him to be the same as the previous priest, but of course they're not. They all have their own character, and they are all quite different. Each one brings his own special quality. It wouldn't do for everyone to be the same. We recall Father Timmins, who was Father Hibbert's curate. Father Timmins was the priest who married us. Of course, there was Father Hibbert himself. He simply was one of us. I remember that he would come down to my parents' house, sit at the table and dive in with the rest of us, eating whatever we were eating. He used to kick his shoes off under the table and really relax. He would take the young people in the parish off to the Socials in nearby parishes. We would all go in his car. He was the one who started up so many of the parish organisations. He was also the one who organised the parquet flooring in the old church.

We remember Father Gostling. He was absolutely brilliant with children. He really seemed to be able to communicate with them. He used to do a Mass in sign language for children with hearing loss. He was marvellous with those children and with any children. He got on extremely well with our son Robert. They got on like a house on fire. He helped Father Gostling with the woodworm treatment of the Stations of the Cross at Horndon Chapel, and with some of the pews in Our Lady and St. Joseph's. Robert learned to play the organ in the church. Molly McDade, the organist, heard him picking out a tune on the keyboard when he was about eleven, and she then taught him. We were delighted because Molly was an old friend and she had played the organ at our wedding.

We were very upset when the old church had to be demolished. We were married there, our children were baptised there, my younger brothers and sisters were baptised there. We all made our First Communions in that church, we were all Confirmed in that church. We were really heartbroken when it was pulled down. When it was rebuilt, we don't know what happened to the big Crucifix which used to be outside the old church. It was really historical. The figure had been repaired and repainted by Molly McDade, who had learned how to do this by working originally with her father. The Knights had done a similar job on the Cross itself. The Crucifix was a landmark for everyone, not just for Catholics.

Peggy Sharp remembers the work of Bill and Sylvia Finnegan

The Christmas Bazaar was held at Saint Joseph's almost every year from 1949 until 2000. The Knights of Saint Columba took a leading role in helping to organise these events, and they held a Grand Christmas Draw which brought in a large part of the money raised.

Bill Finnegan joined the Knights in 1959. He worked tirelessly to provide prizes for the Christmas Draw, going to shops and businesses asking for donations. His wife, Sylvia was the bazaar secretary, and she accompanied him on those treks round the shops. When the Lakeside Shopping Centre was opened they went there as well. This meant that all the Draw prizes were gifts so all the money raised on the sale of tickets was clear profit. The Knights sold books of tickets after all the Masses, making sure that everyone bought some. Some parishioners took books to sell at their workplaces, including Basildon Hospital.

The bazaar was a big event with stalls from the parishioners at East Tilbury and Linford, Horndon and Corringham, the Sisters of Mercy and Stanford. Fortunately there were many helpers, including Maureen and Michael Griffiths, Maureen Walsh, Kit and Pat Parsons from Linford, Connie Appleby and Sylvia Finnegan who made everything on their stalls. These bazaars were very popular with villagers from the neighbouring areas and our own parishioners, and they raised a lot of money for the parish.

The Parish Room which was outside the main halls was used for refreshments. This room had been used for many events, including a Mother and Child Club and various meetings. Unfortunately, it fell into disrepair and had to be demolished.

Bill and Sylvia Finnegan

Bill and other Knights, Bill Frazer, Jack Murphy, Mike Blanc and Bert Janes (to name a few) helped with the decoration of the halls over many years and did a really good job of it. Bill Finnegan somehow managed to obtain a new kitchen for the hall from Magnet, completely FREE.

Only Bill could do that, he was very persuasive in getting things for the parish. Bill died in 2005. That was a great loss to the parish but he will always be remembered fondly for all the work he did for the parish of Our Lady and Saint Joseph.

Tina and Bernadette Hill : Parishioners : March 2012

The Hill family was one of the original families from Corringham, having lived on Lampits Hill Avenue from 1942 until 1988. Our parents, Leslie and Pauline, married in 1939 at Our Lady and Saint Joseph's Church, Stanford-le-Hope. Leslie had converted to Catholicism to marry Pauline. They had three girls, Fay, Tina and Bernadette. Leslie worked in the railway office in Grays and later went to work for Shell, in the wages department at Shell Haven.

When the girls became of school age, Pauline worked as Playground Attendant at Saint Joseph's School, where all three girls went. Later she became Secretary to Sister Mary Aidan. Fay and Tina attended St. Mary's Secondary School in Tilbury and Bernadette made it to Grays Convent.

The Hill family off on holiday, about 1959
Lesley, Bernadette, Tina, Pauline and Fay

Leslie and Pauline took a great interest in working with St. Joseph's Church. Leslie was chief altar server at the time that Father Hibbert was Parish Priest. At Christmas, Leslie and Pauline always had a "ready cut" rug finished, to be raffled at the church Bazaar.

Fay and Bernadette went on to study at Stage School in Romford, and they both made their careers in this field. Fay opened her first Ballet School in Corringham New Town Centre, where she introduced boys, who wanted to be footballers, to ballet. The idea was accepted very cautiously at that time, but it is now very popular and seen as the best exercise for the physique. After marrying and going to live in Sweden, Fay continued to teach ballet. She had three children but sadly she died of cancer in 2003.

Tina worked in several jobs, ending up in British Airways. She retired in 2009 with 41 years service. She is still living in London and enjoying life.

Bernadette married a Portuguese man. Her marriage failed after a couple of years, but she had a son whom she took with her as she travelled extensively in the theatre world. She now has her own Dance School in Los Angeles. Her son lives nearby, with his wife and son.

Leslie died in 1988 and Pauline in 1997. They gave a wonderful childhood to their three girls.

Like all families we have had our "ups and downs" but as our mother always said "As a family we have been very lucky".

Michael Riley : Parishioner : March 2012 : My Family and Saint Joseph's School

My family's association with St. Joseph's began with my grandfather, John Riley, who was among the group of Catholic men who welcomed Father Charles Carless from the train when he arrived to begin his time in Stanford-le-Hope. According to granddad, he provided his kitchen table to serve as an altar for the first Mass in the former barn in Park Road – he was a good story teller but maybe this was true.

John and Annie Riley came to Stanford-le-Hope shortly after their marriage in 1903. John was part of a work force that had moved from Kynoch's main works in Birmingham to a new satellite explosives factory that had been established on the Corringham marshes a few years previously. Kynoch's was a progressive company, building a village for its workers close to the factory ("Kynochtown") and more housing at Digby Road, Corringham ("Kynoch Villas") and it was in one of the latter that my father, Jack, was born. On 14 July 1913, Jack was baptized by Father Carless – the third child to be baptized in the permanent church.

By the following year, John and Annie had moved again, this time to No 2 Butler's Corner, Stanford-le-Hope – the right half of the 300 year old thatched house that once stood on the corner of Corringham Road and what is now Billet Lane. Also in 1914, their eldest son, my Uncle Stan was among those confirmed by Cardinal Bourne during his visit to the new church and school. At this time Stan was attending the Council school but later transferred to St. Joseph's High School. By the end of the Great War Stan, Leonard and Jack Riley were all attending the school. Stan Riley was a member of the St. Joseph's football team and is the boy sitting bolt upright, front row second left, in this photograph from 1920.

This photo of the cast of a School Play (*A Christmas Carol*?) also dates from about 1920. My uncle, Stan Riley, is shown front centre. A few adults are included in the picture but unfortunately none of the names was recorded.

My aunt, Alma Riley, who was born in the thatched cottage in 1919, was at St. Joseph's from 1924 to 1933. She is the girl in the middle of the front row of this class photo which was probably taken about 1929. Again, the names of neither the teacher nor the pupils are recorded.

When war was declared on Nazi Germany on Sunday, 3rd September 1939, my family was at Mass at St. Joseph's. Mass was interrupted twice in quick succession that morning – firstly by the noise of the air raid sirens which were being tested, then by the screaming of my aunt Alma as she ran terrified out of the church door!

Later on in the war, the police called in the school to talk about the V1 attacks. My brother Stan remembers being on his way home for lunch a few days later together with classmate Daphne Turrant and her brother Terry. They had just reached the sandpits when they heard the distinctive sound of a "Doodlebug" passing overhead and then a sudden silence as the engine cut out. Stan started shouting "Lay down flat or we'll all be killed!" but then really got agitated because the others ignored him and carried on walking. Anyway they lived to tell the tale as the bomb glided over Stanford to explode in the fields beyond.

I was a "Babyboomer", starting at St. Joseph's in September 1951. With all the babies born immediately after the war, every available space was in use. The hall was divided by curtains with us 'babies' in Sister Frances's class on one side and Sister Dolores's second class on the other. I remember we also had lessons in the room next to the boiler room. The school buildings were bursting at the seams, but by my third year, our class moved into the first of the new class rooms on the other side of Scratton Road.

A May Procession in the nineteen fifties

In the fifties, my mother's mother had a florist shop at the bottom of the High Street and for many years my mother helped to make the floral crown for the May Procession. When it came to the turn of my class to be involved, I was chosen to carry the crown in the procession which in those days passed along Southend Road to the High Street and then via Central Road, Featherstone Road, Corringham Road and Scratton Road back to the church lawn. The girls liked dressing up like this but I remember being highly embarrassed when my mother and Sister Joseph dressed me in this silk page boy outfit. The other boys (Arthur Wood, Ian Taylor and Robert McAleer) just had to wear blue sashes! And is Robert laughing behind his hand in this photo?

In 1956, my mother took a job as cleaner/caretaker at the school and would remain there for the next twenty years. She got on well with the Sisters, continuing to help around the convent after retirement and even getting my dad involved in doing the odd bit of gardening for them. When Sister Aidan started referring to her as "Sister Gwen" she regarded this as the ultimate accolade!

Margaret Richards (nee Frost) : Parishioner : March 2012

Our family association with Our Lady and St. Joseph's Parish dates back to 1948, when our parents Kathleen and the late Peter Frost were married on 30th July. My grandmother could remember the building and opening of the original church when she was a girl. She also told us how a priest from Grays, Father Carless, cycled from there to Stanford-le-Hope to say Mass in a barn at the corner of Runnymede Road before the building of a permanent church in Stanford.

My mother remembers in her childhood days families and children walking through Stanford and branching off to attend services at their respective chapels and churches. She recalls the war years when soldiers would march through the village, as it was then, to attend services on Sunday mornings and contingents of prisoners of war, many of them attending Our Lady and St. Joseph's Church.

The eldest of four children, I attended St. Joseph's School from 1955, followed by my brother Alan, sister Veronica and much later by younger brother David. The school was then served by the Sisters of Mercy who lived as a Community at the convent – the house adjacent to the former playground which is now a car park. The Headmistress at the time was Sister Mary Aidan, and the teaching nuns were Sister Francis, Sister Joseph and dear Sister Monica. The school secretary throughout our time at St. Joseph's was Mrs. Hill. She shared an office with Sister

Aidan at the top of the staircase next to the School hall; this also backed onto the original church.

I remember hot school dinners with dinner money of five shillings a week – I liked the chocolate pudding and custard but was not so keen on the stew! The food was all served from huge metal trays and deep metal cans. The leftovers were collected once a week by a smelly 'pig van' to be fed to the local pigs.

School days were happy ones. Every year Cadbury's Chocolate Company would run an essay competition based around the growing of the cocoa pod, and the shipping and production of chocolate. The school choir and orchestra, although I think this was mainly recorders, and sports days also come to mind. Every year there was an inter-schools country dancing competition. I took part one year with my partner Stephen Duggan, and when I returned home that Saturday afternoon in May my youngest brother David had been born.

The School Orchestra – with those recorders

Other memories:

- First Holy Communion Day, approximately 1958, all the girls dressed in white with white gloves and the boys looking smart in white shirts and red school tie. Photographs on the lawn where the present church now stands and breakfast in the old School hall – boiled eggs and bread and butter.
- Great excitement on St. Patrick's Day when buckets of shamrock would arrive and each child given some to wear.

- Crates of 1/3 pint of milk being left at the school gates and in winter time being moved beside the radiators to de-ice!

The School Choir

- Our Parish Priest, Father Hibbert, coming over to the playground at lunchtimes with his boxer dog. We always looked forward to seeing them and it was a highlight of our day.
- The school's annual daytrip to Aylesford Priory in Kent for older children, and my first experience of attending Mass in the open air!

Father Hibbert and friends

In looking back at the history of this parish, it should be remembered that the Catholic community of the Bata Estate at East Tilbury have made a big contribution to both school and church over the past years. This stoic community has been batted between the parishes of Our Lady Star of the Sea and Our Lady and St. Joseph over the years, becoming the responsibility of first the Tilbury Parish and then the one at Stanford-le-Hope until the unity of the present day. The families of the estate have represented many nationalities, including Irish, Polish, Czechoslovakian and English. When I was very young, Mass was celebrated in the canteen/dining room of the Bata Hotel, used by the factory workers for their mid-day meals during the week and still smelling of cabbage on Sunday morning.

This was pre Vatican Council when Mass was said in Latin and Father stood with his back to the congregation. We wore our Sunday best to Mass and in those days my sister and I always wore hats. I can remember having new ones at Easter every year.

When the cinema on the estate ceased to function, the building was made into a village community hall and Sunday Mass was then celebrated there at 8.00 a.m., with fasting beforehand of three hours. Confession was also offered before this Mass and my Dad would make sure we were up and ready to attend. Thankfully, it was a short walk from our house to the centre, but on a cold, dark, winter morning with a rumbling tummy I would rather have been in bed. Although it was lovely to get home and have a cooked breakfast waiting – particularly with fried bread – cholesterol was not a word you heard in those days!

I particularly remember Mr. and Mrs. Parsons preparing the altar for Mass and being responsible for the altar linen, also tidying up afterwards, with the men of the congregation putting away the chairs and the younger children eagerly collecting the kneelers for stacking away each week.

Then came a period of great excitement when we were told there would be a purpose-built church for us. Fund raising went on and a piece of land was bought behind the then Bata Hotel. Sadly, the plans fell through and Mass for our community was offered in the shared facility of the Methodist chapel at Linford until very recently, when the parishes of Stanford-le-Hope and Tilbury were combined. Unfortunately, this resulted in many of the older and infirm folk, and those without transport, being unable to attend Sunday Mass.

Over the years, many children from the Bata Estate have attended school at St. Joseph's. In my day we travelled in a typical 1950s coach along the lanes to Stanford. I think it was supplied by Harris of Grays.

These children were our near neighbours: Jimmy, Patrick, Veronica and Sean Parsons, Christine and John Ratajczak, David and Peter Robinson and their sister Debbie, Linda and Vanessa Adamcek, Margaret and Patricia Sullivan, the Payne girls, Georgette, Antoinette, Bernadette and Paulette, along with Carol, Jackie and Kevin Sewell, the Moss girls, Veronica and her elder sister, another Margaret I think, and the Clarke family, Robert, Stephen, Susan and Joanne, Richard and Helena Fedorcio, Ian Hammond and his younger brother, the Siodlak family and many more.

These children not only attended school but also joined the Cub and Scout groups which were run at St. Joseph's at that time. My brothers Alan and David were very active members of 3rd Stanford-le-Hope Scouts – they regularly attended parades and were very serious about badge-work and camping at Mucking and further afield. Although not in uniform, my Dad supported 3rd Stanford-le-Hope Scout Group by serving on the Committee as a long standing secretary, helping with fund raising and also as a member of the selection committee.

Three of our Scouts take a break

I moved away from home in the nineteen seventies, but attend Mass on my visits back. My sister is still a member of the parish and her children, Laura, Antony and Adam, attended St. Joseph's before moving on to local secondary schools.

Betty Farrell : Parishioner : May 2012

I wasn't born in the parish, though I have lived in it for most of my life. I was born in Dublin. My parents died when I was quite young, and I went to live with my mother's sister-in-law and my cousins in Baldoyle.

I went to school as a boarder at Loreto Abbey in Dalkey, because my aunt knew one of the nuns there. I've never forgotten the school. These days there are so many stories and plays about children being unhappy at convent school, but my school wasn't like that at all. The nuns were lovely, very caring.

Peter and I met at a wedding. His older brother married my first cousin. Peter had left school to join the RAF during the war, hoping to be a pilot. He became a wireless operator, which meant that he was also the rear gunner, which was a very risky option. After the War he transferred to RAF Transport Command and was in India at the time of its independence and then served on the Berlin air-lift in 1948/49.

We were married in Ireland, moving to the UK and living in Forest Gate for a while, just two furnished rooms. Our first child, David, was born. Peter got a job with British Rail and later on with Mobil in Coryton. We were offered a Council house in the new East Ham estate in Stanford-le-Hope. We weren't sure, but we decided to give it a try. We moved here in 1957, when Father Hibbert was Parish Priest. He had a great sense of humour.

From the moment we moved here, Peter began to focus his energies on the life of the Church. He had made a decision to do what he could for the Church, in recognition of the way that everything had worked out well for him with his family and new house. Peter had a real sense of social responsibility. He would always support friends and colleagues. It led him into becoming a loyal union member. He also became a member of the Knights of St. Columba. Later on, after our daughter Geraldine was born, I joined the Catholic Women's League and was even able to attend the afternoon meetings with her. When I sat down at the meetings, she would stand quietly alongside me, drinking it all in. She was such a good little girl.

It was our job in the CWL to organise all the refreshments for parish events and activities. We used to joke that we always went out with a tea towel. We would help out when the old church had to be decorated, washing the mould off the walls before they were repainted. We organised so many Jumble Sales. The money raised was always in pennies, but it mounted up to something substantial. Of course, the CWL's work was instrumental in setting up CAFOD, to ensure that money raised for Third World projects went directly to the right people, rather than being diverted through government agencies in other countries, some of whom were prone to corruption. In 1962, CAFOD began to undertake this task, and this year it is celebrating fifty years of its work.

The Youth Club was set up by a group of parents who were also in the Knights. They included Peter, Jack Murphy, Bert Janes, Geoff Helm and Leon Williams. These were usually at the social heart of the parish. At the Youth Club there was a group of boys from Campion School and some girls from Grays Convent. The boys were about two years older than the girls, who were about 14 years of age. The Club was open on a Monday evening in St. Joseph's Hall. Peter would go down early to put out all the furniture and equipment which was stored in a shed at the back. Some of the things were really heavy. Of course, at the end of the evening it all had to be packed away again neatly for the next week. A group of us ladies looked after the young people, and sold them sweets and soft drinks or talked with them when they wanted to talk. But in the days before video recorders, it always seemed that the television programme I wanted to watch was on a Monday evening.

Peter was always on the lookout for parents who could help to run the Youth Club, and he encouraged them to apply for the necessary training for the right qualifications, so that things could be done correctly. I remember he enlisted the help of Ron Spoors, who did so much for the Youth Club. We worked with the Youth Club from the time it began until Peter's death in 1977. I carried on working there for a while, but then my involvement tailed off.

The Youth Club had its own Folk Group and a Drama Group, and they put on concerts to raise money for charity. They linked up with other Youth Clubs, such as the one at Grays, to organise joint discos. There were shinty games at Hassenbrook.

The kids all seemed to like Peter. He was able to remember his own childhood and the mischief he got up to, and that helped him in his relationships with the members of the Youth Club. He was always prepared to get involved, sometimes doing things that might embarrass me. I remember him ice-skating with the young people, and staying on the ice when the speed skaters were practising. He couldn't have done anything better, the youngsters were impressed.

When Peter died, the young people requested and organised a special Mass for him. They all wanted to read at the service. They really missed him.

We often refer to the years when Father Taylor and Father Lynch were in the parish as the Golden Years. Father Taylor was a lovely man, a lovely priest. He was easy to talk with and such a good listener. I felt that I could confide in him because he was so understanding. He was very holy. He never wanted anything for himself. He had an old coat that he used to wear. It was supposed to be black, but it had turned into various shades of green. When we bought the car for Father Taylor, everyone was so willing to contribute because he was so loved.

Father Bart Lynch was a very genuine person. I remember his first Mass in the old church. We used to sit in the Choir Loft at the back of the church, and from there it was possible to see through into the Sacristy. He was leaning down, with his head in his hands. Even from that distance, you could tell that he was saying a prayer. When I got to know him, I mentioned that moment and he said "Well, I didn't know what I was going to see when I came out. All those faces wanting to see the new priest".

After a while, you could tell if Father Bart was going to be saying Mass from the noise in the Sacristy, where he was joking with the altar servers about the performance of their favourite football teams. But when he actually came out to say Mass, he was a completely different person. He was so holy. Many priests have that special air about them when they are conducting their first Masses, and a few priests never lose that sense of wonder, of the miracle that occurs at the moment of consecration. Father David Clemens had that same quality.

Father Gostling supported the Catholic Women's League activities, because his own mother had been a staunch member of the League. He could always be relied upon to accompany us on our days out to Aylesford. Father Taylor would also look in on CWL meetings on occasion, and was always happy to talk with the ladies and answer their questions.

There have been a lot of changes in the Catholic Church over the years. One has been the arrival of Anglican priests, some of whom are already married. It makes me quite sad to reflect that a number of very good Catholic priests in the past had to leave the priesthood because they themselves wanted to get married. I remember meeting Father John Glynn on a Retreat. He was the one who composed that beautiful hymn "I Watch the Sunrise". But now he has left the priesthood in order to get married.

I was School Secretary at St. Joseph's School for over eighteen years. During that time, Sister Monica was Head Teacher, then Sister Philippa and then Mary Pollard. To my mind, Sister Monica **is** Stanford, she's wonderful. I think that the nuns finally left the school because the paperwork just grew too much, and they couldn't do all that and also carry out their vocations in the parish. When I retired, I came back into the school to help out in the classrooms, listening to the children read. But I drew the line at making glove puppets, as I'd never had the knack of sewing and hated it. It was fun being with the children and it does now make me wonder whether I might have missed my vocation, although you have to be a special person to be a good teacher.

Chapter Eleven : A brief look around the church of Our Lady and St. Joseph (*with thanks to parishioner Gareth Outen)*

The first noticeable feature of our church is the Italianate style of the architecture. The design of the new church was the subject of much parish discussion in the early nineteen nineties, when the architect asked for and received the views of the Parish Priest and his congregation. The Parish Council visited many churches to gain an impression of what would be most suitable. The colour of the brickwork is intended to evoke the sense of an essentially village church, with its Italian style a reflection of the architect's particular influences. Father Dick Ashton, the Parish Priest who oversaw the building of the new church, commented when it was completed "Everyone says how beautiful the new church is".

Just inside the entrance to the church, to the right and to the left, are matching ceramic Holy Water stoups. These were made by John Sharp when he was a pupil at St. Anselm's School, Basildon. They were originally made for St. Augustine's Church in Corringham.

On the wall facing the door there is a plaque depicting St. Augustine. This was given by the Greenan family to St. Augustine's Church.

To the left of the main entrance, there is a crucifix that was given to the church by the Nibbs family. It is a memorial for their daughter Sandra, who died on the way home from the Parish Youth Club when she was only fourteen years old.

The body of the church is accessed through the glass doors to the right of the entrance porch. These doors can be drawn back so that the entire narthex or lobby area can be utilised for additional seating during particularly well attended Masses.

The marble panel in the centre of the new altar was taken from the altar in the old church. It depicts a pelican, a symbol of self-giving and often used as an emblem of Our Lord. In the Middle Ages, the pelican was thought to be particularly caring towards its chicks, even to the extent of piercing its own breast to feed its young. The analogy with the story of Christ is all too clear.

In 2007, after a request was made for a Tridentine Mass, it was necessary to widen the altar. Parishioners Roy Bragg and Will Dollard extended the altar by some two feet. Their engineering background ensured that this was a very solid addition to the altar.

A marble panel has been placed in the front of the ambo. This marble panel was also taken from the altar in the earlier church of Our Lady and St. Joseph. The ambo serves as both lectern and pulpit. From the ambo, lay readers read passages from the Old and New Testament as part of the Liturgy of the Mass. The priest will read from the Gospels here and deliver the homily or sermon.

Around the walls of the church are placed the Stations of the Cross, which depict the stages of Our Lord's Passion. This particularly fine collection, in the Bavarian style of wood carving, was bought in northern Italy in the nineteen thirties. The carvings once adorned the little Chapel of the Sacred Heart in Horndon on the Hill. They were refurbished just before the new church of Our Lady and St. Joseph was completed.

A carved figure of St. Joseph stands near the front of the nave. Although created much later than the statue of Our Lady, it was originally situated

in the old church. St. Joseph is remembered especially on March 19th each year and also on May 1st, which is celebrated as the Feast of St. Joseph the Worker.

Behind the altar, on the sanctuary wall, there is a crucifix that once hung in a similar position in the old church. It was given in memory of Mrs. McDade, whose family features so frequently in the early history of the parish.

On either side of the crucifix there are two imposing icons, which depict Our Lady and St. Joseph, the co-patrons of our parish. The Cyrilic script on each identifies the subject. The icons were painted by one of our former Parish Priests, Father David Clemens.

At the base of the east wall stands a credence table, on which the implements needed for the celebration of the Eucharist are placed before the Offertory in the Mass. This table was built by Roy Bragg, using money the parish received as a gift from parishioner Franz Grubba, R.I.P.

The old stone font was removed from Mucking Anglican church when the latter was declared to be redundant. The church at Mucking was in use before the Reformation, and so the font provides a link with earlier Catholic communities in the area.

The font was originally situated in the middle of the church under the skylight (see if you can work out exactly where). Some enterprising and strong parishioners managed to move it to its present position.

In the Blessed Sacrament Tabernacle, our Lord as consecrated host is reserved for the sick and housebound, who are unable to attend Mass and are visited by members of the Church. It is a centre of devotion, and it is customary to genuflect (kneel) to acknowledge our Lord's Presence. The tabernacle was moved from the old church after the fire.

In a ceremony called the Crowning of Our Lady, the statue of Our Lady is decorated with flowers every year by the children of the parish. A garland of flowers is placed on the head of the statue of Our Lady. This takes place on a Sunday in May. The statue was moved from the old church to its present position, and repainted after it had unexpectedly been given a coat of whitewash.

The church organ, a Norwich "Sprowston", was badly damaged during the fire in the old church. It has been extensively restored, and is now used in church services, particularly the 11 a.m. Sunday Mass.

Among the many striking features inside our church are the stained glass windows, a combination of traditional designs from the earlier church, and more modern creations. Some of these feature on the cover of this book. Amongst the modern designs are some beautiful windows created in memory of Jean Helm and the Cluer family and commissioned by Mr. Cluer in 2003/4. The windows were blessed by Father Martin on Easter Monday, 2004. The windows are sensitively designed and crafted. Fortunately, we still have the letter written by the artist, Susan McCarthy, which illustrates the care that goes into the design of such windows and helps us to appreciate the windows more fully.

> Dear Mr. Cluer,
> RE : ST. JOSEPH'S CHURCH, STANFORD-LE-HOPE, ESSEX
>
> Please find enclosed 2 more designs for the stained glass windows in the Chapel of The Blessed Sacrament.
>
> PENANCE
> I have concentrated on the theme of atoning for sins and the attainment of enlightenment and forgiveness through prayer.
>
> The praying hands are intercepted by the Crown of Thorns to remind us that Jesus suffered for the sins of man whilst on earth. The 5 wounds (purple) emphasise this and they are interspersed with beads from the Rosary to assist with our prayers and meditations. The blocks of colour in the background are to represent :
>
> Grey/blue = lost in the murky wilderness of sin and sadness
> Black and white swirls = light breaking through the darkness through the power of prayer
> Clear = enlightenment attained through acceptance and forgiveness.
>
> The amber and white in the background is to show that God's love and warmth is always there, should we choose to accept it.

(This window is dedicated in memory of the Cluer family, and is dated 2004.)

COMMUNION

In this design, the family group has come to the church to celebrate Communion together. The areas of colour in the background represent the Holy Trinity: all three colours relating to the others, i.e. blue + red = purple.

I have kept the outer border clear to allow in maximum light. By using the same glass (where appropriate) as in the other window, the two windows will be strongly related to each other in appearance.

(This window is dedicated to Jean Helm, 1927-2000.)

I hope this meets with your approval.
Yours sincerely
Susan McCarthy BA(Hons)

The traditional stained glass windows, which were once part of the old church, depict a number of religious figures. Starting forward from the right hand rear corner of the church, the first two are Our Lady of the Assumption and The Sacred Heart of Jesus. These are dedicated to the memory of Victor Gill, who died in 1930. The next two are Our Lady of Lourdes and St. Joseph. The last two are St. John the Baptist and St. Teresa of Lisieux, and these are dedicated to the memory of George and Mary Carman and are dated 1939.

The two adjacent windows, more modern in design and more recent in construction, are allegorical depictions of local industry, the river and the spiritual aspects of the area. There is an explanation of the meaning of these windows, created by the artist.

The windows depict Joy and Freedom of the Spirit through the Seven Sacraments of the Church

Modern symbolism of areas near the church is used.
The River Thames is shown at the bottom of the windows.
This is a reference to the waters of hope through the
Sacrament of Baptism.
(The River Hope flows through Stanford-le-Hope.)

The golden cross refers to the
Sacrament of Holy Unction.

Bearing in mind the agricultural nature of the surrounding area,
the yellow areas of wheat represent the
Sacrament of Holy Eucharist.

In the sky are representations of a flame and a dove.
(The flare of the local oil refinery is a flame visible in the area.)
Both the flame and the dove are common depictions of the
presence of the Holy Spirit and represent the
Sacrament of Confirmation.

The grey to white colouration is symbolic in its reference to the
Sacrament of Penance (Reconciliation).

The flowers are associated with the
Sacrament of Holy Matrimony.

The crosses refer to the
Sacrament of Holy Orders.

The windows are dedicated 'In Memory of Doris and Jim Foreman, Special Parents'.

Next to these windows is a plaque dedicated in memory to Hazel Earl 'A kind benefactor to this parish', whose legacy in 2008 helped to clear much of the parish debt.

One of our parishioners, Dave Robinson, has constructed a scale model of the original church of our Lady and St. Joseph. It is accurate to the smallest detail, even to the bicycle left outside the church when the organist went to choir practice. The model is stored for safe keeping at the presbytery, where parishioners may go to see it. Dave is currently engaged in creating a model of the new church (see photographs below|).

The model of the new church in the course of construction

In Scratton Road, next to the church, there was until very recent times the Convent of the Sisters of Mercy. When the Sisters of Mercy withdrew from the parish in 2005 it was a sad loss to us all. Their support helped to establish both the parish and its school, and their work within the community is remembered with love and respect. Fortunately, Sister Monica retains a link with our parish. Although she now lives at the Tilbury Convent of the Sisters of Mercy, Sister Monica continues to be a daily presence in the parish of Our Lady and St. Joseph and the lives of its parishioners.

Appendix (i)

Catholic Priests in Stanford

This book has recorded the history of the parish of Our Lady and St. Joseph from its inception to the present day. However, this does not form a complete picture of the Catholic Church in our area. From the late twelfth century until the English Reformation, the church of St. Margaret of Antioch situated in Stanford-le-Hope was a Catholic institution, and it served a Catholic congregation.

I am indebted to Aubrey Saunders, in whose book *A Short History of the Church and Village of Stanford-le-Hope,* there is a list of priests who have served St. Margaret's from its earliest times to the present day. The following is a list of the priests who served St. Margaret's Church when it was a Catholic foundation.

Date of Induction	Incumbent
Before 1282	Fr. William Haste
1329	Fr. Robert de la Lee
1332	Fr. William de Brauncewell
1336	Fr. Roger Langport
1362	Fr. Erardus de Pratellis
1364	Fr. Thomas de Cubbleote
1379	Fr. Stephen de Nanesby
1383	Fr. John Bennyfield
1384	Fr. Edmund Caldecott
1395	Fr. John Clerk
1398	Fr. John Mary
1427	Fr. Thomas Duffield
1432	Fr. William Hanley
1437	Fr. William Thurlby
1440	Fr. John Bollesor
1440	Fr. Joshua Amwell
1444	Fr. Rad. Pyttye
1450	Fr. John Angrett
1453	Fr. William Bolton
1457	Fr. Thomas Cuthbert
1459	Fr. Roger Petyt
1462	Fr. Thomas Fisher
1470	Fr. Roger Howberthorne
1471	Fr. John Glantham

Date of Induction	Incumbent
1479	Fr. John Brown
1482	Fr. Thomas Blake
1485	Fr. Robert Holme
1488	Fr. William Turner
--	Fr. William Garland
--	Fr. William Raynold
1511	Fr. George Crowmer
1513	Fr. Richard Gybson
1524	Fr. William Fletcher
1531	Fr. John Tendring

The 1534 Act of Supremacy made Henry VIII "the only supreme Head on earth of the Church in England" and signalled the break with Rome.

Perhaps it would now be fitting to add to this list the Parish Priests who have served the parish of Our Lady and St. Joseph.

1913	Fr. Charles Carless
1919	Fr. James Campbell
1920	Fr. Charles Snell
1949	Fr. John Watson
1953	Fr. John Hibbert
1967	Fr. Bernard Collings
1974	Fr. John Taylor
1979	Fr. Bernard McWilliams
1982	Fr. Gerald Gostling
1989	Fr. Richard Ashton
1998	Fr. Martin Nott
2006	Fr. David Clemens
2010	Fr. Paul Dynan

Apart from our Parish Priests, quite a number of priests have assisted in our parish over the years. Some will be well known to the readers of this book, whilst others will perhaps be remembered less clearly.

1932 – 1937	Fr. Laurence Gilmartin
1937 – 1941	Fr. Michael Hopkins
1940 – 1944	Fr. Eric Goldingay
1941 – 1942	Fr. John Boyle
1944 – 1949	Fr. William Evers
1955 – 1956	Fr. Paul Nguiem-Gia-De
1956 – 1957	Fr. John McDermott

1958 – 1960	Fr. Archibald O'Brien
1961 – 1963	Fr. Joseph Haugh
1963 – 1964	Fr. James Robson
1964 – 1969	Fr. John Timmins
1969	Fr. Joseph Bilsborrow
1969 – 1971	Fr. Kester Scrope
1971 – 1973	Fr. Eamonn Magrath
1973 – 1977	Fr. Bartholomew Lynch
1977 – 1980	Fr. Neil Tozer
1980 – 1984	Fr. Joseph Hayes
1983 – 1986	Fr. Peter Connor

Appendix (ii)

Parish Organisations

At the time of the Parish Mission in 1987, a list of parish organisations was drawn up. For many of us, these organisations are known by name, but we do not always appreciate what they actually do. Fortunately, a parish information booklet was produced in 1988. After commentary on the work of the Parish Priest, the Sisters of Mercy and the school, areas that already form the larger part of this book, the parish societies and clubs were considered. Let us see what was written some twenty-five years ago.

Altar Servers

Any boy (*now any child*) who has received his First Communion can be considered for altar serving. Boys meet for practice at St. Joseph's Church, on the first Sunday of every month, following the 11.00 a.m. Mass.

If you think you would be suitable then contact Steve Mundy who will put your name forward to Father Gostling for consideration.

(*The Guild of St. Stephen, as it was known, was formed in the parish by Father John Hibbert. In the Golden Jubilee Brochure, 1963, the Master of Ceremonies was named as Mr. L. Hill, who had presided over the ceremonies since 1945.*)

Choir

The Choir exists to lead the congregation in the sung Liturgy using traditional and modern compositions. Sung Mass is celebrated at St. Joseph's every Sunday at 11.00 a.m. A full sung Liturgy is also used at major feasts such as Christmas and Holy Week.

Choir practice is held on Monday evenings at 7.45 p.m. and new members are always welcome.

Contact Mr. T. Duggan – Choir Master / Organist, or a choir member.

Music at St. Augustine's

If you play an instrument, consider sharing it for Mass.
Contact Peter Preston.

Charities Sub-Committee

The Charities Sub-Committee is a small parish organisation which consists of four members:

Chairman Mr. Dennis Bishop
Secretary Mrs. Teresa Cotgrove
Treasurer Mr. Trevor Cotgrove
Mr. Syd Lawson

We meet every four to six weeks to collect the monies from the collection boxes, from all the Mass centres.

At the moment, some of the money collected is being sent to CAFOD for the Mozambique project. We have undertaken a target of £1,000. We also donate to :

Nazareth House
St. Luke's Hospice
Elizabeth Fitzroy House
Servants of the Paraclete
Manna
Sister Helen

and any other organisation in need. We have also given money to Helen Mundy for the Togo Project.

We would also welcome suggestions should there be any needy organisation parishioners might like to support.

The Catholic Women's League

The Catholic Women's League is a national organisation of Catholic women, founded by Margaret Fletcher in 1906. It is organised into branches at diocesan level and into sections in parishes. There has been a section in Stanford-le-Hope since 1929.

The League encourages women to play their full part in the life of the Church as well as filling a lot of jobs in the background. We support many charities through the branch and nationally, and in this diocese we have two sheltered housing schemes for the elderly. We take an active interest in social problems.

We meet on the first Friday of the month, after Mass, in the Parish Room. New members are always welcome. The Chairperson of the section is Mrs. Maureen Foulkes.

If you would like to know about the CWL, please give your name to Father Gostling and Maureen will get in touch with you.

(This was listed in the Golden Jubilee Brochure, 1963, as the first organisation established in the parish, on November 10th, 1929. Its first Chair was Mrs. Palmer, and she was followed by Mrs. Gill, Mrs. Treston, Mrs. Booth, Mrs. E. Treston, Mrs. Price, Mrs. Cook, Mrs. Yates and Mrs Hall, who was the Chair for a second time. In its early years, the Catholic Women's League carried out parish work and helped distressed families. During the War years they made and sent comforts to the troops. They helped in canteens and with refugee relief work. By 1963, their responsibilities included Bazaar activities, weekly church cleaning and hospital visiting.)

Covenant Scheme

What is a Covenant?

A covenant is simply a promise to support your parish for at least 4 years.

The Inland Revenue are insisting that all covenanted sums must be recorded against the covenanter's number and name, so only those taxpayers who are prepared to provide such proof should make a covenant.

Will a covenant cost me extra tax?

No. Anyone who pays income tax can sign a covenant. Each member of a family who pays income tax can sign a covenant. Even a housewife not paying tax can still covenant provided her husband is a tax-payer.

Why bother to covenant?

You have paid income tax on the money you give to your parish. A covenant authorises the parish to reclaim the tax.

If you would like to know more about the 'Covenant Scheme' then please give your name to Father Gostling who will be only too pleased to put you in touch with those persons overseeing the covenantors.

PLEASE NOTE the 4 years cuts down on administration. If circumstances change you can cancel or alter your Covenant EASILY and at ANY TIME : Making a Covenant makes sense!

Floral Arranging

There is at present a small team of Volunteers responsible for the floral arrangements in St. Joseph's Church.

The team members work on a rota basis and would welcome the hands of any "budding" enthusiast (even if not regularly) to join their force.

If you would like to help – it's one of the most rewarding tasks – then please contact Mrs. Lesley Henderson. Lesley is also available to arrange flowers for every occasion.

Ecumenism

There is at present no local Fellowship of Churches. Local Ministers meet frequently to keep in touch and discuss local events and needs. Our parish ecumenical representative and great promoter is Mr. Geoff Helm.

Many people are involved in ecumenism by sharing common interests with members of other churches.

"Lord that they may be one as we are one."

The Freewheelers Drama Group

The Freewheelers Drama Group has been running now for almost 3 years.

It is a group of men and women, both disabled and able-bodied, who enjoy drama and entertaining others. A few productions have already been seen by the occupants of local O.A.P. complexes, and we have been invited to do more. We have also produced plays for hospital radio.

The 'Freewheelers' meet each Wednesday evening in St. Joseph's Hall (playschool room) between 7.30 and 10 p.m.

Anyone interested in amateur dramatics, including costume design and scenery painting, would be welcome.

Please contact Mr. Paul Sparrowham or Mr. Reg Merritt.

The Harvester

Tuesdays 10.30 a.m. – 1.30 p.m. Red Cross Hall, opposite Post Office, Corringham Road, Stanford.

The Harvester is an informal meeting place, supported and staffed by local Christians as a witness to Christian Unity in Stanford and Corringham. Why not come and join in our hospitality, drinks and cakes available. CHILDREN welcome.

Irish Dancing

The Loretta Webb School of Dancing registered with the Irish Dancing Commission.
Classes are held every week and boys and girls of any age are welcome.

Wednesday evening 7.00 – 8.30 p.m. St. Thomas's, Grays
Thursday evening 7.00 – 8.30 p.m. St. Joseph's, S.L.H.
For further details, contact Pat Maher or Loretta.

Jujitsu

Jujitsu is the ancient Japanese art of self defence, from which Judo and Karate have both emanated. Instruction is by a 3rd Dan, Martial Arts Commission registered coach.

The Club is open to boys and girls between the ages of 6 and 16 years and takes place each Friday evening 6.00 – 7.30 p.m.
Sunday morning 10.00 – 11.30 a.m.
in St. Joseph's Hall.

If you are interested please contact Brian or Marion Herbert.

Knights of St. Columba

It is an order of Catholic men who have banded together to serve the Church, their fellow men and each other in charity and fraternity.

We help our local Parish Priests by carrying out practical work in our parishes.

We assist the Hierarchy in the organising of diocesan and national activities of the Church.

We help one another in sickness or need. We care for our widows and dependants. We pray for the souls of our departed members.

We constantly help each other in the practice of our faith through the Mass and other spiritual activities. We organise pilgrimages and retreats for our members.

If you would like to know more about the K.S.C., please contact G. Sanders, G. Helm, C. Timothy, or G. McNamara.

(*The Golden Jubilee Brochure, 1963, recognised the Knights of St. Columba as the second oldest parish organisation. It was set up in the parish on October 27th, 1946, as Council 367. At that time, there were a few parish members who belonged to Council 81 in Grays. They formed the Council in Stanford-le-Hope, together with returning members of the Armed Forces and some new members in the parish. The Knights did excellent work when they were originally set up, but there were too few in number and the Council became dormant on October 31st, 1951. The Grand Knights of this period were*

1946 – 47	*E. Hagger*
1948	*J. Kettle*
1949 – 50	*W.P. O'Donoghue*
1951	*C.R. Sharp*

On January 5th, 1958, an Associate Group was set up, and this assisted the Parish Priest in his work.

Chairmen of the Group were

1958	*C.R. Sharp*
1959	*P. Payne*
1960	*P.A. Farrell*
1961-62	*C.R. Sharp*

This work consisted largely of organising parish events. Some of the events organised by the K.S.C. were pilgrimages to Walsingham, Aylesford and Ingatestone (in honour of the Forty Martyrs) and a pilgrimage to Lourdes for the Jubilee year. They assisted in the arrangements for the Jubilee 1963.)

The Knights of St. Columba : Council 367 : 1976

Liturgy Committee

The Committee is composed of the Parish Priest and representatives of those directly involved in the liturgy, e.g. Sacristan, servers, readers, choir and organist and any parishioner with an interest in the parish liturgy.

Meetings are held two or three times per year as required. Any parishioners with a keen interest and a contribution to make in this field would be very welcome.

We are always pleased to receive offers to read at Mass. We can provide the necessary training.

Please contact Father Gostling, Sister Philippa or Mr. T. Duggan.

Marriage Encounter

Marriage Encounter Weekend is for happily married couples who wish to strengthen their relationship and love for each other. From here, their love for their family, friends and other people.

It is also for priests; couples relate to each other and priests relate to their congregation. It is fully approved by the Church and even Pope John Paul has been on a 'Weekend'.

There is no actual participation – it's listening to couples and priests giving talks and then sharing with each other, in your own room, what you have heard.

Four talks are given over the weekend:
I
Us
Us and God
Us, God and the World.

A number of couples from the parish have attended the Encounter Weekend and many of us meet monthly to support one another.

After 28 years of married life we felt we would like to 'make' a weekend. It was certainly a turning point in our lives, a wonderful experience.

If you would like to know more about Marriage Encounter please ring Joyce or Ken Clarke.

Mother and Child Club

The Mother and Child Club meets each Wednesday afternoon, with the exception of school holidays, between 1.00 and 3.00 p.m. Anyone with children up to the age of 5 years is welcome.

The group exists to give mothers a chance to get together over a cup of tea, and meet others from the parish. There are toys and activities for the children.

We also have outings and Christmas parties.

For further information, please contact Mrs. Kay Henderson.

Repository

The repository at the back of St. Joseph's Church is open after all Masses at the weekend and at other times as appropriate.

For sale are Missals, prayer books, rosaries, statues, medals, cards and many other religious items.

If there is anything you particularly want but cannot see, please contact Connie Appleby, who will be delighted to offer assistance.

Prayer Group

There is a group which meets for prayer, praise and sharing every Wednesday evening, in the house of Anne Tomlinson, in Rectory Road, Stanford-le-Hope. Everyone is welcome.

If you would like to know more, then please call in and see Anne.

St. Joseph's Pre-School Playgroup

The Playschool was started in April 1978 and has been running successfully for almost 10 years now.

We cater only for the children who later will attend St. Joseph's Primary School. We meet in the old school building, and 15 children attend on each of Monday, Wednesday and Thursday mornings from 9.00 to 12 noon. There is a staff of 3 qualified play leaders at each session.

The starting age is 3 years (there is a waiting list). For further information, please contact Mrs. A. Grant, Playgroup Supervisor.

St. Joseph's Youth Club

The youth of our parish are very important to us. They, after all, are our Future. However, like most 11 – 15 year olds, they are noisy and temperamental! They need somewhere to relax after pressures at school, somewhere to meet with friends, discuss Boys, Girls, make-up, clothes and records.

Where better for them to let off steam than our local Youth Club, which meets on a Monday evening between 7.30 and 9.30 p.m. Here they can get together with their friends, play records (as loud as they like) without any Parental Harassment! We also have table tennis, darts, snooker, cards or the opportunity to just sit around chattering about every day matters.

Over the years the Youth Club have won numerous cups for darts, football, snooker and, more recently, the Parish Challenge Cup!

If you are interested in joining our Club, then please contact Susan Hargis.

To get a flavour of the way the Youth Club operates, here is an article that appeared in *Link*, the quarterly parish magazine, at Easter 1979.

> The Youth Club was formed in 1971 at the request of some of the parish youth. Initially there were twelve members. Over the years the membership capacity has increased to cater for the needs of the parish – at present the maximum number is sixty, which includes the football team. Looking at the attendance record over the past eight years the numbers have fluctuated between eight and forty.
>
> "The aim of the Club is to help and educate young people through their leisure-time activities so to develop their physical, mental, moral and spiritual activities and capacities, that they may grow to full maturity, as persons and members of society and that their conditions of life may be improved." (Constitution: 15/12/1974)
>
> Over the years the Club has had considerable success in various activities. Probably the most memorable sporting event was the staging of "It's a Knockout" in 1972. From a religious aspect the Live Crib, as we know it today, was originally organised by St. Joseph's Youth Club.
>
> Indoor Activities
>
> The Junior Club now meets each Monday evening at St. Augustine's, between 7.00 and 9.00 p.m. This group is aged between 12 and 16. The 16+ group which was formed at the

beginning of this year meets on Thursday evening between 7.30 and 9.30 p.m. Both groups share the facilities which are available, such as table tennis, darts, snooker, table football etc. There is a constant flow of music and the atmosphere is relaxed and happy.

Outdoor Activities

Ice-skating is a very popular event and there are rarely any empty seats on the coach.

The boys always take part in the K.S.C. five a side football competition. This year they were very unlucky not to win the first round. Nevertheless their behaviour on and off the playing area was a credit to the parish of Our Lady and St. Joseph.

The girls take part in the K.S.C. netball competitions – the Senior team did well at Upminster in October last year against some very good opposition. We hope that the under 14 team do even better in Chelmsford when they compete for the Peter Farrell Trophy in March.

The group organised a trip to Grays in January to see the pantomime "Robinson Crusoe". This trip also incorporated the Cubs, Scouts and Guides. In February, 25 members and their friends went to a Diocesan Disco at Tiffanys in Ilford.

Rambling appeals to some of the more hardy members and it is hoped to organise some rambles during the coming months, incorporating a Path Marking exercise.

Exchange Visits

Plans are being made to take a group for a weekend at Buckmore Park in May. This should be a good opportunity for the members to look after the Management Committee without which there would be no Youth Group.

Exchange visits with other clubs are now being encouraged. St. Thomas' Grays visited our club in February, and a return visit to Grays will be arranged in due course. Each year a number of the members attend the annual Youth Pilgrimage to Aylesford. This is indeed a most enjoyable event, as those who went last year will confirm.

The atmosphere in the club generates a feeling of Christian fellowship and as some of our members are not Catholics they must get a favourable impression of our Faith from the attitude of the Catholic members towards them.

A special mention must be made of the invaluable contribution that Peter Farrell made to the Group and to the Youth Service nationally. A special service was organised for Peter following his death and also for Sandra Nibbs, one of our members, who died last April. The group members did the readings, prayers and served the Masses.

Finally, we are always looking for people who may be able to help at the meetings. Whilst the Club always has adults present, it would be appreciated if some of our parishioners could be called upon in case of need. All that is asked for is a little time! You may even have some new ideas for activities!

It must be borne in mind that the Youth of today are the Adults of tomorrow.

Youth Management Committee

The Youth Club was set up in 1971 to serve the needs of the young people aged 12 -16, and later 16 plus, who are part of the parish. It is open to Catholics and non-Catholics alike and, apart from a brief closure at the end of the twentieth century, it has now been running for over forty years.

St. John's Ambulance Brigade

The cadets section of the St. John's Ambulance Brigade meets each Thursday evening between 6.30 – 8.00 p.m. in St. Joseph's Hall.

Any boy or girl between the ages of 8 – 16 years would be very welcome.

Cadets learn first aid, home nursing, and childcare and work towards other proficiency badges such as woodwork or needlework.

For further information, contact Mrs. A. Emberson.

St. Vincent De Paul (SVP)

The parish 'conference' of the Society of St. Vincent De Paul meets on Tuesday evenings at 8 p.m. in the presbytery.

The Society is an international, fraternal organisation of Catholic lay people, men and women, who practise Christianity by helping those in need on a person to person basis.

In this parish, we visit the sick, elderly or disabled people in their own homes.

President George Hasberry
Vice President Mary Dollard

Secretary Syd Lawson
Treasurer Joan Lambert

Please contact one of the above if you are interested.

The **S**ixteen **P**lus **Y**outh **G**roup (SPYG)
SPYG began its existence last year, 1987, after we had a Mission in the church before Easter. During some of the meetings, it was expressed by some youth that they missed a former youth group that used to meet with Sister Helen.

It was decided to restart a group for this age range in the parish and that we would adopt the Young Christian Workers' format for meetings but also be open to our own initiatives for fund raising activities and social events.

During the summer months several of the youth were involved in exams at school so we worked towards a recruiting drive in late September / early October 1987. This finally resulted in a firm group of 10 who regularly turn up each week for meetings in the presbytery on a Monday night at 8 p.m. to 9.30 p.m.

We have already been away for a weekend to Walsingham House in November with Father John Marsland, who just happens to be the National Chaplain for the Y.C.W. It was a great weekend and helped the group to grow together in its early days. We also arranged to do some carol singing on the 23rd December to raise money for the Save the Children Fund. We raised £60 in about two hours and were delighted with the result.

We are now looking forward to doing some 10 pin bowling in the near future and working on some drama production with an eye to raising funds for Sister Helen in Kenya.

Anyone aged 16 and over who is interested in joining us would be most welcome. We even have one extra member from Grays – so it must be worth coming to, I reckon!

Interested? Then please contact Sister Barbara at the convent.

The Deanery Youth Council
The Deanery Youth Council was formed in February this year (1988). It meets every 2 – 3 weeks. The Council consists of representatives from

the parishes of Thurrock and Catholic schools. There is now an average attendance of 10 members.

The meetings are headed by Margaret Magennis. The Council members discuss events which they can organise which would involve the youth of the deanery. The events are spread over each parish so that each has a chance to become more involved in the youth events.

The D.Y.C. was also formed to help other youth organisations if they need it. If help is needed, the group comes together and decides the best way to assist.

Slimming Club

Lose pounds and help us raise pounds for Sister Helen's Mission in Kenya.

We meet each Tuesday between 1 and 3 p.m. in St. Joseph's Parish Room. Tea and Coffee provided – but no biscuits! There is no membership fee, though a donation towards Sister Helen's fund would be greatly appreciated.

If you want to be a 'loser' then pop in any Tuesday afternoon.

The Snowdon Club

The Snowdon Club, which is affiliated to the Essex Physically Handicapped Association, was formed in September 1981 and meets in St. Joseph's Hall, Scratton Road, most Tuesdays throughout the year, from 9.30 a.m. to 2.30 p.m. It caters for physically handicapped adults in an effort to help them lead a fuller life and to provide a break for the helpers at home.

There is a team of experienced helpers who give their time voluntarily and are capable of dealing with wheelchairs and their occupants and, of course, others who are more mobile but still need assistance.

Occupational therapy is available in the form of various kinds of handicraft, plus the usual table games, e.g. scrabble, dominos, cards. Occasionally there is a speaker or demonstration and sometimes a concert party to entertain. Tea and biscuits are provided and a light lunch can be obtained at a small charge.

If you think we can help you or you know anybody who might benefit by joining the Snowdon Club, please contact any of the names listed below for further information. For those who live in the Stanford or Corringham area, transport can be provided for anyone unable to make their own arrangements.

Honorary President	Mrs. Carol Meen
Chairman	Mr. L. Turner
Secretary	Mrs. A. Revell

3rd Stanford-le-Hope (St. Joseph's) Scout Group

The group was started in January 1963 with a scout troop and a cub pack and has since gone from strength to strength. The group now comprises four sections: Venture Scouts, Scouts, Cub Scouts and Beavers, the newest section of the Scouting movement.

Meetings are held every week in St. Joseph's Hall.
Group Chairman : John Hadaway

Venture Scout Unit

This section caters for the 16 – 20 year olds who organise their own activities, which include rock climbing, canoeing, pot holing and parascending as well as weekend camps.

The unit has a leader and an assistant leader and at the present time there are seven members, including several girls. They work towards obtaining the Venture Award and the highest award in Scouting, the Queen's Scout Award. Some also take part in the Duke of Edinburgh's Award Scheme.

Contact Nick Field.

Scout Troop

This section caters for the 10 and a half – 15 year olds who, under the supervision of a Scout Leader and Instructor, take part in many activities organised for them and, sometimes, by themselves. These include night hikes, camping, cooking competitions and back-woodsmanship.

They work to achieve the Chief Scout's Award which is the highest award a scout can gain.

The troop meets on Wednesday evenings at 8.00 p.m.

Contact John Sharp or Nick Field.

Cub Pack

The pack is for boys aged 8 to 10 and a half years and they learn new skills working on their bronze arrow, silver arrow and finally their gold arrow. They take part in many events organised for the local Scouting movement, including archery, handicraft and swimming.

The highlight of their year is the annual camp when the boys live under canvas for a week at one of the district scout campsites.

The pack is led by Akela, the cub mistress, and she is assisted by helpers. At present there are 25 cubs, and they meet on Wednesdays at 6.15 – 8-00 p.m.

Cub Scout Leader : Bev Evans

Beaver Colony

The Beaver Colony is the newest addition to the St. Joseph's Scout Group Colony, arriving on 30th March, 1987.

This section of our group is for boys aged 6 – 7 years and has proved to be a very popular part of the Scouting movement.

The colony is headed by a leader and two assistant leaders. The colony meets on Wednesdays at 5 – 6 p.m.

Beaver Leaders : Jenny Meads and Margaret Sadler

Brownies

"Brownies" are for girls aged 7 – 10 years. The girls learn new crafts and skills and work towards new badge awards. There are many district and pack events throughout the year.

The Brownies meet on Tuesday evening in St. Joseph's Hall, 6 – 7.30 p.m.

For further details, please contact Cheryl.

Guides

Guides are for girls aged 10 – 15 years. The girls take part in many activities and can work towards the ultimate prize in guiding, the Queen's Guide Award.

The Guides meet on Tuesday evening in St. Joseph's Hall between 7.30 and 9.00 p.m.

If you would like to join us then please ring Chris Fields.

(*The formation of the Scouts and Guides at St. Joseph's was reported in the Golden Jubilee Brochure, 1963. At that time it was recorded that the groups had formed just recently and so little could yet be written about them. The Scoutmaster in those days was Mr. Jocelyn, the Cub Mistress was Mrs. Jocelyn and the Guides and Brownies Mistress was Mrs. Wake.*)

The Society for the Protection of Unborn Children (SPUC)

This society was first started when the 'Abortion' law came into force in January 1967. The Thurrock branch was set up in 1978 and has in the region of about 100 members, though sadly only a few are able to attend meetings regularly. Meetings are normally on the last Tuesday of each month. We also now have a Basildon branch.

The aim of the society is ultimately a repeal of the 'Abortion' law. Our work consists of writing letters to MPs, leafleting in shopping centres etc., teaching in schools on the humanity of the unborn child, and what abortion really is. We also provide speakers for public meetings.

The practical side of our work is to help any expectant mother who has difficulties by showing her the alternatives and by putting her in touch with our close associates 'LIFE' who will look after the mother in accommodation during pregnancy and for as long as necessary afterwards.

Another important part of our work is our counselling service. This is to help women who have had an abortion and are now suffering the results. They are treated with sympathy and understanding to help them come to terms with their loss.

Our fund raising activities include coffee mornings, parties, jumble sales, stalls at boot fairs and other social occasions. We are an interdenominational group.

Anyone interested in knowing more about the association can contact Mrs. W. Timothy, Mr. G. Helm, and Mrs. B. Sanders, who will be pleased to give more information.

Woolmarket Arts and Hobbies, Horndon on the Hill

The club is open to ladies who knit, sew by hand, crochet, work tapestry, embroider, draw or paint.

It is a relaxing evening where everyone, as amateurs, helps each other.

The group originated in 1976 as a painting group but now, with 12 – 15 members, it has become a hobbies group.

The cost, including a cup of tea, is 30p. plus 10p. for the weekly raffle. There is no membership fee, just the 30p. entrance each time you attend. Members attend as suits their commitments.

If Horndon is out of reach, then why not start a group in your area?

Any lady is welcome to pop in on Thursday evenings between 7.30 and 10.00 p.m. (Pay 30p. and have a cup of tea!)

If you would like to know more please contact Mrs. Louise Weddell.

BIBLIOGRAPHY

- The Peasants' Revolt : Ronald Webber : Terence Dalton Limited : 1980 ISBN 0 900963 44 1
- A Short History of the Church and Village of Stanford le Hope : Aubrey Saunders : Thurrock Printing Limited : 1989
- Estuary : Land and Water in the Lower Thames Basin: A.K. Astbury : The Carnforth Press, London, 1980 ISBN 0 9507246 0 2
- Thurrock : The Story of the People of Thurrock during the Great War 1914-1918 : Roger Reynolds : Brent Publications, Wickford, 1998 ISBN 0 948706 08 2
- More Front-Line Essex : Michael Foley : The History Press, Stroud, 2008 ISBN 978-0-7509-4951-4
- A Short History of St. Joseph's Catholic Primary School, Stanford-le-Hope : Mary E. Pollard : April 2005
- Secret Essex : Glyn Morgan : Ian Henry Publications : 1982 : ISBN 0 86025 449 6
- Panorama : The Journal of Thurrock Local History Society : Volumes 23, 30.
- Saffron, Cider and Honey, A Town Trail of Horndon on the Hill : W M Tinworth : The Horndon on the Hill Society : 1984
- The Parishioner : Parish Magazine for Our Lady Immaculate, London Road and Holy Name, Lucas Avenue, Chelmsford, Essex : Summer 2004
- Brentwood Diocesan Directory : 2005
- Souvenir of the Opening of the Church of St. Basil the Great: printed by H.B. Butler and Co., Grays : October 1956
- Essex in History : Kenneth Neale : Phillimore : 1997 : ISBN 1 86077 051 7
- Thurrock Public Libraries: the first 100 years 1903-2003 : folder produced by Thurrock Council
- A Century of Thurrock : Brian Evans : Sutton Publishing : 1999 : ISBN 0-7509-2429-2
- Thurrock's Past : Echoes From a Place : Alan Leyin : Lejins publishing : 1997 : ISBN 0 9528789 0 9
- Thurrock in the Thirties : Terry Carney : Thurrock Museum Publications : 2005 : ISBN 0 9506141 8 1